ON THE CLOCK

ON THE CLOCK

What Low-Wage Work Did to Me and How It Drives America Insane

EMILY GUENDELSBERGER

Little, Brown and Company
New York Boston London

Little, Brown and Company
Hachette Book Group
1290 Avenue of the Americas, New York, NY 10104
littlebrown.com

First Edition: July 2019

Little, Brown and Company is a division of Hachette Book Group, Inc. The Little, Brown name and logo are trademarks of Hachette Book Group, Inc.

ISBN 978-0-316-50900-8
LCCN 2019930997

10 9 8 7 6 5 4 3 2 1

LSC-C

Printed in the United States of America

For Rajiv, who is the best

Contents

Author's Note ix

Introduction: In the Weeds 3

Part One: Amazon

One Month to Christmas 15

Three Weeks to Christmas 58

Two Weeks to Christmas 90

One Week to Christmas 94

One Day to Christmas 103

363 Days to Christmas 106

Part Two: Convergys

Week One: Twenty People 126

Week Two: Sixteen People 152

Week Three: Thirteen People 169

Week Four: Twelve People 195

Week Five: Nine People 221

Part Three: McDonald's

Number One 237

Number Two 257

Number Three 277
Number Four 282
Number Five 289
Number Six 305

Conclusion: Out of the Weeds 308
Acknowledgments 317
Selected Reading 319
Notes 323
Index 325

Author's Note

This book is an examination of the day-to-day experience of low-wage work in America in the mid-2010s. There was a lot of totally standard journalism and research involved, but because what interests me most is the *experience,* I worked three jobs undercover to be able to accurately describe that experience.

I mean, *kind of* undercover. I didn't volunteer that I was writing a book, but I also didn't lie or misrepresent myself. Here's how that worked, if you're interested.

About the timeline: The newspaper I worked at closed in October of 2015. I spent part of November and all of December that year in Southern Indiana, across the river from Louisville, Kentucky, working at Amazon. I spent most of the summer of 2016 in western North Carolina working at Convergys. I spent September and October of 2017 in San Francisco working at McDonald's.

About getting the jobs: I applied using my real name and real work history as a journalist who's also had a lot of service jobs. Interviewers were almost entirely interested in the cleanliness of my criminal record and drug test; my prior work experience came up exactly once, in my interview at Convergys. I said I was a writer who hadn't had a steady job since her newspaper closed and laid everybody off a year earlier, which was 100 percent true. I would have been just as honest on follow-up questions had anybody asked them. Nobody did. All three companies seemed desperate to hire enough felony- and opiate-free bodies to keep up with the massive turnover rate built into their business models. Nobody called my references.

About not feeling bad about it: I *might* feel a little bad about taking advantage of careless interviewers or wasting my trainers' time if the massive turnover at each of these jobs was a bug rather than a feature. But high turnover, and the consequent need to hire new bodies quickly and without scrutiny, is intentional. It's central to the way these companies operate. I'll get into detail on that later, but for now, just know that I stayed at these jobs longer than a whole lot of my coworkers did.

About quoting the boss: At Amazon and Convergys, the settings of parts 1 and 2 respectively, I occasionally recorded orientation sessions and other instances when a manager spoke as the voice of the company. Covertly recording your own conversations is legal in both Indiana and North Carolina, where the first two parts take place. California, where the third part takes place, is one of the few states where it's legally fuzzy, so I just didn't do it at all there—quotations in the third part are written entirely from memory and notes I made on breaks. Anyway, the pace at my San Francisco McDonald's was so frantic and the training so minimal that recording wouldn't have been useful, anyway.

About quoting coworkers: I didn't feel right covertly recording my nonmanagement coworkers, even if it would have been legal. When I had a conversation I wanted to use in the book, I'd make a note of it and get back in touch with the person I had been speaking with later, usually after I'd left the job and didn't have to worry about blowing my cover. I'd fill that person in about the book and what it was about and ask if he or she would be willing to try to re-create the conversation on tape. Any extended dialogue scenes with coworkers come from these after-the-fact recordings, which were made with consent.

About quoting others: Experts and sources are fully on the record, just like anything I'd write for a newspaper. I didn't record my interactions with customers; those quotes are from memory.

About names: Some of the names I use for people I met are real, some aren't. I initially let people pick their own fake names, but had to change this policy after the group of guys who appear near the end of the first part all chose names along the lines of Dr. Babydick. It was funny at the time, but it just didn't work written out as dialogue. So, with apologies to Zeb, Eli, and the gang, I chose names for them and everyone else. I tried to pick ones that communicate as much about people's age, race, and culture as their real names do.

About descriptions: I include the race of most people I mention; I think it's pertinent information. I've tried to break my habit of only noting a person's race if she isn't white: if I miss a few here and there, I really am trying.

About the companies: These are the actual companies I worked for, but that doesn't mean this book is meant as an exposé of Amazon, Convergys, McDonald's, or AT&T. The point isn't that these companies are uniquely horrible. It's that these technologies and practices are present in most other low-wage jobs, too. I chose these companies because of how well they've adapted to this system, but the *system* is the problem, not them.

About the paychecks: You *bet* I cashed those checks—I worked my *ass* off. These companies squeezed just as much labor and profit out of me as any of my coworkers, and I didn't work any less hard because I was planning to write about it. Anyone wishing to debate the finer points of journalism ethics may do so after paying off my credit cards.

ON THE CLOCK

Introduction: In the Weeds

What does "in the weeds" mean to you?

I've been asking people that for a couple of years now—it's become a sort of hobby. There's two definitions, and you can often tell a lot by which one a person knows.

First, there's what I call the academic definition: "To be bogged down in the minute or unimportant details of a large project." I heard this a lot in the ten years I spent working in newspapers.

Then there's the waitress definition: "To be harried or frantic because there's more work on your plate than you can do at a reasonable pace." A key part of this definition is a feeling of desperation and hopelessness—being unable to catch up, even though you're working as fast as you possibly can.

I think of this as the waitress definition because that's who I learned it from, at my first real job, scooping ice cream as a sixteen-year-old for $5.15 an hour, the minimum wage in 2000. "Hurry up, kid, I'm in the weeds," snapped an older waitress, impatient to use the cash register I was fumbling with. Her meaning was obvious: she was hustling around at top speed, grim-faced, trying to get her customers taken care of before her tips went down the drain. And I was in her way.

I became very familiar with the weeds that summer. Counter kids spent hours in the weeds each evening, scooping as fast as we could and delaying our bathroom breaks until the line of hot, impatient customers at the window cleared, usually around 10:00 p.m. Afterward, it was bliss to lean my sticky forearms on the counter and relax a little as we waited on the trickle of late-night customers.

But the relief was always short-lived because of another new addition to my professional vocabulary: *If you've got time to lean, you've got time to clean.*

I loathed this cheery little rhyme, coined by McDonald's founder* Ray Kroc and favored by passive-aggressive managers everywhere. It felt like I was being called lazy for taking five minutes to rest after a solid four hours in the weeds, which I found infuriating. *In the weeds* and *time to lean,* it seemed to me, were opposite sides of the same coin and should even each other out.

"This is some *bullshit,*" I thought, with the righteous indignation of a teenager at her first job. I legitimately worked as hard as I could when things were busy. Did they seriously expect me to ask for something to mop the instant I had a second of down time, like some overeager, kiss-ass robot?

After a few weeks, my dad asked how the job was going, and I vented about *time to lean, time to clean.* I'd just read Barbara Ehrenreich's *Nickel and Dimed*—a new release at the time—and had become pretty passionate about labor organization. Dad was less than sympathetic to my new progressive ideals, probably because they came on the heels of what must have been a pretty intolerable Ayn Rand phase.

"They're not paying you to sit around," he told me. "If you're on their dime, you do what they tell you—that's how jobs work. Suck it up."

But I wasn't *sitting,* I protested. It wasn't like I was doing *nothing.* I was supposed to be ready at the window whenever a customer walked up to buy some ice cream—and I *was!* I never complained about working twice as hard when we were in the weeds; it seemed only fair that the pace would slow down when business was slow.

Dad sighed, and gave me some fatherly advice that stuck with me for a long time.

"Well, life isn't always fair, for one. But there's dignity in working hard and doing your job well," he said. Yes, even if that job was scooping ice cream. If you can take pride in doing your work well, that's the key to a happy life, no matter what your job is. Be the best at whatever you do, try harder than everyone else, make yourself indispensable, and you'll succeed. It's the American Dream.

Chastened, I resolved to be the best ice cream scooper I could possibly be. For the rest of the summer, I tried to *be* that overeager, kiss-ass robot. I tried to make my cones beautiful. I made myself smile and be extra friendly

* Well, sort of.

when I was exhausted. I cleaned equipment before being asked to. I even asked if there was anything I could mop.

I kept hoping that if I worked hard enough, the dignity my dad talked about would just materialize, like a runner's high. But it's hard to feel dignified when your right arm is never not sticky or when a jackass crew of boys runs you ragged while pretending not to recognize you from history class.

Anyway, my manager didn't seem to notice my attempts to be the best damn ice cream scooper in the land. All us counter kids were summarily fired at the end of the season, and I moved on to a string of service jobs that took me through high school into college and my early twenties—dishwasher, cashier, receptionist, mall photographer, church pianist, grocery stocker, projectionist, sandwich maker.

When I moved to Philadelphia after college, I continued working service jobs to support myself while trying to break into journalism. I tried to embody my dad's advice by working harder than everybody else—for about a year, I worked five days a week as a receptionist and two days a week as an unpaid intern. I stayed up late memorizing the *AP Stylebook.* I jumped at the chance to do anything editors needed—I practically asked if there was anything I could mop. And, though it felt agonizingly slow at the time, I gradually clawed my way up out of the service sector.

At my first white-collar job—copyediting on the night desk of the *Philadelphia Daily News*—coworkers were confused when I'd say I couldn't go out for a smoke because I was "in the weeds." Here, I discovered, "in the weeds" meant *stuck in the details. Overburdened with work* was a distant second, and it seemed to get more distant the higher you climbed up the career ladder. There was such a class difference between service and white-collar work that those three words actually *meant different things,* as if the two groups spoke different languages.

I was young, insecure about being self-taught, and desperate to fit into the white-collar world, so I started saying I was "swamped" or "on deadline" instead. But I did start noticing the many other ways a *lot* of people with influence seemed to live in a completely different world from the one I knew from service work.

The easiest example to pick on is the "Why don't millennials do X?"

think piece, which often settles on the cultural or technological quirkiness of my generation of consumers. (Okay, readers of a certain age, sing it with me: young people don't buy houses or boats or diamonds or save for retirement because *we don't have any money.*)

I noticed this dynamic a lot in media coverage, too—particularly when you got to the national level. Even now, real, respected people with real, respectable jobs express confusion about things that make me wonder how long it's been since they've had a conversation with anyone making less than $100,000 a year. These vexing puzzles include:

- Why do American employers complain they can't find good workers to fill open positions?
- Why has the life expectancy of middle-aged white Americans fallen off a cliff in the past decade?
- Why is the country ready to riot over jobs—immigrants taking them, trade deals killing them, Wall Street destroying them?
- Why are depression and anxiety so widespread when this is one of the best times to be alive in history?
- Why do people vote against their self-interest?
- If the data says everything's so great, why is America *freaking the fuck out?*

You can make a lot of money explaining away the gap between data and reality in ways that flatter puzzled wealthy people. But if you've had a service job in the past decade, I'll bet that some of the answers are probably as obvious to you as why millennials aren't buying yachts. I'll spend the next few hundred pages trying to make it just as obvious to all you readers, but the short answer? The bottom half of America's labor market *lives* in the weeds. *All the time.*

And the weeds are a terribly toxic place for human beings. The weeds make us crazy. The weeds make us sick. The weeds destroy family life. The weeds push people into addiction. The weeds will literally *kill you.* And people fortunate enough to have good jobs making policy or writing op-eds seem to have no idea how crippled a life with no escape from the weeds is.

When was the last time you asked permission to go to the bathroom? Would you panic over running two minutes late? Is it normal to be constantly monitored at work, to have everything you do timed by the second? When did you last wear a uniform, or have food thrown at you? When's the last time you sold something to pay a bill? Do you have to wait to be searched for stolen goods after you leave work? Have you ever considered DIY dental surgery? Have you gone to work sick because you can't afford to take unpaid time off? Have you had to supply a doctor's note to prove you deserve that unpaid time off? Have you recently overdrawn your checking account, or had all your credit cards declined, or put exactly ten bucks of gas in your car?

Nearly everyone with influence in this country, regardless of political affiliation, is incredibly insulated from how miserable and dehumanizing the daily experience of work has gotten over the past decade or two. Many have *never* had a service job. If I were to give my "in the weeds" poll to everyone with political clout—the donor class, lobbyists, politicians, academics, think tankers, media people—I'd bet everything I own that only a few would know the waitress definition.*

Paul Ryan *might* be an exception. The former Speaker of the House often plays up the time he spent in food service as a young man, particularly the summer he worked at McDonald's, in 1986, as a high school sophomore.

"When I was flipping burgers at McDonald's, when I was standing in front of that big Hobart machine washing dishes, or waiting tables, I never thought of myself as stuck in some station in life," Ryan once told a crowd. "I thought to myself, *I'm the American Dream.*"

But work has changed a lot since 1986. The insane technological advances of the past decades have turned *time to lean* and *time to clean* from subjective things determined by a human manager to objective quantities determined by computers that calculate, monitor, and min-max every second of workers' time on the clock.

A modern McDonald's job, for example, isn't the leisurely activity implied by "flipping burgers." Fast food today is *intense.* In McDonald's phone-book-size operations and training manual, every task has a target time in seconds, as in the assembly of a burger:

---

* My own few years of informal polling support this.

Target order display screen reaction time: 5 seconds.
Target toast time: 23 seconds.
Target sandwich assembly time: 22 seconds.
Target sandwich wrapping time: 14 seconds.
Target order assembly time: 16 seconds.

"Guests should wait no longer than 60 seconds from the time the order is being totaled until the order is presented," the manual advises, and the total time between a guest approaching the counter and receiving her food should never be more than three and a half minutes.

Until pretty recently, it was much too difficult to track and enforce guidelines this specific. Today, though, monitoring equipment integrated into the tools workers use to do their jobs can clock and track nearly any task a worker does in real time. And the street runs both ways—those same systems can be set to harass, nag, startle, or otherwise trigger a worker's stress response every time she lags behind the desired pace. (The next time you're in a busy McDonald's, for example, note the maddening, near-constant beeping of alarms.)

Or look at the copy in a sales brochure for HM Electronics, a major supplier of these sorts of micromonitoring computer business systems for McDonald's and other massive fast-food chains:

> Speed-of-service timers connected to prominent wall-mounted displays give employees the opportunity to compete against the clock and deliver orders within management-set goals. Large timer displays visible to employees help create a greater sense of urgency in completing orders....Incentives and friendly competition among crew members can actually make their jobs more enjoyable and challenging while improving customer satisfaction and increasing sales. By reviewing the timer reports, managers and operators can evaluate employee performance and make the necessary changes.

"Necessary changes" is some pretty amazing business-speak—and who doesn't love an opportunity to compete against the clock and their coworkers for minimum wage?

The other big advance that's made life miserable for low-wage workers is algorithmic scheduling. Work schedules that used to be drawn up by managers now rely heavily on algorithms that analyze historical data to predict exactly how much business a store can expect in the upcoming week. As it's most accurate with the most recent data, this means many workers' schedules vary wildly week to week and are made and posted the day before they start—making it impossible to plan anything more than a week in advance.

Businesses also save a ton of money by scheduling the absolute minimum number of workers to handle the predicted business. And they save even more by scheduling slightly *fewer* people than can handle the predicted work at a reasonable pace. If workers can push themselves to cover the duties of a sick coworker, doesn't that just mean they're not giving it 100 percent the rest of the time? Why can't they work that efficiently *every* shift?

The answer's obvious if you've covered for a sick coworker at a fast-paced job—because you're stuck in the weeds the entire day, and just because you can put up with a miserable day once in a while doesn't mean that the weeds are a sustainable place to live.

From a boss's point of view, though, the weeds are where workers *should* be—at maximum productivity, all day, every day.

The white-collar world tends to be the focus of national conversations about stress and overwork—probably because the people with the clout to affect that conversation socialize with far more lawyers than fast-food or retail workers. Tons of jobs in the white-collar world *are* extremely stressful and closely timed, of course. I shudder thinking of a friend at a big Manhattan law firm whose time is billed in six-minute intervals, or of Paul Ryan, who until recently had one of the most miserable jobs I can imagine. So I can understand why those people might look back on "flipping burgers" as a low-stakes, low-stress breeze. I mean, until recently, my own mental image of service work had fossilized at the last time I held one, too.

But when I look at the favored policies of Paul Ryan and people like him, I see an understanding of "flipping burgers" that's thirty years out of date.*

"What [the left is] offering people is a full stomach and an empty soul," Ryan said in a 2016 speech about how social safety net programs deny

* And that's with every benefit of the doubt for good intentions.

Americans the opportunity for that thing my dad once told me was the key to a happy life—the self-respect and satisfaction that can only come from hard work. "People don't just want a life of comfort," said Ryan. "They want a life of dignity."

And I *do* get that. There *is* a spiritual reward in hard work. I've been lucky enough to have found a career where I *do* find meaning and dignity in my work, so I get to experience it. But in getting out of the service sector, I've been largely insulated from a decade of technological work speedup. So, by definition, have politicians, pundits, donors, lobbyists, and *New York Times* columnists.

And so we offer advice like my dad gave me: Be the best. Take pride in working harder than everyone else. Go the extra mile. Ask for something to mop. And we think it's useful.

As a culture, we put far too much blind trust in data and technology.* Math and logic are beautiful languages. But it's *so* pretentious to pretend that they have adequate vocabulary to accurately describe a human, much less whether a human is happy or miserable. Our brains are the most complicated things in the known universe, with a hundred billion neurons making connections in a mind-bogglingly complex web that constantly changes. Our levels of technology aren't remotely close to being able to accurately describe that mess, and they won't be for a very long time.† Numbers and statistics just aren't up to communicating how something *feels,* even though that's often extremely important information.

That's why I decided to go experience this brave new world myself—so readers can get an idea of what the modern experience of low-wage work *feels* like. I went to work at an Amazon warehouse, a call center, and a McDonald's—three places that are fairly representative of the future of work in America. I spent between one and two months at each, and I worked

---

* Nothing wrong with those things, of course! By the time I started scooping ice cream, I'd maxed out the math classes at my high school, and I've always found the tidiness of problem sets to be a bit of a relief compared to the chaos of things like writing and makeouts and . . . you know, *life.*

† I'm married to a neuroscientist, and the number of things about the brain where the scientific consensus is still ¯_(ツ)_/¯ is *astonishing.*

them for real, with every ounce of my Dad-infused work ethic. And at each one, productivity-enforcing technology constantly corralled me and my coworkers into the weeds like a sheepdog snapping at a herd's heels.

Working in an Amazon warehouse outside Louisville, Kentucky, I walked up to sixteen miles a day to keep up with the rate at which I was supposed to pick orders. A GPS-enabled scanner tracked my movements and constantly informed me how many seconds I had left to complete my task.

Working at a call center in western North Carolina, I was lectured about how using the bathroom too often is the same thing as stealing from the company, and had the minutes I spent in the bathroom tracked in a daily report sent to my supervisor.

Working at a McDonald's in downtown San Francisco, we were underscheduled to the point of a constant, never-ending line of customers—everyone worked at the frantic speed of those in-the-weeds waitresses of my youth all shift, nearly every shift.

I did plenty of research beforehand, and I'd heard *crazy* things about how stressful each job would be—each in its own special way, like Tolstoy's unhappy families. But at each of them, technology made it impossible to escape the weeds. And every time, my thorough research totally failed to prepare me for how dehumanizing the job *felt.*

We're at a strange point in the history of work. Automation of most jobs is only a decade or two away, and human workers increasingly have to compete with computers, algorithms, and robots that never get tired, or sick, or depressed, or need a day off.

Still, in industries that rely on skills that robots still aren't great at—fine motor control, speech and pattern recognition, empathy—the cheapest option is still low-wage human workers. And so many employers demand a workforce that can think, talk, feel, and pick stuff up like humans—but with as few needs outside of work as robots. They insist their workers amputate the messy human bits of themselves—family, hunger, thirst, emotions, the need to make rent, sickness, fatigue, boredom, depression, traffic—or at least keep them completely at bay.

I call these *cyborg jobs*—I have to have something to use as shorthand—and they make up an increasing slice of the American labor market, including most of the postrecession job growth. With labor power crippled by the last few decades of US policy, low-wage workers today have a strong-bordering-on-mandatory incentive to crush those unuseful human parts of themselves down to atomic size. And the pressure's starting to reach unmanageable levels.

How many cyborg jobs are there? It's hard to get good numbers on something that vague, but the statistic I find most convincing comes from a 2013 paper out of Oxford University.[1] The authors tried to calculate how many and what kinds of jobs were so highly routinized that it'd be very easy to replace their human workers with computers or robots—that is, "occupations mainly consisting of tasks following well-defined procedures that can easily be performed by sophisticated algorithms."

They concluded these employed about 47 percent of the US workforce.

So what does "in the weeds" mean to you?

To people with education and influence, "in the weeds" is something academic, about small, unimportant details. It's the footnotes. It's something you observe from the outside.

To everybody else, "in the weeds" is something you experience. It's something you feel. It's your *life*.

It's easy to make fun of that righteously indignant teenager at her first job. Readers to whom this all seems obvious may find the adult me just as naive. I was shocked by the pain-medication vending machines at Amazon, for example, while people familiar with warehousing work might roll their eyes. That's fine. For you, this book may be useful as an exploration of how much better people have it on the other side. Because *every* white-collar person I've mentioned those vending machines to was just as horrified—and they wouldn't put up with any of this for a *second*.

PART ONE

AMAZON

One Month to Christmas

The first time I set foot on the main concourse of Amazon fulfillment center* SDF8, I'm so awestruck I actually stop walking to stare, neck craned back. I've always been fascinated by man-made things so huge they look unnatural—cruise ships, oil derricks, nuclear cooling towers—and SDF8 definitely flips that switch. It feels like walking into an airline hangar. Overhead, a banner that must be as tall as my house hangs from the ceiling, proclaiming WORK HARD. HAVE FUN. MAKE HISTORY.

Amazon.com went live on July 16, 1995, selling books out of a two-hundred-square-foot basement room in an industrial area of Seattle that had once been used for band practice and still had SONIC JUNGLE spraypainted on the door.

By 1997, as founder Jeff Bezos was trying to find funders for Amazon's IPO, the warehouse had relocated to a 93,000-square-foot space on Seattle's Dawson Street. Still, investors were skeptical about Bezos's business plan. "If you're successful, you're going to need a warehouse the size of the Library of Congress," Bezos remembers one man explaining before turning him down.

The modern Library of Congress, the largest library in the world, contains 2.1 million square feet, according to the National Park Service. The

* Amazon is really into giving Amazon-specific names to normal things—it's not a warehouse, it's a *fulfillment center.* You're not a worker, you're an *associate* or an *Amazonian.*

fulfillment center I'm standing in alone contains more than 2.5 million square feet of storage space, and, as of 2019, when this book will first be published, it won't even be in the top ten biggest of Amazon's 175-odd fulfillment and sortation centers in the US.

I knew the numbers about how massive SDF8 was. The actual building is twenty-five acres, thirty if you include the truck bay. It's as long as seven New York blocks, has more than four times the interior space of the world's largest cruise ship, and can hold thirty million items.

But no statistic could have prepared me for actually being here. It's not just big like a cruise ship—it's big like a landscape. Overhead, a Seussian maze of conveyor belts crisscrosses four stories of airspace. Yellow bins glide along them like boats on a lazy river; for unclear reasons, some occasionally appear to hit rapids and shoot off in another direction or go corkscrewing down into a massive two-story machine* squatting at the center of the warehouse like something out of *Akira*. Workers scuttle around its outer levels, ducking in and out of tunnels through the machinery. All over, railings, stairs, and pieces of equipment are painted the same shade of yellow as the bins, giving the place a palette of concrete, steel, and daffodil.

Even the concourse is crowded, and it has to be twenty feet wide. My gawking has started to disrupt traffic, and, embarrassed, I merge back into the confused herd of new hires. We're walking in a long train from the on-site temp office, where we've just received lanyards and white ID badges with our names and photos, to . . . somewhere.

Less confused people with blue ID badges—the mark of the full-time "Amazonian"—flow around us. Most of the year, roughly two-thirds of the more than three thousand workers who keep SDF8 running twenty-four hours a day are "blue badges," while a third are "white badges" like me—temps hired through Integrity Staffing Solutions.

But right now it's "peak"—the crazy holiday season between Black Friday and Christmas when Amazon's business increases exponentially and fulfillment centers hire massive numbers of seasonal workers through a few

* I'll later learn that this is the huge outbound packing complex, where items are put into boxes and shipped.

associated temp agencies like Integrity.* There's maybe a couple hundred of us starting this cold morning.

SDF8 doesn't look like much from the outside. Stuck in the enormous shift-change traffic jam this morning, I could just make out the corner of a big beige warehouse in the predawn darkness, looking no different from the many, many big beige warehouses around here. The southern tip of Indiana, right across the Ohio River from Louisville, Kentucky, is a *logistics hub*—that's an area with a cluster of warehouses at some crossroads of air, truck, train, and river shipping routes. "Locating in Louisville gives your company the ability to move your products to 80% of the world's population in less than 48 hours" is the pitch from the city's economic development group. FedEx, UPS, and the postal service have big facilities here; so do eBay, Caterpillar, Wayfair, and many, many others. The ideal logistics hub also has lots of cheap space, offers business tax breaks, and is home to a lot of underemployed people who used to work in manufacturing.†

The train of newbies keeps walking, now passing an area where hundreds and hundreds of those yellow bins are stacked in shoulder-high towers. Each bin is roughly big enough to hold a small woman with her knees drawn up to her chest, and I immediately, *desperately* want to ride one around the conveyor belts like a roller coaster. Later, when I get out into the mod for real, I'll note that every potential boarding point for a conveyor-belt joyride has several dire signs warning that it will result in the joyrider's gruesome death, so I guess I'm not the only one.‡

And speaking of dumb ideas, I'm now walking while staring straight up at the conveyor belts, so I walk directly into the man in front of me as we bottleneck at a door. "SORRY! SO SORRY!" I yell-apologize, trying to

---

* Around this time, Amazon had 222,000 total employees and announced they'd be creating an additional 100,000 temp positions for peak.

† SDF8, for example, was built in 2012 on the site of the former Indiana Army Ammunition Plant, which made munitions until the Pentagon closed it in 1992.

‡ Reading *The Everything Store*—Brad Stone's incredibly well-researched history/biography of Amazon/Jeff Bezos (New York: Little, Brown, 2013), I'm jealous to read that in a Nevada fulfillment center, "a worker preparing to quit hoisted himself onto a conveyor belt and took a long joyride through the facility. He was subsequently escorted out the door."

speak loud enough to be heard over the din. SDF8 isn't *painfully* loud, but it's almost impossible to hear anything else, like a white-noise machine cranked up to 11. The guy, a tall black man in his early twenties, turns and flashes a grin with a gaping hole where his front teeth used to be. "IT'TH OKAY, I'M THTILL ATHLEEP, TOO," he shouts back as we filter into a room already packed with more new temps.

The chatter in here is almost as loud as the machinery outside. There's way more temps than chairs; lots of people are sitting on the floor. Harried-looking managers pop in every few minutes to grab a random dozen people, apparently forming new training groups.

I housed a coffee on the way here and have had to pee for more than an hour. At the rate they're going, I figure I'll probably have time to find a bathroom without getting in trouble. So I slip back out onto the concourse, feeling like I'm cutting class, and peer around. Way, way off in the distance, I think I see a ladies' room symbol and start walking briskly in that direction, noting landmarks to use as bread crumbs on my way back.

Here's an immense bulletin board.

Here's another group of white badges, some of whom I think I recognize, doing simple stretches in unison.

Here's another banner: WORK HARD. HAVE FUN. MAKE HISTORY.

Just three days ago, I said goodbye to my husband and friends in Philadelphia and drove twelve hours to Louisville. The next morning, I walked into an Integrity Staffing outpost in a beat-up strip mall. The morning after that was orientation. And now... I'm actually *here*. It's surreal.

I had a lot of reasons for choosing Amazon, but the biggest one is that, though the company is enormous and its owner is probably the richest man in the world, its blue-collar facilities are like black boxes. Even a very curious researcher eventually has to give up and accept that everything written about Amazon's blue-collar workers comes from a very, very small amount of original reporting.

The first piece to draw attention was a 2011 exposé[1] by Spencer Soper of the Allentown *Morning Call* after workers in a cluster of Pennsylvania fulfillment centers started passing out by the dozens during a heat wave. Soper worked around Amazon's refusal to talk to him by tracking down and speaking with twenty workers and making FOIA requests, which turned up OSHA complaints like this one:

> On July 25, a security guard at the Amazon warehouse called OSHA and said the temperature exceeded 110 degrees. The guard reported seeing two pregnant women taken to nurses and that Amazon would not open garage doors to help air circulation. "They do have ice pops going around and water everywhere," the guard reported.

One detail that shocked many readers was that Amazon's response to the heat wave involved hiring ambulances to hang around on-site:

> Amazon arranged to have paramedics parked in ambulances outside, ready to treat any workers who dehydrated or suffered other forms of heat stress. Those who couldn't quickly cool off and return to work were sent home or taken out in stretchers and wheelchairs and transported to area hospitals.
>
> And new applicants were ready to begin work at any time.... The supply of temporary workers keeps Amazon's warehouse fully staffed without the expense of a permanent workforce that expects raises and good benefits.

The next peek inside fulfillment centers was "I Was a Warehouse Wage Slave: My Brief, Backbreaking, Rage-Inducing, Low-Paying, Dildo-Packing Time Inside the Online-Shipping Machine." The 2012 first-person account in *Mother Jones*[2] detailed the week reporter Mac McClelland spent working in a warehouse for "Amalgamated Product Giant Shipping Worldwide Inc.," generally understood to be lawsuit-avoidant shorthand for Amazon:

> The culture is intense, an Amalgamated higher-up acknowledges at the beginning of our training.... We don't *want* to be so intense, the higher-up says. But our customers demand it.... The gal conducting our training reminds us again that we cannot miss any days our

> first week. There are *NO* exceptions to this policy. She says to take Brian, for example, who's here with us in training today. Brian already went through this training, but then during his first week his lady had a baby, so he missed a day and he had to be fired.... Okay? Everybody turn around and look at Brian. Welcome back, Brian. Don't end up like Brian.

Then there was a 2015 piece from the investigative wing of the *Huffington Post* titled "The Life and Death of an Amazon Warehouse Temp."[3] It looks at the circumstances around the death of twenty-nine-year-old Jeff Lockhart Jr., an Integrity temp who collapsed while picking at a fulfillment center in Virginia and later died of heart failure.

And that was... pretty much it.

Frustrated, I started delving into Amazonian forums online, reaching out to dozens of people. Nearly all of them truly hated working for Amazon. However, they said, those few pieces hadn't quite captured why fulfillment centers were, as one man put it, such an "existential shithole."

They tended to see the mainstream media's focus on unsafe work conditions and low wages as really off base, for one thing. Everyone said Amazon was strict bordering on obsessive about safety—"It was actually pretty annoying"—and that Amazon paid significantly better than less safe warehouse jobs in their area. "When I see people saying, 'Oh, Amazon, what a shitty employer,' it really makes me wonder if they have any idea how they compare to almost all other employers of unskilled labor," wrote one worker.

Workers also tended to roll their eyes over the response to the Pennsylvania heatstroke story—specifically, to the idea that this was unusually heinous. Even the highest temperatures mentioned in the *Morning Call* sounded pretty standard (though unpleasant) to people who'd worked in other warehouses. High temperatures in the summer are normal, because it's absurdly impractical to air-condition enormous, unshaded, uninsulated warehouses with big open truck bays.

That's kind of a moot point now, anyway—after the bad publicity, Amazon spent $52 million retrofitting most of its US fulfillment centers with air-conditioning. According to one worker, this is going about as well as the laws of thermodynamics would lead you to expect:

> Amazon installed huge amounts of A/C into all of its warehouses and it took the temperature down, like, two degrees in the summer. Massive waste of money, but they did it anyway to try and avoid headlines like these. Public opinion, even if that opinion is grossly ignorant and misinformed, is more important than money.

Workers said the *Mother Jones* piece got closer to nailing the "existential shithole" aspect, but was still a little misleading—the reporter wasn't used to warehouse work and hadn't stayed anywhere near the two weeks it takes most people to adjust to the workload. Of course her experience was agonizing—*everyone's* first two weeks are agonizing.

And as for poor dead Jeff Lockhart Jr., the delay between someone finding him and the 911 call going out sounded understandable to people who'd done the job Lockhart had. His fulfillment center was a million square feet, almost as big as SDF8, and he'd collapsed pretty far from AMCARE.* And anyway, Amazonians said, people sometimes just... die. Sometimes they die at work. It's a shame that the man had a heart condition, but that one anecdote didn't mean Amazon wasn't one of the safest employers in warehousing.† At least, when it came to obvious things like death.

The real problem, I was told, was the subtler plague of injuries from working through pain for fear of getting fired for low productivity numbers. *That's* where Amazon really stood out—repetitive stress injuries.

"Yes. Yes. Yes. There are lots of repetitive stress injuries," said a man in his early thirties who'd been working as a picker in a Tennessee fulfillment center for three years. "I know people who developed various joint problems working there, and I now sometimes experience discomfort in my knees, which was never the case before."

"I saw plenty of older women who literally could not do their jobs any

---

* Amazonian for "nurse's office."

† For just one comparison, look at the October 2018 *New York Times* investigation of a plague of miscarriages among workers in the warehouses of logistics giant XPO (Jessica Silver-Greenberg and Natalie Kitroeff, "Miscarrying at Work: The Physical Toll of Pregnancy Discrimination," https://www.nytimes.com/interactive/2018/10/21/business/pregnancy-discrimination-miscarriages.html).

longer; their knees were not holding up. Mandatory eleven-hour shifts at a ridiculous pace will do that to you," wrote another former worker. Many others mentioned injuries that lingered long after they left Amazon—particularly a problem for temps, who aren't eligible for workers' compensation.

Still—lots of physical jobs will give you repetitive stress injuries. What was different about Amazon?

"The way they make you feel absolutely downtrodden is something that can't be explained to people who haven't worked there," wrote one woman who worked at a Kentucky fulfillment center in 2012 and 2013 in her early twenties. "People say, 'Well, I've worked for such-and-such warehouse, surely it's not that different—' No, it *is* different. It's downright dehumanizing."

"The first time I worked there was so soul-sucking I found myself nearly crying in my car right before I was supposed to walk in," said a man who'd worked as a packer in another Kentucky fulfillment center in his early twenties.

"Worst job I've ever had, and I worked at a goddamn McDonald's."

"I've never seen psychological abuse anywhere like I've seen at Amazon."

"The temp agencies that Amazon uses are atrocious. They absolutely treat you like human waste."

"There's no room for getting tired."

"The pay and benefits are usually good, but it's just not worth it if you don't like being a complete robot."

Everyone agreed that the over-the-top stress of Amazon came from the unrelenting emphasis on "making rate," or hitting your daily individual productivity goals, paired with the company's uncanny ability to monitor workers in real time.

When you clock in at Amazon, the first thing you do is grab a scan gun—a bit like a scanner you'd see at the grocery, but with an LCD screen that tells you what task to do next and starts counting down the seconds you have left to do it. It also tracks your location by GPS—and you take it everywhere with you, even the bathroom. Failure to stay ahead of the countdown—to *make rate*—was grounds for termination, regardless of why.

"Anyone not getting the numbers they want to see, they get rid of them," wrote one worker. "And by get rid of them, I mean deactivate their cards, so they turn up for work and can't enter the building."

"You're at a dead sprint your entire shift," wrote another picker, one of many who said their rates were often set unrealistically high, which forced them to spend entire ten- and eleven-hour shifts in the weeds. "I was a young, average-shaped male, and while I could do it, it was not easy."

"Only one or two employees a day, out of forty, makes rate in the department I work in," wrote another, saying managers sometimes would "revoke talking privileges until people start making rate."

"The job is hard on your body, the company pays as little as it can get away with, and the raise schedule for hourly workers is the worst of any company I have worked for, including big, bad Walmart," wrote another. "Amazon doesn't really treat its workers any better than Walmart, yet largely escapes the negative publicity."

Several other people compared Amazon unfavorably to Walmart, which has overtaken McDonald's as popular shorthand for "the worst possible employer."

Simon Head's 2013 book, *Mindless,* on the rise of productivity-enforcing technologies, spends a whole chapter just on Amazon and Walmart. "When I first did research on Walmart's workplace practices in the early 2000s," Head writes, "I came away convinced that Walmart was the most egregiously ruthless corporation in America."

> In its analysis of the growth of US labor productivity between 1995 and 2000...the McKinsey Global Institute found that just over half that growth took place in two sectors, wholesale and retail, where Walmart "caused the bulk of the productivity acceleration through ongoing managerial innovation that increased competition intensity and drove the diffusion of best practice."

That is, if you had to compete with Walmart, you had to adopt their "best practice" methods of dealing with your own workers if you wanted to stay in business. One of those "managerial innovations" Barbara Ehrenreich mentions in the Walmart chapter of *Nickel and Dimed* is a crusade to rebrand any employee down time as "time theft" and eliminate it entirely. Back in the late '90s, when Ehrenreich did her research, down time monitoring had to be done by humans, like her one manager whose pet peeve was "workers chatting with each other." A decade later, in 2010, Walmart installed an automated monitoring system called Task Manager, which sounds very similar to workers' descriptions of Amazon's scanner system.*

Today, "Amazon's system of employee monitoring is the most oppressive I have ever come across," writes Head. But it's puzzling—worker satisfaction at both Amazon and Walmart is very low. And, at least anecdotally, workers complain about a lot of the same things. Still, Amazon consistently places near the top of lists of the most admired and respected companies in the world, while Walmart never does. Why?

The Everything Store reprints an interesting memo on this topic, titled "Amazon.love," from Jeff Bezos to his senior staff. At the time, Walmart was in the middle of yet another PR crisis over their labor practices, and Bezos mused about why that was:

> "Some big companies develop ardent fan bases, are widely loved by their customers, and are even perceived as cool," [Bezos] wrote. "For different reasons, in different ways and to different degrees, companies like Apple, Nike, Disney, Google, Whole Foods, Costco and even UPS strike me as examples of large companies that are well-liked by their customers."
>
> On the other end of the spectrum, he added, companies like Walmart, Microsoft, Goldman Sachs, and ExxonMobil tended to be feared. Bezos postulated that this second set of companies was viewed, perhaps unfairly, as engaging in exploitative behavior. He . . . applied his usual analytic sensibility to parse out why some companies were loved and others feared.

Bezos then brainstormed a list of traits that make the public think of a company as "cool" or "uncool."† Uncool things: defeating tiny guys,

* Actually, Amazon's early supply-chain and warehousing systems were designed by a former Walmart executive—one of so many high-level execs Amazon poached that Walmart sued, demanding that Amazon "stop targeting Wal-Mart associates and vendors in an effort to duplicate proprietary business systems."

† His point-by-point analysis of cool and uncool reminds me a *lot* of being a thirteen-year-old weirdo trying to logic her way out of the bottom tier of the middle-school hierarchy.

rudeness, conquerors, hypocrisy, mercenaries, pandering. Cool things: the young, explorers, inventing, being polite, taking risks, empowering others, thinking big, authenticity, and *winning*—especially when you're defeating bigger, unsympathetic guys.

Bezos concluded that the most important thing was a public *perception* of the company as a scrappy little guy, a pioneer and inventor rather than a conqueror or a bully. "I actually believe the four 'unloved' companies are inventive as a matter of substance," he wrote. "But they are not *perceived* as inventors and pioneers. It is not enough to be inventive—that pioneering spirit must also come across and be perceivable by the customer base."

Bezos is describing exactly the kind of popular fetish for technology that puzzled me about the support for Uber among so many people who identify as progressives—the idea that innovation, efficiency, and productivity are equivalent to *good*.

And Amazon, like many Silicon Valley juggernauts, *has* managed to retain a public image of the gutsy, innovative startup it once was, even as it eats the lunches of "big, unsympathetic guys" like Walmart.*

Walmart was the apex predator of the '90s and '00s. Today, there's no question that Amazon's taken that crown. Warehousing jobs have started to replace retail jobs in the US as more and more purchases take place online, and Amazon's productivity-enforcing methods will spread across the low-wage labor market of the next couple of decades if they're not constrained, just like Walmart's did.

The situation for Amazon's blue-collar workers at present, then, is a real, honest look at that "future of work" everybody's so interested in. But journalists can't just wander into a fulfillment center to check out the working conditions. Most fulfillment centers are pretty remote, and security is tight—you can't get through the entry turnstiles without an Amazon ID badge or an escort.

It is, however, pretty easy to get a job in a fulfillment center.

A few days from now, when I'm out in the mod on my own, I'll encounter my very first "modesty-wrapped" dildo. For whatever reason, most sexually

* Just a few months before my first day at SDF8, Amazon's market value surpassed Walmart's for the first time. Coverage at the time noted, "You know you're dealing with a real Goliath when it makes Walmart look like David."

explicit products at SDF8 get "modesty-wrapped," or shrink-wrapped in opaque black plastic so workers can't see what's inside. But—come on. I'm not an idiot. I can tell when I'm holding a dildo.

I'll encounter a lot of modesty-wrapped items at SDF8, and *every time* I'm struck with a maddening desire to rip off the black plastic and see what's inside. That's just kind of how I work—I've always had a perverse curiosity that grows in proportion to how deliberately opaque a thing is, whether that thing is a sex toy or the work conditions in Amazon's fulfillment centers.

Companies like Amazon that are *loved*—particularly when they've got that sleek Silicon Valley gleam—just don't get as much scrutiny as companies like Walmart. People with influence are way likelier to be delighted by the speed of Amazon Prime than to know a single person who works somewhere like SDF8. Geography and the no-trespassing policy add more layers of opacity. *Amazon has modesty wrapping*—and it knows it.

When I finally get to a bathroom, I'm pleasantly surprised to find that it's big, and even *clean*. Like, Canadian rest stop clean. I dash into an open stall, relieved. A flyer on the back of the door informs me there will be free pizza at lunch today. *Wow, that's pretty cool of them,* I think, surprised at how much . . . *nicer* everything's been than I'd expected. Then, as I reach for the toilet paper, I notice three messages scratched into the metal of the wall-mounted feminine-product disposal bin:

I HATE THIS PLACE
ME TOO
THIS PLACE SUCKS
DONKEY BALLS

I will think of this little found poem many, many more times before Christmas.

Two months ago, I was senior staff writer at *Philadelphia City Paper,* a small alt-weekly.

One month ago, *Philadelphia City Paper* was sold to a competitor for scrap. We put together a farewell issue on a week's notice, then were all laid off.

I'd wanted to get inside a fulfillment center for a while; suddenly, I was unemployed at the perfect time to do it. Even if nothing came of it, I figured, I *would* at least bank a couple thousand bucks. My ever-supportive husband, Rajiv, told me he could cover our modest mortgage alone for a while, but the idea only made financial sense if I could finagle a free place to stay for a month.

One week ago, I got an offer I couldn't refuse. After a Thanksgiving conversation about the idea, a friend told me his aunt Sue had volunteered a spare bedroom half an hour south of Louisville—rent-free, no questions asked.

As we texted back and forth, Sue warned me that the house would be pretty full—it was her, her husband, and their dog plus her daughter, Katie, who'd moved back in for a few months to take care of *her* new baby daughter, Kaylee. There would be a lot of family around for the holidays and the big Kentucky-Louisville game, too, she texted, presenting this as a potential negative. But even the smallest bedroom of a home with a family and a dog and vicious basketball trash talk sounded infinitely better than spending the holidays alone in a five-star hotel.

Sue's house was only forty-five minutes from fulfillment center SDF8, which seemed to have everything I was looking for—it was *huge,* and only a couple of years old, and had a workamping program. Plus, I'd found some intriguing rumors about a recent bomb threat.

So, four days ago, I packed my car's trunk with books, clothes, and groceries and hit the road for Kentucky.

It's already midnight by the time I finally get to Aunt Sue's; I'd wasted an hour lost on dark country roads with no cell reception. Thankfully, Katie's still up to let me in. She's twenty-five, with a gentle Kentucky drawl and hair the exact shade of red I've always wanted. We briefly discuss our mutual love of her cousin Charlie, an old housemate of mine. A goofy-looking tan dog bumbles around underfoot, looking as if someone sewed the head of a beagle onto the body of a much larger Labrador.

"You'll be in my brother's room," Katie says, beckoning me down the stairs to the basement den, where her boyfriend is holding sleeping baby Kaylee—tiny, adorable, and also red-haired—while watching Fox News on very low volume. He carefully mutes the TV to say hello; onscreen, Donald Trump silently flails above a banner reading TRUMP ACCUSED OF MOCKING NY TIMES REPORTER'S DISABILITY. As he gingerly hands Kaylee back to her mother, I give a whispered explanation of who I am and what I'm doing here.

"Man, my uncle used to work at Amazon—he *hated* that place," the boyfriend whispers when I'm done. I'll hear some mad-libs version of this from nearly everyone I mention Amazon to around here. In the Louisville area, where there are eight Amazon facilities within an hour's drive, it seems that everybody either knows somebody who hated working for Amazon or hated working there themselves.

Katie's one of the latter. As a teenager, she worked in one of the Zappos warehouses clustered near Louisville until the shoe company was bought by Amazon in 2009 for $1.2 billion. Katie says the hype about Zappos treating its employees famously well wasn't exaggerated; she'd loved working there. But once Amazon took over the warehouses, things got bad, so she quit.

I want to hear more, but my twelve hours on the road catch up to me all at once. Katie leads me to a room off the den with a double bed that used to be her brother's. I want to hear more about Zappos and Amazon, but upon seeing a bed, it's as if someone's pushed my shutdown button. I'm asleep the moment I'm horizontal.

The next morning, I go apply for a job. I ask Katie for advice before I leave, but she just shakes her head and says if I have feet, I'll be fine. Any remaining worries are put to rest by the desperate cluster of signs and banners advertising Amazon jobs at UP TO $13/HR! outside the strip-mall outpost of Integrity Staffing Solutions in downtown Louisville.

My impression of Integrity as a minor fiefdom of Amazon is confirmed inside. *Everything* here is about Amazon, from the posters on the wall to the video on the TV. The video, in which real Amazonians testify to how much they love their jobs, is probably meant to counter Amazon's word-of-mouth reputation, but it's pretty ineffective given that the descriptions of the fantastic health insurance segue into alarming descriptions of how much pain I should expect to be in.

"Now, let's be real—this is going to hurt," says one woman. "You'll be tired every day, your feet will hurt, your back will hurt—everything's gonna hurt. But you get used to it." One older woman says she lost twenty pounds from all the walking, posing this as a side benefit.

I look around, hoping to make eyebrows with another applicant about how weird the video is, but the half dozen other people in the waiting area are deep in their paperwork. Maybe twenty minutes later, I'm called up and directed to the first of five computer stations in an hour-long gauntlet of standardized tests.

First, I type in my real name, information, and employment history. Next, I verify that I haven't been convicted of any felonies, particularly theft, about a dozen times. Then I check boxes affirming I'm physically capable of the job requirements, such as:

- *Walking 5 to 15 miles or more (8–12 hrs) per day*
- *Frequently lifting and moving items weighing on average 25–30 pounds during the majority of the workday*
- *Climbing and descending four stories of regular stairs*
- *Regular bending, crouching kneeling and reaching above the head*

Next are still more boxes to check, as I agree that I understand a long list of job-expectation torpedoes:

- *It is necessary for our employees to be flexible in their work schedules*
- *You may have to work a schedule that is not your first choice*
- *Working nights, weekends, and holidays may be required*
- *Overtime is often required (sometimes on very short notice)*
- *You may have to work overtime when it is not convenient*
- *Temperature in the warehouse varies between 60 and 95 degrees and will occasionally exceed 95 degrees*
- *Work schedules are subject to change without notice*

- *We operate 24 hours 7 days a week. If a holiday falls on your scheduled work-day you will be required to work it*
- *Our ability to provide excellent customer service for our customers during the months of November and December is critical for the success of our company. We do not typically allow any scheduled time off such as vacation or personal days during these months*

After verifying one last time that I really, truly, absolutely have not been convicted of any felonies of any kind, I'm directed to the next station for a battery of questions about myself.

On half of these, the correct answer is obvious. To what degree is it okay to take a longer break than you're permitted? Pretend to be sick when you don't feel like working? Does everyone steal from work once in a while, Y/N?

But the other half are oddly philosophical, and kind of hard. *Do* I believe people are generally honest? *Is* it okay to tell a small lie if nobody is hurt by it? As I click my way through the endless questions, I picture my answers rattling around in some remote algorithm like dice in a cup.

Finally I get to which job I'd prefer, though I'm almost certainly going to be put in picking or packing regardless of how I answer. Packing is standing in place for ten hours, grabbing orders off a conveyor belt, and sealing them into shipping boxes; picking is walking around finding the items people have ordered and sending them off on a conveyor belt to be packed. Picking is generally regarded as the least desirable job at Amazon, with packing a close second.

My busted right knee can tolerate lots of walking much better than lots of standing. Plus, as I understand it, packing stations are offset so you can't talk to each other, whereas I assume you sometimes run into other pickers out in the shelving system. I select picking as my first choice.

This mildly surprises the woman I'm eventually called up to speak with half an hour later. She shrugs as if to say "Your funeral," and asks whether I'm looking for day or night shift—day is 6:30 a.m. to 6:00 p.m.; night is 6:30 p.m. to 6:00 a.m. "Night pays a dollar extra," she adds, but I opt for day's $10.50 an hour. She tells me, somewhat apologetically, that even a volunteer picker who can start tomorrow isn't going to get a schedule with two consecutive days off right away. She hands me a list of potential schedules, out of which having Tuesdays and Thursdays off seems like the least bad option.

And, to my surprise, that's it. My interviewer types as I suck on an oral drug test, then puts it in a biohazard bag and congratulates me, the newest employee of Integrity Staffing. She hands me a folder of documents and tells me orientation is at nine tomorrow, and my first shift will start at 6:30 the morning after that.

"Try to get there early, and *definitely* don't be late," she says. *Don't end up like Brian,* I think.

I'm so paranoid that I get to orientation half an hour early the next morning. The hotel hosting SDF8's orientations is flanked by an RV park and a highway bypass, and the thick fog coming off the nearby Ohio River* makes everything look pretty bleak. Inside, a schedule taped to the wall of the basement-level ballroom identifies my orientation session as the first of three today. I plunk down in a back row and fiddle with my phone as maybe a hundred people gradually filter in, taking up a third of the folding chairs that face a large projection screen.

At 9:00 a.m. on the dot, a man with a Cuban accent and endless nervous energy bounds to the front, dims the lights, and calls up his first slide—the words WORK HARD. HAVE FUN. MAKE HISTORY.

"Another day in paradise!" he says cheerily. "Good morning, everybody! How are you doing?" *Great,* some people respond, less cheerily. The man introduces himself as Miguel and assures us that the day is only going to get greater, because we're going to be learning about Amazon.

Miguel says he came to this country from Cuba† ten months ago and

---

* The Ohio River serves as the dividing line between Kentucky and Indiana; I'll be crossing it every day to get to SDF8, which is in Clarksville, Indiana.

† The Louisville area has seen a huge wave of Cuban immigration over the past decade—there's even a Spanish-language magazine here called *El Kentubano.* I'd guess a third of my fellow newbies were speaking Spanish to one another on our first day. That's the last time I'll see most of them, though—we're sorted into

got a job as a picker at Amazon seven months ago. Since then, he's risen to an office job, in payroll. Well, he adds, at least he'll be starting that job as soon as peak's over and he doesn't have to do two to three orientation sessions a day, which he's been doing for almost two months now. *Ooh, trouble in paradise,* I think.

"The first thing I learned about Amazon is there's *no sitting!*" begins Miguel, pacing back and forth in illustration. "No matter what you're going to be doing in the building, you will *always* be on your feet. You will be walking or standing for eleven hours.

"Yet today you're sitting here, and you're going to get paid! Isn't that nice enough, for a start? That deserves a hand; give them a hand!" We muster some applause for our employer.

The next slide shows a corner of a nondescript beige building. "That will be what you're going to be working in. We call it SFD8, or the Ocho. Now, they call it *fulfillment center**—you know why they call it that way? Because in that building, dreams, desires, wishes are fulfilled." The sacred responsibility of making customers' dreams come true, he tells us gravely, will now be on our shoulders.

Next slide is policies and procedures. "The first one is going to be attendance," says Miguel. "We expect you to work the full shift, including any scheduled overtime. You can expect us to tell you about required overtime as soon as we can, and no later than the start of the lunch break during the shift on the day before.

"Now, some of you might be looking for full-time job opportunities with Amazon. Which I'm not saying you're gonna get. But you *might* get," Miguel says, his tone suggesting that a full-time blue badge is a prize only to be claimed by the übertemp.† The best way to show we really *want* that blue badge, he says, is perfect attendance.

English- and Spanish-language training groups later that morning, and the Spanish-speaking workers seem to get trained for a different set of jobs from the English speakers.

* Nobody who works at Amazon ever uses the *W* word.

† Amazon says it generally converts 10 to 15 percent of temp workers to full-time after peak—that's roughly as selective as Dartmouth, Georgetown, or Cornell.

Miguel directs our eyes to the hotline number on the folder on our chairs. If we're going to be late or sick, we *must* call in at least two hours before the start of our shift. If we're no-call-no-show two days in a row, we won't just be fired—we'll be blacklisted. Our relationship with Amazon will never progress beyond the white badge.

"We will not consider excuses for being late outside of approved exceptions," says Miguel. Temps don't have sick days or vacation: instead, we have a point system that Miguel explains was developed to give us as much freedom with our schedules as possible.

"You have six points: if you're at six points, your assignment with Amazon will end," says Miguel. "Try to keep your points low—that way you will have flexibility in case of an emergency." Miguel clicks forward to a slide listing the many ways we can rack up points.

"Say I'm late to my shift or late returning from lunch less than an hour—how many points do I get?" asks Miguel. *Half,* we chorus, reading the answer off the screen verbatim.

"If it's more than an hour?" *One.*

"Now, if I leave work up to an hour before the end of my shift?" *Half.*

"And if it's over an hour?" *Whole.*

"What if I don't come to work?" *Point and a half.*

"What if I don't come to work and also don't call out?" *Three.*

"If you do not finish your shift and walk off the job without telling anybody?" *Termination.*

"Let's say it's Saturday, 4:00 p.m. You've been working since Tuesday. You think you cannot make it anymore, your feet are killing you, you want to go home. And you're free to go home!" Miguel smiles, spreading his arms wide as if he's Oprah handing us all free cars. "Of course, you will get a point, because you're leaving two hours before the end of your shift. But like I said, the points are there for you to *use.* You can go home." He doesn't bother to say that any time we take off will be unpaid. That, I guess, is obvious to everyone in this shabby hotel ballroom.

I knew that this was how it worked beforehand, but it still catches me a bit off guard. If some HR director at a newspaper had tried to sell me on "being able to stay home sick without pay without getting fired, up to a point" being a legit job perk, I would have laughed him out of the room.

But over the next month, I will be legitimately shocked at how many of my coworkers see Amazon's small allotment of unpaid time off, or UPT, as generous.

There's a few exceptions to the six-point rule—you can get some time excused with a doctor's note or proof of a close relative's death. You can apply in writing in case of other emergencies, but those are very, very rare, Miguel says. "I have a doctor's appointment, I have court—it has to be more serious than that. Use your points."

We will clock in and out by scanning our white badges four times a day. "Lunch is gonna be a thirty-minute break, unpaid, and you will also get two fifteen-minute breaks, paid.

"Now," Miguel asks us, "what is it that you are not going to like about the breaks?"

A former worker raises his hand. "Your break doesn't start once you get out the door. It's your last item you scan—that's where your fifteen minutes starts. And it takes you ten minutes to get out the door, so you've got five minutes to get back and make your first scan."

Miguel nods at this correct answer. "Breaks are measured from last scan to first scan. So if your break starts at ten, then ten is when you make your last scan. And then by 10:12, or 10:13 at the latest, you head back in to your work area.... You know," he pauses, "the easiest thing in the world is taking too long a break."

The former worker pipes up again. "You're gonna get tired and lose track of time."

Miguel nods. "You will be coming back at 10:19, 10:20. If you do that, then—"

"The coach is going to be there. Guaranteed. *Guaranteed,*" the man again interrupts.

"It's more than just guaranteed," says Miguel. "They'll want to know the reason you took those extra few minutes. If this happens for a reason, then you will be fine! But if you don't have a reason, then you will not be fine. You are going to be *fired.*" Miguel seems pleased with this odd turn of phrase, as if he came up with it himself.

"Now, they have asked me to talk about TOT—Time Off Task," he continues. "Say they're paying you to listen to me, but instead of that you're on your phone. Are you on task or off task?" *Off task,* we mumble.

"Or you're talking to your closest neighbor. Are you on task or are you off task?" *Off task.* Miguel smiles encouragingly. "I'm going to put it this way so you can understand how it should be fair on both ends," he tells us.

Say you worked a full forty-hour week, but Amazon only paid you for thirty. Wouldn't they be stealing from you? Wouldn't you be mad? *Yes!* we chorus.

So then doesn't Jeff Bezos have a right to be mad if you're clocked in for forty hours but only actually working for thirty? Aren't you stealing from *him? Yes,* we agree, with less enthusiasm.

And, unlike other places we may have worked, Amazon will *know* if you're only on task for thirty hours. "Amazon knows how your day is spent," Miguel says. The company can track every second of a worker's productivity throughout the day. "We have a saying in Spanish—*Siempre va a te ver.* That means *There's always an eye out there on you.*"

The "eye" isn't cameras—it's the scanner guns former workers talked about, which wirelessly upload your location and how long it's been since your last bar-code scan in real time. If you're going too slow, the scanner will display a message telling you so. If you go too slow too often, a "coach" will come find you to tell you in person.

"Jeff Bezos has a lot of managers to make sure that things work exactly the way he expects them. These managers get reports every day with your Time Off Task. Maybe this report is saying that today, when you were supposed to work eleven hours, you worked eight and a half—and the rest of that time you were talking, you were in the break room, you were doing whatever you were doing that was not exactly what you were being paid for. That time when you're not scanning anything? That will add up."

A bunch of hands shoot up. What if you have to use the bathroom? What if you need to get a drink of water? What if you need help with something? What if you need to go to the nurse?

"I don't say it's about *killing* yourself!" Miguel says, quieting us down. "You're not supposed to have to *kill* yourself. But it's not about killing *time,* either. If you're there killing time, someone will kill... *your assignment.*" He again seems pleased with this odd turn of phrase, and moves on to the topic of safety as if it were an answer.*

"Now, Amazon is committed to providing you a safe working environment," Miguel continues. "But it's *everyone's* responsibility to work in a safe, responsible manner and to call out unsafe situations." Failure to do so, he says, will result in disciplinary action up to and including termination. He then runs through a very long list of the unsafe behaviors that might get you fired—no riding around on the conveyor belts, no running (even if you're late), no horseplay. ("Why? We are not horses! *Right?* So leave horseplay to the horses.")

It's also important to keep the warehouse clean and tidy for safety's sake. Just picking up a scrap of paper on the floor might save someone's day, Miguel says. "I'm not gonna go as far as saying that you're saving somebody's *life,* but you might be saving somebody's *day*—and somebody's paycheck. *Right?* They slip on it, they fall down, they get injured—they don't get a paycheck."

This is one of those weird quirks of the US employment market. If a full-time employee is injured in the course of doing her job, she's eligible for workers' compensation—government-mandated employer coverage of medical costs and money to make up for injury-related lost wages. But freelancers, independent contractors, and seasonal or temp workers—like all of us here for orientation—are just out of luck.

We have a personal responsibility not to injure ourselves by overworking, cautions Miguel. "If you're experiencing pain or discomfort, keep in

* Months after I leave SDF8, the number of minutes workers are allowed to spend in the bathroom is clarified on the huge bulletin board for employee questions and feedback:

Question: "Are we expected to only use the restroom on breaks/lunch? I was told by my manager that he could only excuse 18 mins of my TOT for RR breaks. 18 mins for a 10hr shift is RIDICULOUS. It takes that long for 1 RR break from the 4th floor!"

Answer: "You are welcome to use the restroom whenever needed. It is a suggestion and try to use the restroom around breaks/lunches to reduce the potential for long periods of time away from the work area. 18 mins is the standard time used at this point but we take each situation into consideration."

mind that this might be because you're injured," in which case we should report to AMCARE.

"*But!* You could also just be sore. You *know* you're going to be sore, right?" He raises his eyebrows and gets a weak laugh. "When I first started at Amazon, I was picking for a month and a half, and for a month and a half I was sore. By the end of the week, my whole body was killing me," says Miguel. "So: keep in mind that you're going to be sore. Just push through."

I am again unclear on where the line is between taking responsibility and pushing through. In my limited athletic experience, I've gathered that if you'd say a body part is killing you, you're *not* supposed to push through. You're supposed to ice it and rest.

Miguel also stresses the importance of getting enough rest, though it's still unclear to what degree rest and Time Off Task are the same thing.

"How many hours' sleep do you get every night?" he asks. He starts counting down from eight, asking us to raise our hands at our own number. Most get five or six. Everyone marvels at the one older guy who says he gets nine. "You're the luckiest one I've had here in two months, and I'm in here two orientations a day and sometimes I have 350 in just one of them!" says Miguel to general laughter. "I would love to be able to sleep like that! Give him a hand, everybody!" He gets a warmer round of applause than earlier ones.

Then Miguel pauses, seeming to have lost his train of thought. "The funny thing about it is that, where I come from, they talk about this country as the American Dream. Then we come here and we find out we cannot sleep! *Right?*" He raises his eyebrows again and waits a beat, apparently expecting a laugh. None comes. It's a weird, awkward moment. *Serious trouble in paradise,* I think.

We move on to hazmat protocol, which takes an eternity, then some very '90s videos about discrimination and harassment, then one final review of the long list of offenses that can or will result in termination:

Stealing
Not wearing your badge
Using your badge to swipe in anyone but yourself
Smoking in the building

Stealing
Smoking in the parking lot
Riding the conveyor belts
Failing a randomly administered drug test
Refusing to allow security to search you
Lending someone your badge
Sneaking in a cell phone or MP3 player
Sexual harassment
Stealing
Violence or threats of violence
Bringing weapons, drugs, or alcohol into the warehouse
Being high or drunk while working
Not following safety rules
Stealing

Not stealing is emphasized a *lot.* SDF8's security guards have the right to search us at any time. We aren't allowed to bring anything that's sold by Amazon into the warehouse with us, because how would security be able to tell whether we really owned it? And if we're caught stealing, we won't just be fired—we'll also be fined $500 and handed over to the police.

If any of us worked at SDF8 last year, Miguel says, we'll be happy to hear that they've just gotten rid of the metal detectors at the exits, which makes leaving the building a lot easier these days. The new high-tech replacement system can tell the difference between innocent stuff that used to set off the alarm—car keys, jewelry, change, pens, bras—and forbidden items like cell phones, MP3 players, cameras, flash drives, and memory cards.

He doesn't mention that this change happened soon after Amazon got a lot of bad press over a class-action lawsuit that went to the Supreme Court in 2014. From *Integrity Staffing Solutions, Inc. v. Busk:*

> Petitioner Integrity Staffing Solutions, Inc., required its hourly warehouse workers, who retrieved products from warehouse shelves and packaged them for delivery to Amazon.com customers, to undergo a security screening before leaving the warehouse each day. Respondents, former employees, sued the company alleging...

> they were entitled to compensation...for the roughly 25 minutes each day that they spent waiting to undergo and undergoing those screenings.

Whatever. I'm relieved. One worker I'd emailed with said he'd once set off the metal detector with a single foil gum wrapper, and my right knee's held together with metal screws. I wasn't pleased with the idea of being searched every single day, which would make it hard to bring in a pencil and paper, much less the voice recorder I'd hoped to smuggle in to take notes while walking. But...

Wait—can a security system tell the difference between electronics in a car key fob and electronics in a memory card? I'm pretty sure it can't. I hope beyond hope that this new "high-tech system" is just security theater.

"Now, this is a slide everybody loves the most," Miguel finally says after nearly two hours. "You know why that is? Because *it's the last one!*" It's identical to the first: WORK HARD. HAVE FUN. MAKE HISTORY.

I snap awake when my alarm goes off at 4:00 a.m. the next day. Being up at this hour feels absurd, but I figure it'll give me enough time to shower, dress, have breakfast, drive the forty-five minutes to SDF8, and *still* arrive with half an hour of padding. I walk out the door with my lunchbox and a travel mug of coffee ten minutes ahead of schedule, but my smugness fades as I see that everything, including my car, has been aggressively coated in ice. It's been a mild winter so far, but *of course* it's freezing two hours before sunrise. *You idiot.*

Panic brewing, I start the car, blast the heater, dig out the scraper, and start to hack away at the seemingly impermeable ice. I finally pull out of the driveway fifteen minutes behind schedule.

During the day, the twisty backcountry roads between the McPhersons' and the highway are lovely. Before sunrise, they're a terrifying combination of thick fog, unfamiliar hairpin turns, bad Google Maps connectivity, and ghostly deer sightings. I fall further and further behind schedule, so I speed like a maniac once I get to the highway, which is, thankfully, deserted at this ungodly hour. I wince as I bite into the bed of a fingernail, only now noticing I've spent the last twenty minutes gnawing my nails into stubs. I've made up some lost time as I close in on SDF8, but then Google Maps abandons me in the middle of a confusing traffic circle, and I somehow end up on a highway going the wrong direction.

I literally scream with frustration as I try to get myself turned back around, praying that I haven't screwed this up already. Adrenaline floods my body, wiping away all thoughts except *Don't end up like Brian. Don't end up like Brian. Don't end up like Brian.*

This nail-chewing panic over potentially being five minutes late wasn't part of my newspaper jobs, but I also don't remember it from my service jobs in the late '90s and early 2000s. At the time, a manager would weigh a worker's overall job performance against her reasons for being late and decide whether it's a big deal. Here, judgment is supposedly binary, dispassionate, and automatic—you either clock in on time or you don't.

My phone announces that I've arrived at my destination with seven minutes to spare just as I reach the butt end of an enormous traffic jam. Police lights flash way up ahead—an accident? Maybe my lateness will be overlooked if something's blocking the road and making *everyone* late.

By 6:27, I've inched up to the three squad cars at the entrance to the parking lot. There's no accident. The policemen are directing traffic, like they do every day. *There's 2,500 parking spaces and only two shifts: of course there's a massive traffic jam.*

I find a parking spot blessedly quickly, grab my lunch, and sprint for the on-site Integrity Staffing office, which signs indicate is on the opposite goddamn end of the seven-block-long building. I catch a WORK HARD. HAVE FUN. MAKE HISTORY. sign out of the corner of my eye as I run, right next to a sign strictly prohibiting running in the parking lot.

Here's a moment I won't realize is significant until later: I'm being presented with a choice about which rule to break. I can break the safety rule, keep running, and *maybe* make it on time. Or I can walk the rest of the way and be late, but safe.

Running will *maybe* get me fired. The consequences of being late, I've been told, are automatic. So I make the only logical decision, which is to keep running.

This will be a recurring theme of my month at SDF8.

I stumble into Integrity at 6:32, sweaty and gasping. But as I look around, it's chaos. Dozens of new recruits mill around aimlessly, and everything seems to be moving at the speed of a checked-out DMV. In other circumstances, I'd be irritated that I ran all that way for no reason. But after that horrible, stressful hour in the car, all I feel is relief that I'm not going to end up like Brian.

After an hour of paperwork and waiting in lines, someone comes along to herd several dozen new recruits and me down a corridor. As I step out of the hallway and onto the concourse, I get my first look at the inside of SDF8. Then I go try to find a bathroom.

After I find my way back, I eventually get put into a training group and sent off to "Safety School," where a couple dozen of us spend hours learning and practicing the proper way to do everything—stretch (do it on your own every couple of hours), push a pick cart (use two hands and stop to look both ways at the end of the aisle), lift something heavy (legs, not back; turn, don't twist), pull out a drawer (use a stepstool if it's above shoulder height), escape a fire or tornado (even then, *don't run*), etc.

Finally, we're put into groups of five to go out into the shelves and learn to pick. My trainer is Michelle, a young black woman with two braided pigtails under a pink baseball cap. The machinery is so loud in this part of SDF8 that you have to yell to be heard, so Michelle just gestures for us to follow her and shouts out places as we pass them—the bathroom, the AMCARE medical center, the cafeteria, the other cafeteria, the painkiller vending machine.

Wait, *what?* I pause to peer through the glass and find that this vending machine does indeed seem to be stocked with single-dose foil packets of pills. I have many questions, but don't want to ask them via yelling at the top of my lungs, so I table them and hurry to catch up with the group.

After a couple of minutes, we arrive at a quieter open area at the corner of a four-story shelving system that stretches as far as I can see in two directions. It looks like a vanishing-point drafting exercise, or something drawn by M. C. Escher.

"This"—Michelle points at the shelving system—"is East Mod." The five of us white badges will be picking here most of the time, she says, though we may sometimes be sent to West Mod, on the opposite side of the building.

We introduce ourselves: Jasmine is a quiet black college student who worked peak last year and already knows what she's doing; she wears glasses and radiates competence. Teena is a tiny blond teenager constantly on the lookout for a cousin who's also in here somewhere. Darryl is a skinny black twenty-year-old who just moved to Louisville from Detroit with his mom. He's a big talker and immediately finds a comedy partner in Yolanda, a middle-aged black woman with an even bigger personality. The next two days of training are always teetering on the edge of turning into the Yolanda and Darryl Show. Michelle has to drag the group back on task, but even when she's annoyed by their constant joking, she's clearly as charmed as I am.

"This is the standup area: this is where you all will meet back up whenever we part ways," Michelle says, gesturing to the open area on the edge of the mod. After our two days of training, we'll join all other East Mod pickers here for standup meeting twice a day—at the beginning of the shift and after lunch. She then checks her watch and tells us to go to lunch and meet her back here at 12:30 on the dot.

I'm the only smoker in my group, so I break off and take my lunch toward the outdoor smoking area I saw by the Integrity offices. It takes me five minutes to walk there, and I realize just as I arrive that my cigarettes are still in my purse, all the way back on the other side of the building. It's already 12:10; it'll take ten minutes to get there and back, which would leave five minutes to smoke and eat. As I dither about which I want to do more, smoke or eat, I hear a voice over the chatter talking about how more people at Amazon should practice yoga.

Curious, I sidle up to the picnic table where the yoga preacher and her congregation of three are eating. They're all white, tattooed women around my age—late twenties and early thirties.

"Hi...uh...it's my first day, and I don't know anybody yet. Could I sit with you?" I ask, feeling like I'm back in high school. "And, uh, maybe bum a cigarette from someone? I'll hit you back. I just left them way down there," I say, gesturing at the distant east end of the building.

They laugh and tell me to sit my ass down as the yogi passes me a menthol. I thank her fervently as she introduces herself as Blair. Blair's wiry, with a lot of nervous energy and a pixie cut. She looks down at my lunch—rice with sludgy Indian food from a shelf-stable foil bag. "Oh, my god, *are you a vegan, too?*" She looks disappointed that I'm not. It's apparently a lonely life being vegan in southern Indiana.

All four women are white-badge pickers like me, but in West Mod. They inform me that there's a smoking area on the east side, too. Feeling dumb, I ask what else I should know as a new picker.

"Stretch!" Blair exclaims. "I'm always telling everyone to stretch, but they never listen to me!"

"It gets *really boring* sometimes," says another woman, which everyone immediately confirms.

"Yeah...how do you keep yourself from going nuts?" I ask. This is a common icebreaker at SDF8. A lot of people sing or dance. Blair likes to see how fast she can go.

"Yeah, and you're making the rest of us look bad," says the woman next to her, only half joking. Blair primly says she doesn't care—she's getting that blue badge no matter what.

After lunch, I speedwalk to the other end of the building in time for my first standup meeting, during which a blue badge leads a couple hundred of us in five minutes of stretches while a manager speaks into a megaphone. I don't catch a single word of it, but everybody else seems to get the message when it's time to start. They pick their scanner guns up off the floor and do something that causes a chorus of beeps. Pickers then begin streaming out into the mod, vanishing from view as they go up staircases and turn corners.

After lunch, we learn how to navigate the mod. The first thing you'll do every morning, Michelle says, is grab a scanner gun. She holds up her own. It looks just as it'd been described to me—like a cordless, handheld scanner in a grocery store, but with more buttons and a square LCD screen.

Michelle scans the blue badge hanging from a lanyard around her neck—BEEP—then demonstrates how to push a long sequence of buttons in order to request work. She tells us not to worry if we don't remember it all at first—the sequence is printed on a laminated card in our orientation packets that we can hang off our lanyards.

Michelle's scanner now reads SCAN A NEW TOTE—tote, we learn, is the Amazonian term for one of those omnipresent yellow bins—above an intimidating-looking alphanumeric code:

P-3 A198 D221

This string is the coordinates of the one item among millions we're about to go find, Michelle says. It may look crazy at first, but it's easy if you pretend you're finding someone's apartment. That letter *A* tells you you'll be in East Mod—that's like a state. *P-3* means you'll be on the third floor of the mod—the floors are like different cities. The two three-digit numbers give the apartment building's address—221 198th Street. The *D* means you take the apartment building's elevator up to the fourth floor—you open the fourth drawer from the bottom. Then the item's barcode is like the apartment number.

"Okay, now we're actually going to get a pick cart and learn how to navigate," says Michelle. We follow her up the stairs to the third floor, Yolanda and Darryl joking loudly about how they're never going to get this in a million years and how they need an oxygen mask for all these stairs.

"How you feeling, Emily? You're the only one not complaining," Michelle says. I blush and say I'm just sleepy—and I don't mind walking too much, anyway.* She raises her eyebrows.

"You do? Well, I hate it."

"Yeah? I figured walking would be a lot easier than standing all day," I say.

"Yeah, I agree with that—I could *not* stand in place."

"Do they ever play music in here or anything?" I ask. The mod isn't *quiet,* exactly—the ambient hum of the fans, fluorescent lights, and occasional conveyor belts is actually pretty loud. But it *feels* silent, as if we're at the bottom of the ocean.

Michelle shakes her head—no music.

"So what do you do to keep yourself from going *nuts* out here?" I ask.

---

* I'd actually spent the previous month working my way up to walking eight miles a day all over Philadelphia in my special warehouse shoes, hoping it might make the first weeks less awful.

Michelle laughs, and so does Jasmine. They admit to singing to themselves a lot—plus you do sometimes run into other pickers out in the mod.

"Every once in a while I'll make conversation with somebody about something," says Jasmine, "because people, they'll talk to you about *anything.*" Michelle nods knowingly.

"Like, it gets bottled up?" I say.

"Yeah!" says Jasmine. "It's almost like jail—like, after you've been inside so long—"

"And you can't see the outside," Michelle finishes. "Unless you find a window, which is, like, *impossible.*" We're now pretty deep into the mod, surrounded by thousands of pieces of modular, double-sided, floor-to-ceiling cardboard shelving. It's incredibly visually busy—nearly every surface has a color-coded sign on it. I can't see either end of the corridor we're on. I know if I just walked straight in any direction long enough I'd eventually get to an edge, but it still feels creepy, like you could get lost in here forever.

"Yeah! People will talk about—I mean, *anything* and *everything.* Stuff you pick, stuff you see, events going on...they'll talk about *any* of them," says Jasmine. "Some of them don't know when to stop! It's, like—*okay, I do gotta go pick...*"

I laugh. "You just have to keep moving?"

"Yeah, sometimes you gotta take a walk. You can't just open a book to everybody—they'll keep turning pages."

Michelle shows us taped-off areas where we can find and return pick carts. There's space for one of those omnipresent yellow bins on the top and one on the bottom, and a small stepladder hanging from hooks on the end. She grabs one, tests the wheels, then starts pushing it. We follow.

There's three types of "roads" for navigating the mod—"highways" wide enough for two carts and a few "superhighways" around eight carts wide running east to west. Running north to south are a few "highways," but mostly narrow "alleys" between shelves where the items are actually stored. Each is only wide enough for one cart at a time to maximize storage space, and shelves loom claustrophobically on both sides.

We suddenly emerge into a much wider corridor flanked by tall stacks of those yellow plastic totes. More totes glide along a loud conveyor belt running down the center of the corridor. Michelle has to raise her voice to be heard over the white noise of the belt.

"Okay, you wanna grab one of these totes from any of these locations," she shouts, taking one from the top of a stack and putting it on her cart with a loud clunk.

"Now, if you ever forget anything, always check your screen, because it's telling you exactly what to do," she continues, showing her own scanner around. "Right now, it says, 'Scan new tote.'" She scans the bar code on the front of the yellow tote—BEEP—and we follow her to a quieter spot.

"Okay, now let's take a closer look at our numbers. Our first number is 198, so it's the number in the purple, and that's gonna be the street. You know, like Tenth Street, the street Amazon lies on?"

"I'm not from here," says Yolanda.

"I'm not, either, but—"

"Is it far from the bridge, then?" asks Darryl.

"I'm learning," says Yolanda.

"No, it's—"

"The bus was going all *kind* of detours this morning," says Darryl.

"I got a ride this morning, but tomorrow morning I'll ride the bus," says Yolanda.

"See, my mama, like, she ain't even crossing the bridge. She drop me off *at* the bridge! Like, 'You can get *yourself* across there. I'm not going across there!'" Even Michelle laughs at Darryl's impression of his mom before firmly cutting off the Darryl and Yolanda Show.

"Anyway!" she half yells. "The first number is in the purple, the second number is in the black. So we look for 198..." The explanation continues for quite a while. It's a lot to remember. Yolanda sighs, saying all this is going to give her a migraine.

I get migraines, too, and we commiserate as we walk. Like mine, Yolanda's migraines can be triggered by dehydration, so she's really pleased about all the water coolers we pass. She says this is a really nice warehouse—she used to work in the Caterpillar one down the street and passed out from heatstroke three times in there last summer.

We eventually bumble our way to the correct coordinates, count up from the bottom, scan the bar code on the proper drawer—BEEP—and pull it open. Inside is a bizarre selection of twelve or fifteen articles of clothing; no two are the same.

Michelle explains that a while back Amazon figured out that "chaotic storage" made the most sense—if a picker needs to get a pair of medium black socks, it's much faster to find black socks among a bunch of dissimilar items than to find a medium in a drawer full of black socks of all different sizes.

"Now"—Michelle shows us her scanner again—"here's the description, at the bottom, of what you're picking." The item we're looking for is an Ugly Christmas Sweater, medium, green. It's obvious where it is, but Michelle picks up and scans a hat instead—DEE-DOO-DEE-DOO. The tritone beeps clearly mean "Nope!" The scanner directs Michelle to scan the drawer again—BEEP. This time she picks up the bagged sweater, scans its bar code—BEEP—and tosses it into the yellow tote. I'm a little charmed to see that the LCD screen says THANK YOU! before instructing Michelle to scan her tote again—BEEP—and giving her the coordinates of the next item.

That's pretty much all there is to picking. We take turns finding items under Michelle's supervision for the rest of the day. When the yellow tote gets filled to the two-thirds mark, we push the cart over to the nearest conveyor belt, close the tote out on the scanner—BEEP—send it gliding off to parts unknown, then start a new one—BEEP. Sometimes the scanner has us go drop off a tote with only a couple of items in it. I ask if this has something to do with Amazon Prime; Michelle says probably, but she really doesn't know.

The next day, my alarm goes off at 3:45 a.m., and this time I *do* arrive early. I kill some time investigating the weird vending machine from the previous day. It's full of single-serving packets of generic over-the-counter medicine—mainly mild painkillers like Tylenol and Advil, though there's antacids, too.

After standup meeting, my group reassembles around Michelle, minus tiny blond Teena. Maybe she decided this wasn't for her; maybe she failed her drug test; maybe she overslept and got fired. People disappearing without explanation will be another constant theme of my time here.

The second day of training is the same as the first. Honestly, one day would have been enough. The system just doesn't leave many possibilities for screwing up. As Michelle says, if you don't know what to do, just check your scanner—it'll tell you.

We work on trying to get fast enough to beat the clock, which manifests itself visually as a blue bar at the bottom of the LCD screen that gets shorter and shorter as your remaining seconds tick by. By the end of the day, I can beat the clock most of the time. I'm also slightly obsessed with a man I keep seeing around the mod wearing these amazing bright blue velvet harem pants. He walks incredibly fast and appears to be friends with Michelle, because they always wave and smile, though his pick path never gets close enough to ours to actually make talking possible.

The next morning is my first real shift. I arrive half an hour early feeling confident. Picking is *easy*. And I'm sore, but it's not as bad as I'd expected—I mean, we walked pretty much nonstop all day yesterday.

At standup, we stretch for a few minutes while a guy talks at us through a megaphone that makes him sound like adults do to Charlie Brown. I still have no clue what he's saying. But the meaning again becomes obvious when everybody picks up their scanners and requests work in a chorus of BEEPs, so I do, too, and stream out into the mod with everyone else.

East Mod is almost entirely stocked with clothing, though there's an area with bright yellow shelves of miscellaneous tiny junk on the first floor. Even deep in the mod, where everything's the same monotonous cardboard brown, it's hard to get used to how the shelves seem to stretch on forever in every direction.

After a few hours on my own, I've gotten the hang of East Mod's grid system and no longer have to pause to think about which direction to turn. After that, I don't really need to think at all. All I need to do is keep walking.

But there's plenty to stop and gawk at. After lunch, the scanner takes me through an area where coats on hangers stretch out in both directions like an infinite dry cleaner's. Then my pick path takes me right to an edge of the mod's third floor: the shelves abruptly end in a breathtaking panoramic view of the rest of SDF8, which somehow looks even more vast from this high vantage point. I spend a few minutes of Time Off Task gazing through the safety bars at all the antlike workers below going about their mysterious jobs.

All day, I'm charmed that my scanner thanks me every time I drop a yellow tote off at the conveyor belt. Watching it sail off into the distance gives me a weird feeling of satisfaction, like I really *am* helping customers fulfill their dreams. *You're welcome!* I think.

Traffic isn't terrible on the way home, and I get back to the McPhersons' around 7:30. Katie saved me a plate of leftovers; Kaylee dances around happily in one of those bouncy-baby rigs in the kitchen as we chat and I eat.

Katie's curious about what it's like over there. When she was at Zappos, she says, it used to feel almost like a family. She was friends with everybody she worked with; their bosses were cool and would get everybody pizza when they had to come in for overtime. They'd even have video game tournaments and stuff. "They really tried to make sure we were having *fun,* not just getting a paycheck," Katie says. "They actually cared whether we stayed."

Counterintuitively, Zappos used to offer its workers a lump sum to quit, even in the warehouses. The amount of money started at $2,000 and increased the longer you'd been there. The theory was that this would weed out people who didn't really want to be there and that it would keep the culture positive. It apparently worked—Katie turned the money down twice, and so did most people. CEO Tony Hsieh later wrote in *Delivering Happiness,* a history of Zappos, that less than 1 percent of Zappos employees took the offer.

This is why, Hsieh writes, he used to let journalists roam free around Zappos buildings. "Unlike most companies, we don't give reporters a small list of people they're allowed to talk to. Instead, we encourage them to wander around and talk to whoever they want. It's our way of being as transparent as possible, which is part of our culture."

Katie quit not too long after Amazon acquired Zappos and began changing its warehouses into fulfillment centers. "It was just . . . different. It wasn't fun anymore. It was go, go, go all the time, like we were just robots to them."

I start to respond but get ambushed by a yawn midway through the sentence. It's barely eight. When did I get so *tired?* It didn't *feel* like I was doing that much, and my step counter said I'd only walked six miles. But I can't keep my eyes open. I barely get my shoes off and into bed before I'm asleep—teeth unbrushed, face unwashed, fully clothed.

When my alarm goes off for my second full day of picking, it is the worst my body's felt in my entire life. And I'm not unfamiliar with pain. As a kid, I went through years of complicated corrective surgeries on my legs, followed by some nasty physical therapy. I've broken bones. I get incapacitating migraines. Playing rugby in college, I was once matched up against a woman named Rhonda the Tank.

This is worse. It feels like I've been hit by a garbage truck. *Everything* hurts. My feet are the worst, but my back, shoulders, arms, and neck feel terrible, too. My hips, knees, and thighs ache from all the squats to pick from floor-level drawers. My right wrist, hand, and fingers ache from operating the scanner gun. My right elbow aches from pulling open hundreds of drawers. I even have a throbbing headache.

I groan involuntarily as I force myself to swing my legs over the side of the bed. The carpet feels like it's made of knives when I put weight on my feet, but I force myself to limp upstairs to the shower. Even before I've made coffee, I swallow a double dose of Advil and toss the bottle in my purse for later. I will need it.

At SDF8, I pop Advil like candy all day, not even bothering to track when my last dose was. I don't talk to anyone at break or lunch; I'm too tired. My head pounds, and I feel generally *dull.* By the end of my shift, I'm almost staggering from the stabbing pain in my feet and trying to lean some of my weight on my cart as I push it, as if it's a walker.

The next morning, I wake up feeling even worse. The day again goes by in a blur of pain and exhaustion, but I do remember checking my step-counter bracelet with morbid curiosity at the end of the day to find that, again, it only recorded about seven miles. This time, I'm *positive* the step counter is wrong. *Maybe it's not swinging back and forth because my hands are pushing the cart? Whatever. Who cares?* I fall asleep in my clothes again.

The next morning, I somehow wake up feeling even worse.

I make it through lunch, but an hour later the stabbing pain in my feet has spread up through my legs and hips. Every time the scanner has me squat down to get something from a low drawer, it's a little harder to force myself back up to standing.

Finally, I do a full squat to retrieve an item from a bottom drawer and my body mutinies. *Stand up,* I order my legs for the hundredth time today, but it's as if they've gotten fed up with all the abuse and hung up on my brain. *Stand up, you idiot,* my brain screams as I slowly topple backwards into a sitting position, but it's just not happening. I sigh. *Might as well rub my feet as long as I'm down here.* I start to take off my shoes and am slightly horrified to find that my feet are so swollen they're straining my shoelaces. Untying the laces feels sinfully good.

The "sinful" part is reinforced by my scanner, which has started notifying me that I have zero seconds remaining to pick my next item. *Fuck you,* I think, reaching above my head to drop the horrible thing on my cart, out of sight. I try to rub some life into my horrible-looking feet. *How many minutes of this can I get away with before some Time Off Task algorithm alerts a manager? If you're deep in the mod, it can take fifteen minutes to get to a bathroom and back—if I keep it under fifteen minutes, maybe it'll just look like a bathroom break.* I desperately want to believe this, so I do—in retrospect, I realize that the scan gun's GPS would have given me away.

I reach for the little bottle of Advil in my sweatshirt pocket and find I'm down to my last two. *How did that happen?* I consider taking one now and saving the other for later. But if I cared about Future Emily, I wouldn't be giving her future stomach ulcers from massive overdoses of ibuprofen. I swallow both pills.

Several minutes later, my brain reasserts control over my legs. I relace my shoes as tightly as I can and haul myself to my knees, then my feet, and proceed in a zombielike shamble to the next stop on my pick path.

Of course, those last two Advil wear off with three hours left on my shift. I curse Past Emily for a selfish bitch as the stabbing pain in my feet starts up again. Eventually I have to get something from a bottom shelf and again find that I can't get back up.

This time, I almost nod off with my back against the cardboard shelves. *Get up, you idiot!* I yell at myself, alarmed. *Don't end up like Brian!*

The thought of getting fired and giving up is awful. The thought of getting fired and starting all over again next peak is awful. The thought of going three more hours without something for the pain is awful. The thought of going home with my tail between my legs because I can't do a job that hundreds of thousands of people do every day is awful. I sit on the floor weighing my awful options, and to my shock, I actually start to cry.*

Jesus, what are you doing? I desperately try to pull it together, but the further shame of crying in public—and at work!—only makes things worse. Nobody walks by, though. That's one upside of the isolation—nobody to catch you crying on the floor.

It's pretty clear that whatever algorithm plots our pick paths around the warehouse is brilliantly engineered, immensely complicated, and set to keep people from getting within speaking distance of one another. The mod, though it's comparatively swarming with pickers during peak, is a very lonely place. I catch glimpses of people pushing carts or sorting through bins off in the distance, but I rarely get close enough to another human long enough to say hello, much less chat.

Keeping us isolated makes logistical sense because the alleys between shelves are so narrow. But it also eliminates the opportunity for inefficient workplace chatter, which I'm convinced is a goal rather than a side effect. When I'm sent over to learn packing one day, the workstations are set up catty-corner from one another, making it impossible to talk.

I am undeniably more productive than I've been at other jobs where I was able to talk to my coworkers. Not just as a journalist, either—none of my service jobs a decade ago was anywhere near this isolating. The novelty of getting up to speed and the agony in my feet have kept my mind occupied so far, but I can already tell that boredom and loneliness are going to be a... *something.* You know. What's the word? A *problem.* They're going to be a *big problem. Wait, what was I thinking about again?*

---

* Crying on the job is a common theme on forums for Amazon workers, regardless of gender. Again, I so wish I had room for all the bonkers stories I read and heard, but since space is limited, here's just one example:

I worked for a catering company contracted by Amazon to feed a Thanksgiving meal to every Amazon employee on every shift. This was a 24 hour gig.... Each shift had three or four groups, and there were at least two people from each group that would be crying/sobbing during their entire lunch break.... Their fellow Amazon employees seemed totally unfazed, and acted as if this was nothing out of the norm.

I jerk awake. *Okay,* I say to myself, beginning to panic. *Okay. Okay. I'm out of Advil. What am I going to do?*

Then I remember the painkiller vending machines. Supposedly they're free with a swipe of your ID badge, which is good, because we're not allowed to bring our wallets inside. I've seen other vending machines around the mod, but the only one I'm positive I can find is back by East Mod's standup area, a five-minute walk from where I'm sitting.

Get up get up get up, I yell at myself. *You cannot lose this job!* I drag myself to my feet, wincing, and limp toward where I hope there's a staircase to the ground floor.

But when I finally arrive at the vending machine, it doesn't recognize my badge. I thunk my forehead against the glass in despair, staring in at the rows of little foil packets. *So close. So far.*

A woman notices me being pathetic and comes over. "Let me guess—it's your first week," she says, pity in her Kentucky drawl. She's white and middle-aged, with the blue badge of a full-time Amazonian and the air of lower management. I tell her it's my third day out of training, and she grimaces.

"Yeah, well, the second day's worse than the first and the third's worse than the second. But I promise this is as bad as it gets. If you can make it through the first two weeks, it gets easier. It really does." She looks genuinely sympathetic. "Is the machine not working with your badge? It should..." She takes my ID and tries swiping it herself, with the same result. She frowns. As she tries a few more times at various speeds, I ask about the vending machines, which are apparently new.

"They put them in last year after peak," she says. There had been problems with lines of dead-eyed, ibuprofen-seeking zombies like me building up outside AMCARE, enough to snarl up foot traffic on the twenty-foot-wide main concourse. Because nearly everybody just wanted over-the-counter painkillers, management installed these vending machines around the building last year. *Et voilà:* no more traffic jams, and workers get free drugs a short walk away. Win-win.

The woman gives up and hands me back my badge, rolling her eyes. "You go see AMCARE about your badge after work; they'll fix it for you. In the meantime, what do you want?" she asks, swiping her own badge. I select ibuprofen and thank the woman from the depths of my soul. She smiles and taps the badge on her chest.

"Everyone with a blue badge was once right where you are now," she says as I tilt back my head to dry-swallow the pills. "It really does get better. You just have to get used to it.

"Be careful about overusing those, though," she warns as I start limping back toward the stairs to the third floor. "I have to take four to get the effect of two now."

Near the end of my shift, I turn into an alley to find Yolanda sitting slumped on the floor next to her cart—eyes closed, back against the shelves, unmoving. Initially, my brain shrieks an alarm, thinking of poor dead Jeff Lockhart—but, I mean, I probably looked just as corpselike twice today. It's still a relief that Yolanda responds when I ask if she's okay.

She moves the tiniest possible amount, as if she can barely muster the energy to rotate her head and open her eyes. There's no sign of the lively goofball from training—Yolanda looks like a toy whose batteries have run down. She waves off my concern, saying she just needs to sit down for a spell. But after I turn the corner at the end of the aisle, I never see Yolanda again. She's just *gone.*

It's sleeting and completely dark when I hobble out to my car at the end of the day, feeling about ninety years old. I seriously consider curling up in the backseat and sleeping until my next shift, but grudgingly decide that, even with the blanket from the trunk, it'd be too cold. Instead, I blast the heat and rest my forehead on the steering wheel.

What are you even doing here?

I really wasn't prepared for this much pain. It's one thing to walk ten or twelve miles—or however many miles it actually is, because it's *not* seven—and another thing entirely to do it, plus hundreds of squats, five days a week. Rhonda the Tank was rough, but I didn't have to wake up to get flattened by her the next morning, and the next, and the next.

My phone pings as it finishes downloading my daily step count from my bracelet, which today I hooked onto a shoelace instead of my wrist. I check it, and... *yes,* my first few days of data *were* incorrect. *Really* incorrect. Today, my bracelet recorded more than thirty thousand steps. I start giggling helplessly as I work out the math. That's more than fifteen miles.

Fifteen! Fucking! Miles! It's the funniest, most horrible thing I've ever heard.

Crazy people laugh alone in their cars, I tell myself, trying to take deep breaths. But I can't seem to stop.

I have it so much easier than nearly all my coworkers. At least half the East Mod pickers look past retirement age. Most younger people have kids, and they talk on smoke breaks about doing chores and making dinner after their shifts. There's even a few very pregnant women picking, which flabbergasts me every time I see one out in the mod. I thought my ridiculous-looking warehouse shoes would help me blend in, but everybody else wears sneakers that are cheap, old, or both. I see an alarming number of Chuck Taylors, which would give me shin splints in thirty seconds. Despite all my research, I'm embarrassingly unprepared for what "normal" means outside the white-collar world, and I've grossly misjudged what $10.50 an hour is worth to a lot of people.

I'd expected the pain. I'd expected the monotony. I hadn't expected so many people to regard this as a decent job.

Because Amazon *does* pay better than comparable jobs in the area. And I'd known, academically, that 80 percent of low-wage workers in the private sector don't get any paid time off. I hadn't really *understood* it, though. Unpaid time off still sounded like a laughable benefit to me, but tons of my coworkers were grateful for it, saying it really did give them more flexibility than most other jobs. White and blue badges alike say they'd take the worst job here over the best job in fast food, a sector discussed with a universal shudder. And if you hustle enough to get that blue badge, the health insurance is good, and there's even the possibility of earning paid time off.

I went in expecting to find that Amazon's system was uniquely strict. But if you don't have a college degree, special skills, or a pristine criminal record, most jobs you can get will use the same kinds of productivity-managing equipment and techniques as Amazon does, though maybe a little less efficiently. It's *normal* to have your thirty-minute lunch timed down to the second. It's *normal* to work through pain and illness. It's *normal* to have *time to lean, time to clean* enforced by constant monitoring and beeping.

My stomach groans, and I realize I'm starving—*my* new normal. I grab the bag of healthy snacks I've started keeping shotgun to pacify my stomach on the drive home—the urge to stop at a McDonald's halfway has been almost overwhelming lately.

I eat a carrot. My stomach gives me the side-eye.

I eat a handful of carrots. *Dude,* my stomach gurgles.

Fuck it, I think, putting the car in reverse. *I didn't fall asleep. I stood back up. I deserve McDonald's.*

As I inch out of the massive parking lot, I spot Darryl in the large huddle of people at the bus stop. It's freezing and miserable, and we're going the same way. I consider stopping to give him a ride.

No. Fuck Darryl. I don't care.

I don't want to make small talk. I don't want to delay my bedtime for however many minutes I'll have to go out of my way. I don't want Darryl to get the wrong idea, and I don't want to feel obligated to give him rides in the future. I *just don't care.*

And I want McDonald's, *right fucking now.*

So I pretend not to see him.

I find it hard to explain the needling shame I still feel about this. It's not a big deal, and I'm positive Darryl wouldn't hold it against me. But I like to think of myself as someone who'd offer a nice kid a ride home after a truly shitty day of work. Right now, though, exhaustion has shrunk my circle of empathy to the point that it's barely big enough for myself. I didn't know that could happen, and it's not pleasant. I guess I never realized that this might affect more than just my body.

As traffic crawls past the bus stop, I'm overwhelmed by a surge of desperate gratitude—for my car, for the credit card I'll use at McDonald's, for my low-interest mortgage, for decades of regular dental care, for my college degree in two impractical subjects, for my husband's ability to pay our bills while I try to shoot the moon, for my naive ideas about "normal," for my ability to shrug and think, *Fuck Darryl.*

I came to SDF8 to try to *understand* what it feels like to work in a fulfillment center. But the thing I really and truly *understand* now is that, regardless of how broke I may be, I'm the upper class. I always will be. I won't ever really *understand* what it feels like to work here, because I know that I get to leave.

You idiot.

I take one more look at Darryl in my rearview mirror. I could still go back. But in the place I'd usually feel empathy, there's just a shameful, overwhelming relief, and the words *I get to leave.*

Three Weeks to Christmas

If this were a completely accurate representation of my month at SDF8, the next forty pages would consist entirely of complaints about constant pain, waking up at 4:00 a.m., walking between thirteen and sixteen miles per day, being too tired to talk to anyone, eating a lot of McDonald's, rarely seeing the sun, and passing out the minute I get home from work.

I'm so exhausted that Rajiv leaves a whole week's worth of increasingly concerned voicemails before I call him back. The only time we can talk is after I get off work, and though I feel guilty, I lack the energy to hide the fact that calling him feels like yet another task I have to complete before I can sleep.

"Huh…that's…pretty nice of them, I guess?" Rajiv hazards when I tell him about the painkiller vending machines. My husband's a very logical thinker, and he's not *wrong,* exactly. I appreciated the *hell* out of those free Advil.

But he's fucking *wrong!*

Rajiv and I don't fight much, especially about dumb stuff like this. We're usually pretty good about talking through things before they get to fight territory. But today I'm too exhausted to drill down, locate the miscommunication, and explain so he can understand how I feel. Instead, I resent that he won't just take my word that it's *fucked up.* If I had the energy, I'd be pissed off. Since I don't, I just get sullen.

Later, on a day off, I apologize and pose the situation as a multiple-choice question:

Q: Your warehouse workers work 11.5-hour shifts. In order to make rate, a significant number of them need to take over-the-counter painkillers multiple times per shift, which means regular backups at the medical office. Do you:

A. Scale back the rate—clearly, workers are at their physical limits
B. Make shifts shorter
C. Increase the number or duration of breaks
D. Increase staffing at the nurse's office
E. Install vending machines to dispense painkillers more efficiently

Seriously—what kind of fucking sociopath goes with E?

But that's just how Amazon is—all about thinking outside the box. After just one week at SDF8, it's so obvious how "hire ambulances to wait around so workers with heatstroke can get to the hospital faster" seemed like a clever, innovative solution to someone.

You can track the onset of my semipermanent bad mood through my voice memos. Notes from the first couple of days are detailed and useful—I try to measure East Mod by counting my steps; I describe the process of picking; I talk about products my scanner sends me to get, whether I'm making rate, all the crazy equipment. I also record a few longer, diary-style reflections like this one, made en route to my third full day of work:

> *It is 5:29 a.m. Today will be my... my fourth day? I started Thursday, so... no, today will be my* fifth *day. It's kind of all blurred together— I'm so tired.* [PATHETIC LAUGH] *Both because I have to get up at four to make it there on time and just the sheer workload.*
>
> *Yesterday seemed unusual— like, other people were commenting on how weird the pick paths were at lunch. The scanner kept sending me back and forth from one end of the mod to the other. It was driving me nuts.... I need to figure out how long that is. It definitely takes a long time to walk. The timer gave me more than two minutes to walk somewhere yesterday.*

That is, the pick paths usually keep you within a smaller area of the mod instead of sending you from row 1 to row 250 then all the way back to row 1, which gets exhausting real fast. I try to work out those usual boundaries out loud as I drive:

> *There's three conveyor belts that divide the mod into four parts, and usually you don't cross under the belts. Then, east–west, the numbers go from 100 to 1,000... or does it start at zero?*
>
> [LAUGH] *No, it definitely starts at 100, because the 100 row is on the edge of the mezzanine, and that's where I dropped a cock sock down, like, three floors into the standup area yesterday. It just fluttered down super slowly, like the feather from* Forrest Gump.

After the first week, there's a hilariously steep drop-off in memo length and quality. My voice sounds dead, and I take a much more just-the-facts approach:

> *Friday morning—making, like, 90 rate on the first floor.*
>
> *Got sent over to work in West Mod today; it took a minute to get used to navigating there because it's a mirror image of East Mod, so my internal compass is backwards.*
>
> *I ran into Blair the vegan; she picks super, super fast—it's crazy how fast she walks! She says all the West Mod pickers are pissed at her because she keeps winning Power Hour. (Note: figure out what Power Hour is.)*

The next week, nearly all my notes are just two-second clips of me angrily whispering "*Fuck* your [product whose existence I resent]." Many of these come from TEK0, a.k.a. the section of bright yellow shelving on the first floor that stores miscellaneous items. I reproduce some of these memos here:

> "*Fuck* your sexy candy corn costume."
> "*Fuck* your enormous bag of ping-pong balls."
> "*Fuck* your angel communication journal."
> "*Fuck* your feces-themed board game."

"*Fuck* your eco-friendly jeans."

"*Fuck* your Beautiful Celtic Dragonfly Zodiac Wall Clock by Brigid Ashwood."

"*Fuck* your shapewear."

"*Fuck* Derrida."

"*Fuck* your Michael Kors bag."

"*Fuck* Minecraft."

"*Fuck* your Alexander Del Rossa Women's Super Plush Microfiber Fleece Bathrobe Robe."

"*Fuck* your fucking Amazon gift card—seriously, what kind of asshole orders an Amazon gift card off *fucking Amazon?*"

There's one outlier in the "fuck your" period—a very long recording in which, after recording my objections to a TARDIS throw blanket, I accidentally continue to record for a couple of hours. Later, I fast-forward through this accidental tape just in case, listening for anything other than the white noise of the mod and my scanner gun's beeps. Half an hour in, I catch a short blip of my voice. Rewinding, I'm *very* embarrassed to discover that it isn't speech—I am *whimpering.* I make the incredibly pathetic noise several more times in the recording.

By the end of my second week, I don't even have the energy to get pissed off about stupid products. I just stop recording.

Doesn't Jeff Bezos have a right to be mad if you're clocked in for forty hours but only actually working for thirty? Aren't you stealing from him?

What is an honest day's work? How long does it last? How hard do you work? What are you owed in exchange?

I like to picture the history of work as two titans, Labor and Capital,*

* For my purposes, "Capital" refers to the small group of people who own the resources needed to make things or provide services that can be sold for a profit—a car factory, fields of strawberries, a McDonald's franchise, a hotel, an angel

locked in a centuries-long wrestling match. Whoever's on top at the moment gets to define "an honest day's work."

The general understanding is that as society advances, work gets cleaner, easier, less dangerous—generally *better.* Pushing a cart at SDF8 isn't easy, but it does seem much easier than hunting with a spear, or toiling in some baron's fields, or mining coal during the Industrial Revolution. In comparison, nominal air-conditioning, safety obsession, and slightly above average pay seem like things to be grateful for.

I found this viewpoint in a lot of online discussions of working conditions at Amazon, which inevitably seem to devolve into accusations of laziness and ingratitude:

> Amazon is definitely not as hard as all of you crybabies are making it seem, I have worked construction jobs and in furniture warehouses that are 10x harder than this for less pay and I still had nothing to complain about, just grateful to have a job.
>
> if You think Amazon is bad, try McDonalds you McBitches
>
> You've got to be fucking kidding me! I work in a warehouse thats at least 110–120 most of the summer with toxic solvent vapors from open buckets of ink all year round and a management team that thinks that "the first guy that complains is a fag" I'd love to work for Amazon.

All these oh-please-my-job-is-*way*-worse Stockholm syndrome posts are surprisingly common for a society where work has only been getting better and better.

---

investment—and the money to pay people who work at turning those resources into more money.

"Labor" refers to most of the rest of us, people who work for someone other than ourselves. These people trade a day's worth of their energy to someone else—peasants tilling the fields, assembly-line workers making cars, kids flipping burgers, maids cleaning rooms, coders developing an app—in exchange for money.

And more than anecdotal evidence suggests that, though American jobs have gotten safer, people's *experience* of them is at an all-time low. We're less likely to get killed or maimed at work than ever before, true. But we're also at record lows for job satisfaction, job security, free time, and feeling in control of our lives.

For just one example, a recent study by the *Harvard Business Review* and the Energy Project surveyed twenty thousand workers across twenty-five industries and found that American workers have never felt unhappier or less secure at work, with only 37 percent satisfied with their jobs.. The authors wrote:

> It's a depressing but undeniable reality: the vast majority of employees feel depleted, diminished, disenfranchised, demoralized, and disengaged at work.... For 200 years, since the dawn of the Industrial Age, the model for how to work has been the machine, and more recently, the computer.... Machines are valued for their speed, efficiency, and predictability. They make no demands. When they break, they can be repaired or replaced. Computers run even faster and do more. The assumption in organizations has been that people ought to be able to operate in the same way.[4]

Still, says the Stockholm syndrome patient, look at the alternatives. Hunting for food? Subsistence farming? Coal mining? Quit your whining.

Now, I would make a terrible farmer. But I would like to question this assumption that the way we work in the modern world is actually *better* for us. Work was hard before modern technology, no doubt. But it wasn't exactly *stressful*. And there's a really big difference between *difficult* work and *stressful* work that comes down to *time to lean, time to clean*.

The boss is a pretty recent invention on the evolutionary timescale. Let's skip past the majority of history, when we lived in egalitarian bands of nomadic hunter-gatherers where everybody shared. People generally didn't even have bosses during feudalism—not in the modern way we think of a boss as someone who directs your work and pays you a regular wage. Most people worked for themselves—most as farmers, fewer as artisans—even if some noble came by to take much of the fruits of their labors. Even as capitalism began to replace feudalism in the sixteenth and seventeenth centuries, few people had the sort of regular labor-for-wage arrangement we'd regard as a job today—and if they did, it was for a very small business.

Then came the Industrial Revolution.

There's a bit from an old *Simpsons* episode that keeps coming to mind as I drag myself around SDF8. Homer, for some reason, has been promoted to manage a team of engineers. When he's brought in to meet them, they're all typing away, looking cheerful and competent. Unsure what to do, Homer hazards, "Are you guys working?"

"Yes, sir, Mr. Simpson!"

"Could you, um, work any harder than this?"

"Sure thing, boss," says one, and they start typing noticeably faster.

Later, Homer is congratulated for raising productivity by 2 percent. When he goes to tell the engineers the good news, he finds them looking haggard and unable to muster much enthusiasm. "I'm sorry. We're just a little tired, sir," explains one.

At the beginning of the industrial era, in the late 1800s, factory owners were roughly in Homer's position. Companies had been growing larger and larger, which made it harder and harder for Capital to understand what Labor actually *did* all day. Owners were much less likely to notice when workers were slacking off, making it hard to pin down whether any one individual was doing an honest day's work.

If, like Homer, your employees were willing to work themselves to exhaustion just because you asked nicely, you were in good shape. But the loyalty a former apprentice might feel toward the employer who'd taught her a craft just wasn't there when the boss was some distant rich guy she'd never met.

Without those motivations, it became very difficult for owners to keep track of how much (or whether) any one employee was working, resulting in situations like this:

> As the scale of the factory increased, it became harder to supervise all employees and ensure that they were doing a fair day's work for a day's pay....It was common for time-keepers to be unable to

> account for up to 20% of the men who were clocked in. In one shipyard, one man was charged with making loud hammering noises on the hull of the ship while the remainder of the work crew played cards.[5]

After a while, owners hit on the solution of piecework—paying workers a set price per task completed or item finished rather than a certain amount per day. The idea was to set the rates per piece so that diligent workers who gave 110 percent could earn more money at piecework than the daily rate.

This didn't work very well. First, workers noted the obvious: every time they took the bait and sped up, management inevitably dropped the amount paid per task, and the "110 percent" pace became the new normal. Not being idiots, piece-rate workers tended to band together and "soldier," or collectively work at an agreed-upon pace that was more relaxed than what they were technically capable of.

Second, it's a lot harder to measure shovelfuls of coal than finished artificial flowers and petticoats—the industries that first started paying piece rates. What if one man shovels coal faster but another lifts more with each shovelful? What if one man works slow and steady and another works furiously but takes a lot of breaks? Should two men be paid the same if they're equally tired at the end of the day, or if they shovel the same weight? And even if you could figure that out, how would you keep track of that much data—much less make sense of it—when you keep records in pen and ink?

On top of that, skilled workers were even harder to manage. Fred Colvin, *American Machinist* editor during this era, wrote in his memoir that, during those early years of industrialization, "the budding science of metallurgy was looked upon as a secret art."

> Every job of heat-treating, or of hardening and tempering, took on the nature of sorcery and black magic.... There was much solemn hokum about the carbon composition of various steels, the proper ingredients to be used in the hardening bath, and even the kind of weather that should prevail during the ritual.[6]

If it's difficult to replace a skilled machinist, it's nearly impossible to replace a skilled machinist who's the only one who really knows the arcane quirks of every piece of equipment you own. And since skilled workers also tended to be the most senior, they were often the ones organizing and enforcing the pace of work—not factory owners.

So how did Capital get Labor in the sleeper hold that produced SDF8? It started back in my hometown of Philadelphia with Frederick Taylor—father of scientific management and the most important forgotten man in US history.

Frederick Winslow Taylor was born into a wealthy Philadelphia family in 1856. Expected to go to Harvard, he instead chose to go into industry by taking a job as a lowly machinist's apprentice at Midvale Steelworks. As young Fred worked his way up to head engineer, he observed widespread soldiering among his coworkers.

"The natural laziness of men is serious," Taylor would later write in his 1911 magnum opus, *The Principles of Scientific Management,* "but by far the greatest evil from which both workmen and employers are suffering is the systematic soldiering which is almost universal."

He really meant "evil," too. Taylor was an early true believer in the idea of efficiency and productivity as savior. Increases in labor productivity at factories employing his "scientific management," he believed, would raise the wages of the workers, which he saw as the only realistic way of ending poverty and class conflict.

Scientific management, or Taylorism, was a new system of eliminating all mystery from factory work, whether it was how fast workers were *really* capable of going or the "sorcery and black magic" methods of skilled workers. To do this, Taylor used a relatively new technology—the affordable, accurate stopwatch—to measure and analyze previously subjective tasks. It was the birth of literal micromanagement.

First, Taylor would pull the best, strongest "first-rate men" and pay them extra to work as fast as possible while he watched, timing their motions to fractions of a second. From this, he'd determine the "one best way" of doing a task, use that to calculate how much a first-rate man should be able to do in a day, then use *that* to calculate a new piece rate for all workers.

Taylor generally set his new rates somewhere between "extremely ambitious" and "ludicrous," which might explain why everyone hated him.

The best-known story about Taylor involves pig iron* and a Pennsylvania Dutch laborer he called Schmidt. The story made Taylor famous, and he'd been fond of telling it in public for years before publishing it in *Scientific Management* under the heading "The Story of Schmidt"—he even wrote Schmidt's lines out in dialect, so you can hear the dumb accent he'd be using if he were telling it in person. It goes like this:

In 1899, early in young Taylor's tenure as an efficiency consultant at Bethlehem Steel, the price of pig iron rose, which meant the steelworks needed ten thousand tons of the stuff loaded by hand onto freight cars.

This is what that entailed: There was a pile of pig iron, a freight car, and a twenty-foot plank ramp between the pile and the car. A worker would pick up one ninety-two-pound iron bar from the pile, walk with it up the ramp, and hand it off to another man waiting inside the train car. Then he'd walk back down the ramp and get another, for the next ten hours.

When Taylor began his experiment, the average worker at Bethlehem loaded about thirteen tons of pig iron a day, a little below the fifteen tons academics estimate was an average day's work for free laborers throughout history.[7] Taylor took the simplicity of the task as an opportunity to prove to skeptical clients that his system could be used to analyze and optimize absolutely anything:

> Nothing has as yet been said about the science of handling pig iron. The writer trusts, however, that before leaving this illustration the reader will be thoroughly convinced that there is a science of handling pig iron, and further that this science amounts to so much that the man who is suited to handle pig iron cannot possibly understand it, nor even work in accordance with the laws of this science, without the help of those who are over him.

---

* Pig iron is a crude intermediate step between mined ore and refined steel—it's metal that's been put through a furnace and formed into standardized bars, or "pigs," for easier accounting and storage.

That's another thing about Fred Taylor—he often claimed to respect and feel kinship with the men he'd labored alongside during his apprenticeships, but he *constantly* talks shit about them, and seems to regard them as almost another species:

> One of the very first requirements for a man who is fit to handle pig iron as a regular occupation [is] that he shall be so stupid and so phlegmatic that he more nearly resembles in his mental make-up the ox than any other type.... He is so stupid that the word "percentage" has no meaning to him, and he must consequently be trained by a man more intelligent than himself.

That's the heart of Taylorism—the belief that workers given free rein will *always* default to the sort of soldiering Taylor observed working his way up from apprentice, which he saw as laziness and stupidity rather than self-preservation. He thus encourages the removal of "all possible brain work" and agency from the hands of workers—even the minimal amount involved in deciding how to best carry a heavy iron bar up a ramp without hurting yourself.

Stopwatches and data gave Taylor a sheen of objectivity, and he sold his methods as pure science, the antidote to the "sorcery and black magic" that gave skilled workers so much power over the operations of factories. In hindsight, though, Taylor just seems to be substituting his own sped-up rules of thumb. He often played fast and loose with numbers and had an extremely unscientific habit of rounding to nice clean multiples of five. Here's how Taylor determined how fast workers should be loading pig iron, from Robert Kanigel's indispensable biography *The One Best Way:*

> On a comfortably cool Monday, ten of the best men in the regular yard gang were ordered to work as flat-out fast as they could, for the time it took to load one car. They did it, literally running up and down the planks, in fourteen minutes: 16½ tons' worth. That worked out to seventy-one tons per man per day. Timings of individual men, some probably by Taylor, stopwatch in hand, followed. He recalled, "It took me about a day and a half to be sure what those

> people could do"—which he set at seventy-five, not seventy-one, tons per day.
>
> Of course, the men were drained.... "It was quite evident," wrote [Taylor's assistants], "that this gait could not be kept up for any considerable length of time." Yet, somehow, this wildly artificial figure became the basis for fixing piece rates. Through reasoning entirely opaque a century later, Taylor lopped off 40 percent, to allow for rest and unavoidable delay, and set forty-five tons per day as each man's daily stint. This was at least double—and probably closer to triple—what laborers had been able to manage throughout history.
>
> What was the basis for the 40 percent allowance that led to Taylor's standard? Why not 60, or 80, or 10 percent? The report that [Taylor's assistants] prepared later grants no insight. The stopwatch timing, the careful "observations," the pages of numbers and calculations, might feebly suggest "science." But the 40 percent was sheer witchcraft.[8]

However he arrived at his numbers, Taylor now had to convince the yard gang to work at maximum physical capacity all day, every day. It wasn't going to be an easy sell, he knew—introducing the new pig-iron piece rates all at once would lead to revolt. So Taylor initially asked for volunteers, tempting them with the possibility of earning 50 percent more than the day rate of $1.15. At the new rate of 3.75 cents per ton, anyone who managed to load Taylor's full forty-five tons would earn $1.69. Anyone still loading the factory's previous average of thirteen tons, though, would earn less than fifty cents.

Taylor's ideal first-rate man, then, had to be strong, hardworking, and not particularly good at math—he'd be doing the work of four men for the pay of a man and a half. Taylor found this man in twenty-eight-year-old Pennsylvania Dutchman Henry Noll,* made famous in *Scientific Management* as "Schmidt." Taylor writes:

---

* Not much is known about Noll outside of what Taylor writes about him, but historical photographs reveal him to be kind of a hottie.

[Schmidt] was a little Pennsylvania Dutchman who had been observed to trot back home for a mile or so after his work in the evening about as fresh as he was when he came trotting down to work in the morning. We found that upon wages of $1.15 a day he had succeeded in buying a small plot of ground, and that he was engaged in putting up the walls of a little house for himself in the morning before starting to work and at night after leaving. He also had the reputation of being exceedingly "close," that is, of placing a very high value on a dollar. As one man whom we talked to about him said, "A penny looks about the size of a cart-wheel to him." This man we will call Schmidt.

The task before us, then, narrowed itself down to getting Schmidt to handle 47 tons of pig iron per day and making him glad to do it. This was done as follows. Schmidt was called out from among the gang of pig-iron handlers and talked to somewhat in this way:

> *"Schmidt, are you a high-priced man?"*
>
> *"Vell, I don't know vat you mean."*
>
> *"Oh yes, you do. What I want to know is whether you are a high-priced man or not."*
>
> *"Vell, I don't know vat you mean."*
>
> *"Oh, come now, you answer my questions. What I want to find out is whether you are a high-priced man or one of these cheap fellows here. What I want to find out is whether you want to earn $1.85 a day or whether you are satisfied with $1.15, just the same as all those cheap fellows are getting."*
>
> *"Did I vant $1.85 a day? Vas dot a high-priced man? Vell, yes, I vas a high-priced man."*
>
> *"Oh, you're aggravating me. Of course you want $1.85 a day—everyone wants it! You know perfectly well that that has very little to do with your being a high-priced man. For goodness' sake answer my questions, and don't waste any more of my time. Now come over here. You see that pile of pig iron?"*
>
> *"Yes."*
>
> *"You see that car?"*

> *"Yes."*
>
> *"Well, if you are a high-priced man, you will load that pig iron on that car tomorrow for $1.85. Now do wake up and answer my question. Tell me whether you are a high-priced man or not."*
>
> *"Vell—did I got $1.85 for loading dot pig iron on dot car tomorrow?"*
>
> *"Yes, of course you do, and you get $1.85 for loading a pile like that every day right through the year. That is what a high-priced man does, and you know it just as well as I do."*
>
> *"Vell, dot's all right. I could load dot pig iron on the car tomorrow for $1.85, and I get it every day, don't I?"*
>
> *"Certainly you do—certainly you do."*
>
> *"Vell, den, I vas a high-priced man."*
>
> *"Now, hold on, hold on. You know just as well as I do that a high-priced man has to do exactly as he's told from morning till night. You have seen this man here before, haven't you?"*
>
> *"No, I never saw him."*
>
> *"Well, if you are a high-priced man, you will do exactly as this man tells you tomorrow, from morning till night. When he tells you to pick up a pig and walk, you pick it up and you walk, and when he tells you to sit down and rest, you rest. You do that right straight through the day. And what's more, no back talk. . . . Do you understand that? When this man tells you to walk, you walk; when he tells you to sit down, you sit down, and you don't talk back at him. Now you come on to work here tomorrow morning and I'll know before night whether you are really a high-priced man or not."*

This seems to be rather rough talk. And indeed it would be if applied to an educated mechanic, or even an intelligent laborer. With a man of the mentally sluggish type of Schmidt it is appropriate and not unkind, since it is effective in fixing his attention on the high wages which he wants and away from what, if it were called to his attention, he probably would consider impossibly hard work. . . .

> Schmidt started to work, and all day long, and at regular intervals, was told by the man who stood over him with a watch, "Now pick up a pig and walk. Now sit down and rest. Now walk—now rest," etc. He worked when he was told to work, and rested when he was told to rest, and at half-past five in the afternoon had his 47 tons loaded on the car. And he practically never failed to work at this pace and do the task that was set him during the three years that the writer was at Bethlehem.... One man after another was picked out and trained to handle pig iron at the rate of 47 tons per day until all of the pig iron was handled at this rate, and the men were receiving 60 percent more wages than other workmen around them.

The Story of Schmidt, like many stories Taylor told, is misleading. First, his habit of rounding to multiples of five is in full effect. And, according to notes from the time, Henry Noll wasn't specially selected. He was just the only one out of dozens of men who tried who could regularly meet Taylor's goals.

Because the other workers at Bethlehem Steel *did* in fact notice that this was what they "would consider impossibly hard work." Ten of the fifteen men who volunteered for Taylor's experiment asked to switch back to the day rate after only three days. They were fired. Others who replaced them just physically couldn't do it and quit or just stopped showing up. From notes taken at the time:

> We found that [Gruen] was not fitted for such heavy work.
>
> Roth on this day loaded 43 tons, earning $1.63, but after this day did not return to work.
>
> Koch and Howarth [claimed] that they could not earn a fair day's wages at this work.

Journalist Upton Sinclair, whose *The Jungle* was the catalyst for reforms in the meatpacking industry, wrote a horrified letter to *American Magazine* in response to its publication of the excerpted Story of Schmidt. "I shall not soon forget the picture which he gave us," wrote Sinclair, of Schmidt and his fellow workers at Bethlehem Steel, "induced to give 362 per cent more service for 61 per cent more pay." Why, he asked, should they "receive $1.85 for the work, instead of, say, $2.85"?

Taylor responded in a letter to the same magazine the next month, explaining that in his experience, if you pay workers too much, they "work irregularly and tend to become more or less shiftless, extravagant and dissipated. Our experiments showed...that for their own best interest it does not do for most men to get rich too fast."

The less obvious but equally important effect of Taylorism was breaking the power that skilled workers held over the pace of work and the operations of factories. He began disassembling skilled jobs into multiple smaller unskilled jobs, often designing specialized tools to replace a skilled worker's "sorcery and black magic" knowledge base. There was no mystery in the "one best way," and that removed the job security of skilled workers, further shifting the balance of power toward factory owners.

Division of labor wasn't new. The productivity benefits of having many workers collaborate on a multistep manufacturing process had been famously described more than a century earlier by Adam Smith in 1776's *The Wealth of Nations,* a founding document of the then-new system of capitalism. Smith famously uses the example of a pin* factory—like Taylor with his pig iron, Smith chose pins specifically because they were seen as "very trifling" to manufacture:

> One man draws out the wire, another straights it, a third cuts it, a fourth points it, a fifth grinds it at the top for receiving the head; to make the head requires two or three distinct operations; to put it on, is a peculiar business, to whiten the pins is another; it is even a trade by itself to put them into the paper; and the important business of making a pin is, in this manner, divided into about eighteen distinct operations.
>
> [Ten workers] could, when they exerted themselves, make... upwards of forty-eight thousand pins in a day. Each person, therefore...might be considered as making four thousand eight hundred pins in a day. But if they had all wrought separately and independently,

* "Pin" in this case meant "nail," not the kind of pin used in sewing.

> and without any of them having been educated to this peculiar business, they certainly could not each of them have made twenty, perhaps not one pin in a day.

What's less well known about *The Wealth of Nations* is that Smith also describes the ill effects of monotonous, highly divided labor on the day-to-day *experience* of workers:

> The man whose whole life is spent in performing a few simple operations... has no occasion to exert his understanding or to exercise his invention in finding out expedients for removing difficulties which never occur. He naturally loses, therefore, the habit of such exertion, and generally becomes as stupid and ignorant as it is possible for a human creature to become.
>
> The torpor of his mind renders him not only incapable of relishing or bearing a part in any rational conversation, but of conceiving any generous, noble, or tender sentiment, and consequently of forming any just judgement concerning many even of the ordinary duties of private life....
>
> But in every improved and civilized society this is the state into which the labouring poor, that is, the great body of the people, must necessarily fall, unless government takes some pains to prevent it.

That sounds a whole lot like *depression* to me—just before the concept of *depression* existed. And the idea that highly divided labor was *by its very nature* monotonous, alienating, and depressing for workers is, basically, Karl Marx.

Smith's theory of markets works on the assumption that the profits of higher labor productivity would obviously be passed along to workers as higher wages—giving them an incentive to put up with the monotony of subdivided work. And in the late 1700s, that might have worked. Businesses were much smaller back then—Smith's pin "factory" had just ten workers, who'd be doubly motivated by working alongside a boss they knew personally and sharing in the profits.

That system has a ceiling, though. Once a company grows to employ more than a couple hundred workers in more and more complicated jobs, it becomes increasingly difficult to know all of them personally, much less keep track of and control them all. The more efficiently you subdivide job duties, the unhappier your workers become. And a workforce of miserable, bored, hard-to-supervise workers quickly leads to soldiering, or situations like the shipworkers playing cards all day while one guy makes a lot of noise with a hammer. At the turn of the century, growth and division of labor were approaching that point of diminishing returns.*

But Taylorism had no ceiling. Its combination of objective-seeming data analysis, specific productivity goals, monitoring, and deskilling was the system that growing factories had been desperate for. By conceiving of workers as numbers in an equation rather than individual humans, Taylor made it possible for companies to expand enormously, employing thousands and even millions of workers without losing control over them.

Taylorism revolutionized American industry. Production rates at factories that hired him often tripled or quadrupled, and our wild manufacturing capacity is exactly what enabled the US to take its spot at the forefront of the post–World War II world. As I said, Taylor's probably the most influential American whom not many people remember—as history goes, business management just can't compete with war and politics.

But even at the time, Taylor was controversial. As you may have guessed, workers despised "Speedy" Taylor and his stopwatches. After Bethlehem, Taylor spent a decade on the road as a management consultant, and others began to brand themselves as efficiency experts and spread their own versions of scientific management.

Taylor's results could be incredible, but he left a trail of discontent behind him. Men complained of overwork, exhaustion, and the mind-numbing monotony of this new kind of work.

"No tyrant or slave driver in the ecstasy of his most delirious dream ever sought to place upon abject slaves a condition more repugnant," said one very dramatic labor leader in the midst of a 1911 strike at Boston's federal Watertown Arsenal. It had been catalyzed by Taylor's pronouncement that

* There were some exceptions to this rule in closed systems where workers couldn't just quit their jobs—for example, railroad and mining "company towns" and, obviously, slavery.

a molding process usually taking fifty-three minutes would now take less than half that long.

But even more than the stopwatches, Watertown workers deeply resented Taylor's inherent premise that they were lazy morons who would just screw around or mess things up if given any freedom at all. They wrote in a plea to their boss: "It is humiliating to us, who have always tried to give the Government the best that was in us. This method is un-American."

Taylorism nominally fell out of favor in the 1930s, and in modern parlance the word has a negative connotation along the lines of "eugenics" or "lobotomy." But Taylorism's central premise that workers are lazy, stupid, and *never* to be trusted became the undercurrent of American management, from Ford's assembly lines to Taco Bell's decree that every car at the drive-through be greeted within four seconds of pulling up.

The technology available today allows for the kinds of individual, minute levels of supervision and control Taylor could only dream of. The digital ghosts of his stopwatches and "one best way" have infiltrated previously hard-to-quantify sectors of the US workforce, digitally deskilling and speeding up work. Techno-Taylorism has gotten the most attention as it starts making inroads into high-wage jobs such as law, medicine, and journalism, but it's already a way of life in the low-wage sector—fast food, call centers, nursing, elder care, etc. It's very difficult for modern unskilled workers to avoid working in a techno-Taylorized environment defined by mistrust and contempt.

This is because technology also multiplies Taylorism's second prong—deskilling. "If you don't know what to do, just check your scanner—it'll tell you" is Michelle's golden rule, and it's true. Nearly every drop of "brain work" has been wrung out of this job, like so many others. Cashiers used to have to be able to do math in their heads to give people change; today, many registers automatically dispense the appropriate coins. Call-center workers rely on elaborate scripts instead of understanding the systems they work within. London's taxi drivers, who once had to study for years to pass the Knowledge, are being displaced by Uber drivers with GPS maps.

As more and more skill is stripped out of a job, the cost of turnover falls; eventually, training an ever-churning influx of new unskilled workers becomes less expensive than incentivizing people to stay by improving the experience of work or paying more.

And so we get the modern low-wage workplace, where Capital has had Labor in a headlock for quite a while. I can't think of a better example of what happens when employers have total control of what "an honest day's work" means than "time theft," pain-med vending machines, and the never-ending countdown of my scanner.

I may just be naive, but I really *do* think Taylor's goal of ending poverty by increasing efficiency was genuine, though the man often comes off as a callous jerk. He thought his methods would eventually drag the lower classes out of poverty and into a better future, even if they went kicking and screaming.

When done properly, Taylor writes, scientific management can "promote harmony between workmen and the management"—the cliché that a rising tide lifts all boats. If you were to graph his ideal outcome, productivity and real worker compensation would rise in parallel, like this:

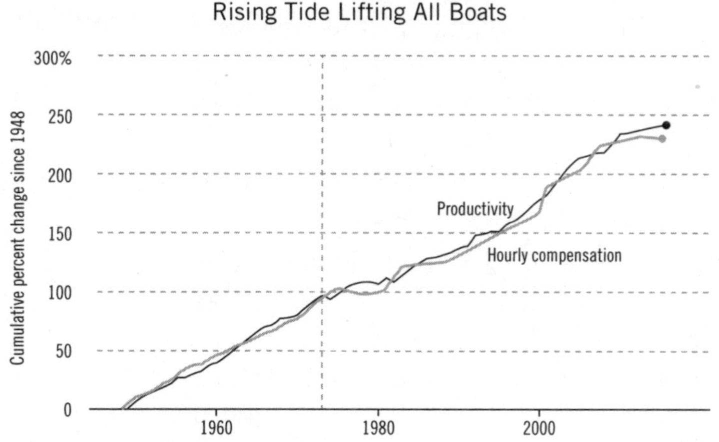

But then Taylor has a rare moment of self-doubt. "In the other case," he cautions, it "may be used more or less as a club to drive the workmen into doing a larger day's work for approximately the same pay that they received in the past." That is, productivity will steadily increase, but management *won't* cut workers in on the profits by raising wages. The graph of *that* situation would look more like this:

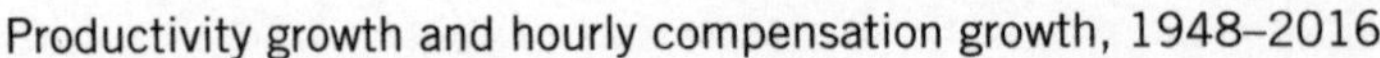

Productivity growth and hourly compensation growth, 1948–2016

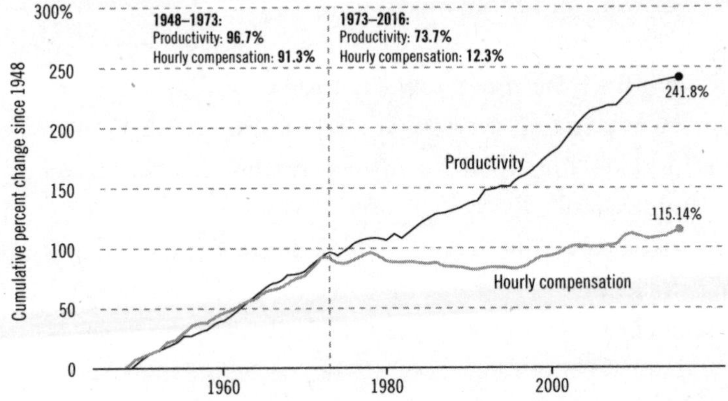

The above is the actual graph of the productivity vs. adjusted-for-inflation average compensation of nonmanagerial workers in the US.[9] Note how it goes according to Taylor's plan at first, but then something in the early 1970s abruptly uncouples labor productivity and worker compensation. The tide continues to rise, but it stopped lifting all boats almost fifty years ago.

What happened in the early '70s? I think about this a *lot* as I walk around SDF8, because I'm desperate for puzzles to take my mind off my aching body and the hours of monotony, which are really starting to get to me. And this actually *is* a legit economic mystery. It's like an Everlasting Gobstopper: I can suck on it *forever.*

The most obvious thing would be business deregulation and the decreasing power of labor unions, but then wouldn't the split have started with Reagan in the '80s? *I guess Carter did his fair share of deregulation...*

Maybe it marks the *real* beginning of global trade. The US basically had a twenty-year head start on everybody else after World War II because so many countries got so wrecked. Maybe the early '70s are just when the rest of the world had recovered enough for things to get back to normal.

The early '70s are definitely when Japan had rebuilt enough to become a force to reckon with. That's about when the Toyota Production System started eating American manufacturers' lunch—something I know from looking up all the Japanese terms like *kaizen* and *muda* that still show up without explanation in signage all over SDF8. And Nixon went to China in '72, though Mao didn't die until... what, '76?

There might have been more people in the private workforce after the end of the Vietnam War and the draft—maybe the women who'd taken the places of men who were sent off to fight in Korea and Vietnam didn't necessarily want to leave when those soldiers rejoined the private sector, and that's about the time double-income households started becoming the norm.

Then there's technology. The silicon computer chip was invented in the late '50s, but it took until 1971 for Intel to come out with the first widely successful commercial version.

What would Taylor think of all this? is another hypothetical to distract myself with. My scanner gun is his vision incarnate—my own personal stopwatch *and* pitiless robo-manager rolled into one. Amazon's system constantly watches, times, deskills, *and* micromanages hundreds of thousands of workers in real time, all day, every day.

Would Taylor be horrified that his fears about the abuse of his ideas had come true? Or would he jizz in his pants?

I force myself to keep walking through those first weeks at SDF8. And, as the nice blue-badge lady promised, it *does* start to get a little easier. I slowly regain the energy to do things outside of work other than sleep and self-pity.

I'm not doing any of the work I'm supposedly here to do, though. I haven't touched my pile of books, and I've written almost nothing—I'm just so exhausted. It's as if I have a set amount of willpower each day, and I use it all up just putting one foot in front of the other all day. I get so panicked about my lack of progress that I force myself to set up a phone interview with an expert on opioid addiction, hoping this baby step will prime the writing pump.

I can't overemphasize the presence of the opioid crisis in the Louisville area. It's *everywhere*—from the front page of every newspaper to the billboards along my commute to the bed I sleep in. It used to belong to Katie's younger brother, who'd gotten addicted to Oxycontin after a difficult brain surgery and made the classic transition to heroin after his prescriptions ran out. His room was only available for me because he was in jail after a years-long downward spiral. The pain of the situation was omnipresent in the McPherson household.

It seemed obvious to me that SDF8 ran on painkillers. And if two Advil could quickly turn into four Advil, how quickly could four Advil turn into codeine, Vicodin, Oxycontin, heroin? Maybe Louisville had been hit so hard by opioids because, with all these warehousing jobs, there was just more . . . *pain* here.

Usually, I'd do more research before taking this vague a theory out in public, but now it's everything I can muster to just call the first person I see quoted about opioids in a newspaper—Robert Walker, of the Center on Drug and Alcohol Research at the University of Kentucky. He specializes in the rise of prescription opioid addiction, particularly in the nearby ground zero of Appalachia. I hope he'll just tell me I'm right, and point me at scientific backing to support my theory.

Instead, Walker gently tells me it doesn't really work that way, and recommends a bunch of books to read. I remember glancing over at my piles of untouched books, already standing as shameful little monuments to my laziness and procrastination.

It's not the injuries and physical pain, Walker says. It's more the stress, and the despair.

"When you're working in a life role with high demand and very minimal resources, you get very high levels of toxic kinds of stress. The job that you're in is classic—you have no control over the demand that's placed on you for productivity for any given hour that you work there. That is a contributing factor to the innate biological desire for *relief.* And that desire is part of what motivates the substance abuse," he says.

I'm fascinated. "You know, since I started, I've—you know everyone's inner four-year-old that just wants McDonald's?"

"Yup!"

"Since I've started this job, I have a *lot* less control over my four-year-old. Like—'Whatever, screw it, I'm going to McDonald's.' Is that related?"

"That's *right!*" he says, excited. "That is *exactly* the same thing! Some people will turn to cigarette smoking, others it's overeating, others it's overdrinking, for others it's drug use."

Then he says something I haven't been able to get out of my head to this day: "The human mind is designed to *not feel bad.* It does not *like* to feel bad. And it will tend to do things that it can to correct for feeling bad. And, unfortunately, things like drugs, alcohol, tobacco, and food—particularly carbs—make us feel *better.* It's a native tendency to self-medicate into a better mental state, to get rid of this overwhelming negativity.

Even when you control for things like access to health care, Walker says, there's a big link between a feeling that you lack control over your life and all sorts of health problems—not just addiction, but cancer, depression, obesity, and heart disease.* The plagues of modernity are rooted in our human instinct to *not feel bad,* to grope around for whatever pleasure we can when everyday life provides none—even if those pleasures are terrible for us.

What many people do is "begin to experience their lives in this hopelessness, a lack of belief in the future—and those are very strong predictors for substance dependence." This, Walker says, is why so much of the War on Drugs has been like "whack-a-mole"—it's only addressed the side effects of our attempts to escape *feeling bad,* rather than seriously looking at *why* so many people feel so bad.

"Like, in Appalachia—if anyone wants to take this substance abuse problem seriously, they will build an interstate and a decent highway system through the area so that people can build businesses there. It's ridiculous to think that treatment or greater law enforcement is going to have any effect on the drug abuse problem there, because it's driven by core economic and life issues. It's a depressing place to live. And people don't like to stay depressed, so they do things to get away from it."

After this conversation, I notice how much stuff I'm doing to get away from life. I hang out with Katie a lot when I'm not at SDF8 or sleeping—binge-watching *Firefly,* discussing boys, even going to the mall for Christmas shopping and getting photos of Kaylee with a constipated-looking Santa. But we keep things mostly sedentary. Staying awake through a whole movie is still about as much as Kaylee and I can handle. I continue making no writing progress.

One day, the three of us are watching *The Muppet Christmas Carol*† when I start laughing almost involuntarily—that same weird, desperate giggle that

---

* For a much more detailed look at this, check out *The Status Syndrome* by Michael Marmot.

† Indisputably the best Christmas movie.

made me think *Crazy people laugh alone in their cars.* Katie looks over with questioning eyebrows—it's not even a funny scene.

It's the end of the workday on Christmas Eve, and clerk Bob Cratchit (played by Kermit the Frog) is timidly hoping his boss, Scrooge, will let him spend Christmas Day with his family. The Muppet adaptation actually hews pretty close to Dickens's original text:

> At length the hour of shutting up the counting-house arrived. With an ill-will Scrooge dismounted from his stool, and tacitly admitted the fact to the expectant clerk in the Tank, who instantly snuffed his candle out, and put on his hat.
>
> "You'll want all day to-morrow, I suppose?" said Scrooge.
>
> "If quite convenient, sir."
>
> "It's not convenient," said Scrooge, "and it's not fair. If I was to stop half-a-crown for it, you'd think yourself ill-used, I'll be bound?"
>
> The clerk smiled faintly.
>
> "And yet," said Scrooge, "you don't think *me* ill-used, when I pay a day's wages for no work."
>
> The clerk observed that it was only once a year.
>
> "A poor excuse for picking a man's pocket every twenty-fifth of December!" said Scrooge, buttoning his great-coat to the chin. "But I suppose you must have the whole day. Be here all the earlier next morning."

"What's so funny?" asks Katie.

"Holy shit, dude," I say, wiping my eyes. "Scrooge *literally* has a better time-off policy than Amazon."

As the weeks go by, I eventually can go a whole shift without sitting down on the floor. I still pop Advil all day like it's my job, of course, but the sharp agony in my feet has dulled into a more tolerable kind of pain. I usually can make rate, and I don't walk out.

On bad days, I think about Henry Noll—what *his* body must have felt like at the end of one of those forty-seven-ton days, and how he eventually drank himself to death.

But though my performance reviews are good, I'm no Schmidt.

I do *know* a Schmidt, though. The next time I see her, I tell her why I'm here, and we make a dinner date for later in the week. At a vegan restaurant.

Blair bursts in an hour late, apologizing for some sort of emergency with her son. I actually didn't mind waiting. Sitting in a chair with nothing to do now feels like a pleasant luxury, and being in downtown Louisville makes me feel less homesick.

I also didn't bother waiting to eat. My new Amazon metabolism means I'm constantly ravenous, and I've already ordered and wolfed down a bunch of fried tofu isotopes. We order some more and get to talking.

Blair's one of very few people I've met who actually enjoys being a picker. She started at SDF8 a little before Thanksgiving through Integrity, but it's not her first time picking.

"I actually used to work for Zappos ten years ago—before Amazon bought them, when they were the small guys. I was one of under a hundred employees back then, when they couldn't foot the light bill for the whole warehouse and all the pickers wore aprons," Blair says. Like Katie, she says Zappos was much more fun than SDF8, though much less efficient—"There weren't elevators and conveyor belts; you did everything by hand."

Blair eventually left Zappos to have her son and since then has mostly worked in the restaurant industry. She applied at Amazon this year because she'd heard it was a good job with good insurance if you were willing to work hard.

"Had you heard Amazon ran things differently than Zappos?" I ask.

"People made it sound *awful!*" Blair says. "It scared the *crap* out of me!"

"Those videos in the Integrity office were *nuts,* right?"

"And orientation! *You must be able to walk over twenty miles in a day! You must be able to stand on your feet for over ten hours a day! You're not allowed to sit down in the warehouse, ever!*"

I laugh, recounting how many times I've had to sit on the floor. Blair hasn't. She follows all the rules to the letter—she really, *really* wants that blue badge.

I find her worries about this silly. Blair's an ideal worker, way better than I am—and I've personally been assured by three young men with Integrity clipboards that conversion is in my future. Blair rolls her eyes, saying they tell everyone that so they won't quit before Christmas. I'm a little deflated, but still try to convince Blair she's golden.

"Didn't you say you won the Power Hour again today?"

"Uh-huh. I always do," she says proudly. She's won it so many times that she's lost track. I ask her to tell me what the hell Power Hour is; I still can't understand most of the megaphone announcements at standup.

She explains that it's an incentive: if you can make a hundred picks or whatever in that hour, you win a prize.

"What exactly do you *win?* Other than eternal glory?"

"Right," Blair says with a giggle. "I'm mainly doing it for the thrill of the hunt. I want to know I can *win;* I want to know I can *conquer.* And I want to be noticed, hopefully, by management. The actual incentive is just a vendor dollar, usually."

She has to explain vendor dollars, too, and I'm dumbstruck.

"So—wait. Let me get this straight. The prize for going as fast as you possibly can for an hour is a dollar coupon for some—but not all—of the vending machines in the building?"

Blair shrugs, saying she's seen it go up to two and even three dollars. "And someone figured out you can put it in the machine and get change back, so you can get a regular dollar—that's what a lot of people do." Plus every time you win, they enter you in a drawing for various Amazon gift cards, which can be worth up to $500. "That's really cool, especially since the number of pickers is dwindling. I think that's why people are mad at me—my odds are a lot better to win that gift card."

I think of Henry Noll, Taylor's living proof that a man *could* regularly lift forty-seven tons a day. Henry Noll, who often had to have an armed guard escort him home from Bethlehem Steel so angry coworkers wouldn't rough him up.

Blair says it's nice to talk to me even if I *am* a journalist, because she hasn't bothered to make many friends during peak. "I'd heard they had a crazy turnover rate because of the workload and the long hours, so I was, like, 'Don't get attached.' I got buddy-buddy with one girl in my training session because I could tell she was serious, like me—but nobody else. And we were looking around at standup yesterday, like, 'Where *is* everybody?' She was, like, 'Do you see anyone else from our training group?' And I was, like, *'No one.'* Not one person from our entire group of—it was over five hundred people."

I raise an internal eyebrow at the idea that Blair could remember the faces of more than five hundred people in her training group. But that level of turnover does sound plausible. Darryl's★ the only other person from training I see around anymore, and I barely recognize any faces at standup after two weeks. The Amazon newsletters posted weekly on the bathroom stall doors have sidebars of fun statistics, including how many new hires there were the previous week. Even during these final few weeks of peak, it's been around twenty-five new blue badges and between four hundred and five hundred new white badges hired every single week. A 99 percent turnover rate for pickers since Thanksgiving isn't that implausible.

"I do think the hours are long—I've never worked such long days," Blair says, not even in food service. "But honestly, I feel like it's a dream job." Like me, she's fascinated by SDF8's size and complexity. It's good exercise, too—her insomnia is *cured.*

Mostly, though, she takes pride in being good at her job. Her numbers, she says, are usually double or triple what other pickers can manage. That doesn't happen for her at every job—she actually *technically* qualifies for disability.

"Between my Asperger's, which is technically classified as autism spectrum disorder, and hearing loss and ADHD and PTSD—that lovely storm of me—that's what qualified me," Blair says. "But I just couldn't accept a handout. I love knowing that the government had my back, but I was, like, 'My mind might be a little special, but my body's fine. I can physically work.'

"And I love that I've found a job that actually utilizes the way that I *am.* My eidetic† memory—I've never really been able to use that at a job before.

★ When our pick paths get close every few days, Darryl always yells, "Hey, *Philly!*" and wanders over to chat for as long as I'm willing to ignore my scanner—the mod's isolation seems to be especially rough on extroverts. He's much more willing to ignore his scanner than I am mine—he claims he heard Time Off Task only matters if it's more than fifteen minutes at a time. I tell him I'm pretty sure that's not right, but he just teases me for worrying about him.

† Photographic.

Like, at the grocery store, I remembered *all* the codes, even for other departments that weren't mine. They'd be coming to me, like, 'What's the code for artichokes?'" Blair laughs. A photographic memory is *very* useful at SDF8, she says. When an item code she's encountered before comes up on the scanner, "there are images attached, not just numbers. I'm remembering the bar code, and its picture, and its feel—that's one of the things that makes me so fast."

I'm a little taken aback. Maybe Blair *could* really remember all five hundred pickers in her training class.

"I don't think the other pickers really understand—they accuse me of cheating all the time! But I can't help that I was born this way! Like, don't hate on me! I'm finally happy! Finding a job where I'm mentally and physically happy—that's hard for me."

When she logs in to her scanner and gets the coordinates of her first item of the morning, her work brain turns on. And her work brain doesn't have room for anxiety. "As soon as I have that first location, that doesn't stop repeating in my head until I'm there. And once I'm almost there, the image of the item I'm about to pick doesn't leave my brain until I have it in my tote and the next location pops in. There's not even time for me to think about anything else, unless I want to suck at my job. I've noticed that any time I'm ruminating or thinking about my personal life, my numbers start to go slower.

"And I love that I go to work, I clock in, I do my job, I clock out. That's it! I've never had a job like that. All the other departments have their shit together! The sanitary team, for instance, cleaning the bathrooms and stuff—I'm a clean person, and every other job I've had I always ended up being the unpaid janitor, you know? I tend to take work home with me. Especially the restaurant industry—it's like you become part of the fibers of the restaurant. But I don't feel like I'm part of the fibers of Amazon. I know Amazon would exist fine without me, and I kind of like that. I *like* being a number."

"I just can't imagine trying to do this job and be a parent, too," I say.

"It's been really hard. I'm extremely close with my son," Blair says, then sighs. "Luckily, I have a very supportive mom; she keeps him for me. I had to wake up at three in the morning and leave the apartment at four to catch the bus, and my son gets on his bus at 7:30. It just wasn't working. So my mom was more than happy to let him stay with her for now.

"That's usually the first place I go when I get off work—I go there and do normal mom things. I just had to have a very frank talk with my son..." Blair trails off, staring down at her plate. "Luckily, he's ten, and he understands that I'm just not going to be around a lot right now, and that it's going to get a lot better after December." Her pain is so obvious and raw that I switch to a happier subject.

"So once you do get that blue badge, what does your ideal future with Amazon look like?"

"I want to beat the world record!" Blair says, her face lighting up. I laugh. "I'm not kidding! I was thinking about it—what's the world picking record? Well, for a human. Because I know those Kiva robots, what they can do—they're gonna put everyone out of work!"

In 2012, Amazon bought Kiva Systems, a robotics company specializing in automating the process of picking and packing in warehouses, for $775 million. SDF8, which opened in 2012, is "seventh generation." The eighth-generation fulfillment centers that opened after 2014 integrate robot and human workers to make picking a stationary job. The robots are orange and kind of cute, like bigger, stronger Roombas balancing drawers on their heads.

"The video I saw, they're, like—shelves that move," says Blair. "They move and dance about the warehouse and communicate with one another; they bring the shelf that has the right item to a human picker. They even face it the right way, so all you have to do is—BEEP!" She perfectly reproduces the noise of the scan gun we hear thousands of times a day.

Blair is right to worry about robots eventually replacing her. All Amazon's metrics and ticking clocks and automatic penalties *are* meant to constrain the inefficiencies of human workers so they act more like robots. Nearly everything human about us is inefficient compared to a Kiva robot—our emergency-prone families, our boredom, our need to use the bathroom. If you think Amazon won't replace its human workers the instant it's technologically feasible, you're kidding yourself.

"But there have been so many items I've been able to pick because of my human intuition," protests Blair. "Like, I can see the tiniest hint of color reflected on a cellophane package five bins up above my head and know that that's the right item. Or I can feel it with my hands and be, like, 'Yeah, this is chiffon.' A robot can't do that. It's my dream to keep those robots away."

"So you're going to be Amazon's John Henry? That didn't work out so great for him," I say. Blair gives me a quizzical look.

The waitress stops by to check on us and we realize we're both still starving. We order a second dinner. As we wait, I recount the story of John Henry as best I can remember.*

John Henry is an American folk hero, possibly based on a real African American railroad worker who died helping to dig the Chesapeake and Ohio Railway's Big Bend Tunnel in West Virginia in the 1870s. At the time, tunnels had to be manually cut through rock. The biggest and strongest railroad workers, called steel-driving men, would use heavy hammers to pound long steel rods as deep as twelve feet into the rock of a mountain. The holes were then filled with explosives and detonated. In the legend, John Henry was the biggest and strongest of the steel-driving men. He supposedly wielded two twenty-pound hammers, one in each hand.

One day, the railroad brought in a steam drill to replace the steel-driving men. John Henry, out of pride or an instinct for job preservation, challenged his boss to let him race the machine, one on one. The boss agreed, and all the railroad workers gathered to watch the battle between man and machine.

John Henry and the steam drill were neck and neck for hours, but as they neared the finish line, the drill finally broke. John Henry kept going and won the contest, but he'd pushed himself too hard—as he struck the winning blow with his hammers, his heart gave out and he fell over, dead. The folktales never really get into what happens after that, but history would suggest that the boss repaired the steam drill and fired the remaining steel drivers as if the contest never took place.

Blair shrugs. It's a sad story, but not a great parallel to Amazon. A steam drill might be able to pound holes in rock or push a cart around a warehouse faster than a human, yes. But a robot definitely can't recognize chiffon by sight or touch or pick up oddly shaped sex toys without dropping them. We

* My recall at the time wasn't perfect; I've substituted a more accurate version.

giggle about the farce of modesty wrapping and the astonishing volume and variety of dildos we've picked.

"Oh, my god, I dropped one the other day and it, like, *bounced!*" says Blair with a laugh.

"If a dildo bounces in the forest and there's only robots around to see it, is it still super funny?" I ask.

I don't want to burst Blair's bubble, so don't mention that Amazon is one of the world's biggest drivers of automation technology and that robots are getting exponentially better at overcoming their limitations.

When I get home, I look up whether there's a picking world record; there actually *is* an annual Amazon Picking Challenge that awards $80,000 in prizes. Grand prize goes to the designers of the robot that comes closest to, essentially, being able to recognize chiffon by its look and feel and pick up dildos without sending them bouncing across the floor. The robots are getting really good at it.

Two Weeks to Christmas

It's 6:45 a.m., and I groan—actually groan out loud—as I log in to my scanner and find myself assigned to the fourth floor. *Again.*

Nobody likes the fourth floor. Sometimes, when pickers log in and draw an assignment on four, they'll log out and back in again, rerolling the dice until they get any other floor. My suspicions about my probability-defying number of fourth-floor assignments were confirmed when we all got scolded for rerolling at standup a couple of days ago.

Here are some of the many reasons to hate the fourth floor:

- **Stairs.** All the bathrooms and break rooms are on the ground floor, and three flights of stairs is no joke when your body hurts this much—plus, it adds to your Time Off Task.
- **Metrics.** Four is where they store oversize items—puffy winter coats, enormous Michael Kors bags, improbably large Carhartt overalls. The drawers up there are double-wide, so the distance between picks is twice as long—at least, it definitely *feels* that way. Your rate also gets kneecapped by all the extra trips to the conveyor belt and back, because a single fuzzy bathrobe or puffer coat can fill a bin to the brim. I almost never make rate on the fourth floor. The rate is ninety per hour (or whatever it is today—it's always changing), whether we're picking small miscellany from the tiny yellow TEK0 cubbies on the ground floor, where, bored, I clocked 140 one day

seeing how fast I could go, or big stuff up on four, where I average between fifty and sixty.*

- **Heat rises.** It's not so bad in December, but the fourth floor is the only place in SDF8 where I get sweaty. I can't imagine what it must be like up here in the summer.
- **It's dark, lonely, and kind of creepy.** Since the whole grid is bigger up here, pickers are even more widely spaced out than usual. You don't realize it on the lower floors, but the mod's fluorescent lights turn off after five minutes or so if they don't sense motion nearby. There's so few people on the fourth floor that each picker basically blazes a light trail into the darkness as she walks. From above, it must look like that Snake game on early Nokia cell phones.

But there's one upside to the motion-sensor lights—they make it clear when there's nobody within earshot and I can sing at full volume. This is no small thing, because I'm starting to lose my mind with boredom.

My body is grudgingly adjusting to the job, but my brain isn't. I've started dreading the monotony even more than the pain. There is literally nothing to do out in the mod but pick. I'm desperate for an audiobook, music, a conversation—*anything* to do with my brain while my body picks.

It's hard to communicate how big a deal the boredom is—it's much easier to write about pain. But I'd never considered quitting because of the pain. The long days of lonely monotony bring me close to walking out more than once.

I get desperate. I pose myself still more hypothetical questions that should take a while to consider, like "What's the most specific human

* Given Amazon's obsessive attention to detail in every other facet of their logistics pipeline, I'd guess they probably *are* factoring in which floor we're on. But if that's the case, they're not telling us.

emotion that would still be recognizable in all cultures?"* I assemble extremely specific playlists in my head.† I play car games with myself.‡

But anything that requires prolonged thought or attention is hard to keep up, I find. Something about picking uses that same part of my brain. The only thing I can do without losing the thread of one or the other is sing. So I sing until I'm hoarse, every day. I have literally taken to memorizing new songs so my repertoire has more variety.

Honestly, though, I've stopped caring who overhears me, which nullifies the only benefit of the fourth floor. I consider rerolling to see if I can get a different assignment, but...whatever. I should embrace the Christmas spirit and let the people gunning for that blue badge, like Blair, have the assignments that'll help their metrics.

As we head out into the mod after standup, I find myself climbing stairs next to the blue velvet harem pants guy. I keep meaning to talk to him, and not just because of the pants—whenever I see him, he's always walking super fast, just like Blair, and always seems to be in a great mood.

"I like your pants," I say. He says thanks, they're his favorite, and introduces himself as Eli.

"Hey—whenever I see you out there, you look like you're having a good time. Can I ask what you do to keep yourself from going nuts?" I ask.

"I count đồng," Eli says.

"Dong?" I say, taken aback.

"Dồng," he repeats, smiling. "It's the currency in Vietnam." He'll be traveling around Vietnam, Thailand, and Laos for five months after peak. "I like to convert the wages into the currency there. Like—*I've made three million đồng today!*"

The crowd on the stairs thins out as we climb past the second floor.

---

* Everything I come up with is put to shame by a smoke-break conversation in which single mothers of very different backgrounds bond over their horrified fascination with how much their teenage sons scratch their balls.

† Songs with a glockenspiel, songs with just a first name as the title, songs where someone yells "YEE-OW!," etc.

‡ I even get all the way through an Amazon-themed "I'm going to the picnic" one afternoon, from Advil to a Zero-tolerance policy about stealing.

"Hey," I say, making a spur-of-the-moment decision. "This is weird, but I'm actually a reporter working here for this book I'm writing—can I maybe talk to you after work sometime?"

"For sure!" says Eli. He's here as a workamper, someone who travels the country doing seasonal jobs, so he's down at the RV park across the street from where we had orientation, with the rest of the workampers.

Eli's in his early forties, much younger than the average workamper. Most are retirees who, for whatever reason, sold the house and bought an RV but can't actually *retire*-retire. So they drive around the country following a nomadic circuit of seasonal work—the previous stop for many of them was the late September sugar beet harvest in Minnesota and North Dakota. Amazon's CamperForce program specifically recruits workampers for peak at some sites, including SDF8, and pays for their campsite rental as an incentive.*

Eli says he came to work peak with a bunch of friends, and in the evenings they usually hang out around the campfire down at the RV park. He invites me to stop by sometime. They'll be easy to find—they're the ones without RVs. I say I'll bring a sixer as Eli turns off at the third floor, waving. *The ones without RVs?*

* For more about workamping, check out Jessica Bruder's *Nomadland: Surviving America in the Twenty-First Century* (New York: W. W. Norton, 2017).

One Week to Christmas

Even though the pain and lethargy are getting better, it still takes me a week to muster the energy to visit Eli and his friends after work. I see what he meant—they're a small sub-encampment of tents wedged between the rows of dark, silent RVs. I follow the sound of voices to a campfire next to a big white van. There's a cluster of small tents nearby, and I spot Eli bustling around a larger tarp-and-stakes outdoor kitchen that reminds me of my time in the Girl Scouts.

The five guys passing a bottle of whiskey around the campfire are younger than Eli—late teens to midtwenties, I'd guess. And while Eli's vibe is hippieish and cheerful, his friends are clearly "travelers"—also known as crusties, also known as crust punks, also known as gutter punks, also known as oogles, also known as homeless, transient young people.

Some travelers panhandle, which can give the impression that they all do. But many, like these guys, live more like Depression-era hobos crossed with '70s anarcho-punks—hitchhiking and riding the rails around the country in search of work. They often follow the same seasonal circuit as the workampers, just less comfortably. I can't believe they're sleeping in tents—it's warm for December, but my car still frosts over every night.

I go say hi to Eli, who's looking a bit maternal as he assembles little mini pizzas for everyone. Eli's worked peak through Amazon's CamperForce program three times, twice in Kansas and now here. He met most of these guys working in Alaska this summer, and at his suggestion, they all came down to camp together for peak. I've definitely seen some of these guys out picking in East Mod, though I haven't really talked to any.

I put my beers in the communal area, take a stump-seat around the campfire, introduce myself and my project, and offer around a big bag of homemade Christmas cookies my mom sent. The guy to my left introduces himself as Zeb and takes one with an enthusiastic "*Fuck,* yeah, thank you!" He takes a bite and closes his eyes in bliss. Zeb is missing half a front tooth, but unlike a lot of people with front-and-center dental issues, he isn't shy about smiling or talking. He really loves to tell stories—sometimes to the point of monologue. When I ask how they all met in Alaska, he launches into the tale, with occasional interruptions from the others.

You see, salmon processing plants need a ton of extra labor every June and July, when the fish return to their birthplaces to spawn. The permanent population of Naknek, Alaska—"The red salmon capital of the world!"—is less than seven hundred people, so companies will fly out, house, and feed workers willing to come up for the summer season.

"So a lot of us up there are drug addicts and alcoholics being sober for the first time in who knows how long," says Zeb. "Up there, an eighteen-rack of beer costs $38. I personally showed up with seven cents in my pocket, and you don't get paid until the very end—so we were all just *fucked.* We had to learn how to communicate sober. It was very strange and enlightening and horrible and miserable and beautiful and great." He gives another asymmetric grin. "That was the first time I'd been sober for an extended period of time since I was thirteen years old."

I ask what the job was like, and all the guys start talking simultaneously, like an enthusiastic high school class. It's pretty charming, honestly. I get the idea they don't get asked nonjudgmental questions about their lives very often.

"We were all flown in as—"

"—just laborers—"

"Yeah, there's these fish that are coming in, and they first go into this machine called the Iron Butcher, which Damien ran—"

"I ran it, too—"

"It decapitates and guts—"

"Naw, they don't have their heads already—it takes the *fins* off, and it scoops the guts out. But you know, it's not perfect—"

"—a hundred and thirty fish a minute!"

"—my face got, like, *covered* in blood—"

"It's, like, a hundred years old, and they haven't built a machine that's more efficient. The only person that can work on it is this old-ass Vietnamese dude who's been doing it his whole life—"

"—there's no instruction manual for it, either—"

"—it's really loud and heinous and scary as *fuck*. Some dude got half his hand cut off—"

"It's literally raining blood, because there's fish up on these conveyor belts two stories up above you getting their heads chopped off, and you're up to your ankles in blood down below—"

"And you're *trapped,*" says Zeb, wresting back control of the narrative with great effort. "They pay for the flight there, the flight back, your food, and your place to stay. But if you quit ahead of time, they charge you for all that, so basically you're trapped on a fucking island. You can't hitchhike out or anything. You're stuck."

"*Fuck,* man," I say, fascinated.

The youngest guy, Neal, laughs. "Were you guys still trying to sell me on this place?"

"Yes," they all say in unison, and laugh.

Neal has a ponytail almost to his waist and looks much less weathered than the other guys. *No way is he over eighteen,* I think.

"It made a lot of us sick," Zeb continues, "because this machine, it gets gunked up. When we did a deep clean, we found remains that had been in there for god knows how long that were gray and sludgy and disgusting, and they smelled *so putrid.* That was giving us what they all called the—what was it?"

"The Naknek Hack!" Even Eli chimes in over his shoulder from the kitchen tent.

"Right!" says Zeb. "Something about the fish rotting in there gets into your lungs, and it made us all sick. Not to mention the sleep deprivation—we were working sixteen hours a day."

"Jesus," I say. "So Amazon is...kind of cake, then?"

The guys jump all over each other in their eagerness to communicate what an easy, bullshit job picking is.

"So was Naknek the worst job you've ever had?"

"No," says Matthias, a serious guy with dirty-blond dreads.

"Without a fucking doubt," says Zeb.

"This was the first real job I've had," says Probably Teenage Neal.

"I thought being in a call center was worse, psychologically," says Damien, the bearded, soft-spoken guy to my right, passing me the bottle of whiskey. I take a pull and pass it along to Zeb.

"I feel like a fucking robot here," says Zeb, "but this is eleven-hour days, indoors. That's *nothing*."

"I dunno, my feet are *fucked*," says the last traveler, a quiet guy who goes by Kalin. I ask what happened.

"Just walking? I guess I went too hard the first couple weeks, and maybe my shoes are weird. But my feet are, like, *mincemeat*. I used to walk twenty miles a day with a backpack on and not change my socks, and they *never* looked as fucked up as they are now." He sticks out a leg for my perusal; his shoes are beat the hell up.

"Hey, what's up with *your* shoes, those heels?" Matthias suddenly asks me. "I saw them when you were out smoking one day and I was gonna comment on them, those badass shoes."

"Oh, they have little springs in the heels—like Inspector Gadget shoes?" I stand and bounce on the heels a little to demonstrate.

"Oh *hell* yeah—like moon boots!" says Zeb. "That's fucking awesome!"

"My knee is all fucked up, and these are supposed to make walking on concrete less bad for it," I say. "It's funny, people ask about them all the time—I expected at least *somebody* to have seen them before, 'cause they're specifically made for warehouse work. But people seem to just wear normal shoes here."

"Can I be honest with you?" asks Matthias. Sure, I say. "I've seen you a number of times over the past month, and I really did think that you were stuck up."

I laugh. "Because I didn't talk to anybody?"

"Yeah, there were a number of times that I wanted to try to, but you were just...I've done it, too, just, like—walk a straight line."

"Yeah!" says Zeb. "I said something to you in passing in an alleyway once, and you looked *so* pissed off, like I offended the shit out of you just by saying hello."

"Aw, I'm sorry! Can I tell you a secret?" I say. I take off the old black ski cap I wear every day and show them the tiny MP3 player and earbud sewn inside. There are oohs and aahs.

It was a last resort. The hours of monotony and loneliness were pushing me to the edge. Most days, I felt like I was going to go crazy by lunch. Finally I rigged up this system to covertly listen to audiobooks, operating the controls at the base of my neck. The risk of being caught was lower than the risk that I would have a bad day, walk out, and never come back.

"I have to keep it turned up really loud so I can hear it even when I'm near a fan or conveyor belt, and sometimes people say things to me that I can't hear," I explain. "But I can't take the headphone out without it being really obvious."

"No, I totally see where you're coming from!" says Zeb, laughing. "I'm glad you talked to us today, because at first I was, like, 'Wow, that girl's a *bitch,*' and I was never going to say a fucking word to you."

"I mean, when I first showed up, I *did* have my 'Don't fucking talk to me' face on because I was so tired, and grumpy as *fuck,*" I say. "I had a desk job before this, so at first I *constantly* felt like shit and kind of hated everyone and everything. Like, the scan-gun countdown—I was so stressed out!"

Matthias laughs and says that I'm clearly working *way* too hard. Metrics only matter if you're trying to get a blue badge. Early on, he says, they really *would* come find you after ten minutes off task, "but now, they need us there more than they're paying us." He's spent the past week testing the boundaries. "You know—'Let's find out where the line is for Time Off Task; let's see when they come and find me.' My record is forty-eight minutes off task before lunch," Matthias says, almost proud. "That was the last time they came to talk to me."

"What were you *doing?*" I say, both horrified and impressed. I'd been curious, too, but my experiments were *much* tamer—mostly just more leisurely trips to the bathroom.

Matthias shrugs—just talking to people he ran into, nothing crazy. "Then I started following Zeb's lead on 'third break.' Right at 5:05, like clockwork every day, I'd be gone for ten minutes, twelve minutes, fifteen minutes. And nobody said *anything*."

"I think at the end, they just gave up on us," says Zeb.

"Ugh, you workampers, you're leaving in, like, five days—whatever," says Eli, distributing mini pizzas.

"Not only that, they were saying that the facility as a whole was already operating at 110 percent—at that point, what the hell does it actually *matter?*" says Matthias, affecting a cheery, brainwashed tone. "We're *Making History! Exceeding Expectations!*"

"Yeah, I go really fast, so I feel like I can sit and talk for five minutes here and there, you know?" says Eli. Like Blair, he frequently wins Power Hours.

"Seriously, though, am I missing something about Power Hours?" I ask. "The prizes seem terrible." There's general agreement that Power Hours are indeed fucking stupid.

"You increase their productivity by 30 percent and you get a fucking soda," scoffs Zeb.

"You know how it says 'work hard, have fun, make history' everywhere?" says Matthias. "I have a theory that the 'make history' part is about how Amazon is a sociological experiment on how far a corporation can push people. Like, *How much can we get away with mistreating human beings for one single fucking dollar?*"

Eli, ever positive, says it isn't about the prizes for him—he just likes doing a good job, and Power Hours are at least something to *do*. Why not?

"Well, yeah, okay—but *why?*" Matthias says, turning to Eli. "You're working even harder for no reason, just because they *asked?*"

"I dunno. It's an easy job, and it pays pretty good." Eli shrugs. "I'm gonna walk out of here in two months with four grand in my pocket. I have fun every day; I meet good people. Sure, my feet hurt a little bit. But other than that, I enjoy it. I see Amazon as a means to my holiday. And that makes it easy."

"But you are less than a fraction of a percentage of the people that they employ at Amazon—you have an end in sight," Matthias points out.

"Oh, *absolutely!*" Eli agrees quickly. "I wouldn't want to do it for a year! It's just my fun money for my trip, and that's why it doesn't bother me." *He gets to leave, too,* I think.

Damien passes me the bottle of whiskey again. I take another pull and pass it on.

"Could any of you work at Amazon for real, without an end date?" I ask.

"No no no no no no no no no *no,*" says Matthias emphatically. "No way, no way."

"I don't think so," says Probably Teenage Neal.

"I could probably do another month if I needed more money for my trip, but that's still an end date," says Eli.

"People that don't have an end date..." Zeb says and shakes his head. "I heard this lady talking on a smoke break, like—'Yeah, I'm trying to move out of the city, and it looks like things are working good at Amazon, so I'm thinking of buying a house around here in the country.' I'm thinking, 'You are moving your whole entire life, purchasing a house and land out here because it's close to Amazon.' That is fucking *insane* to me. Like—Amazon doesn't give a *shit* about you. You're a cog in a machine to them. And there is *nothing* satisfying about this job, nothing challenging. I get no joy out of this job at all."

"I like it a little bit more than Zeb does," says Eli, "but without an end date—*no.* I like knowing that however bad the job is, it's going to end. That's peace of mind. You can do *anything* for a couple of months."

It suddenly starts to rain, and most of the guys run for shelter in the RV park's men's room. I take cover under the kitchen tarp with Eli.

"I've been traveling since I was nineteen," he says. "Not like how these guys do, hopping trains and shit, but I've been to nineteen countries. I see jobs as a means to my end. I make probably ten grand a year, and I feel like I'm living like a rich man. How many millionaires go on five-month vacations? I'm giddy as hell about the next five months. I have no idea what it's going to bring—I have an entry flight and an exit flight and three countries to explore."

It sounds amazing, and I tell him so.

"I retire every year! Why wait until you're sixty-five? I don't know if I'm gonna be in good health—my brother's fifty, and he's falling apart! I'm gonna live every year the best I can. There's so many people stuck in their ruts—not happy, going to work to pay bills for houses and cars they can't afford. Taking money way too seriously makes them hate their jobs, and then they hate their life."

What about kids? I ask.

Eli shrugs. "I don't have any kids. And I don't have a house. I have no bills—well, I have my cell phone and the insurance and upkeep on my van, but the job in Alaska takes care of that for the year, and Amazon is for my flight and some spending đồng. I feel like I'm living a dream, and I never want to wake up."

It does kind of sound like a dream to me. But it means living entirely in the short term, like our hunter-gatherer ancestors. In this dream, you never have kids, save money, put down roots, get old or sick, or need to take care of your elderly parents. It's a dream of having every roll of the dice come out in your favor, forever.

It makes me think of that mean-spirited fable about the grasshopper and the ant—Grasshopper plays his fiddle all summer while Ant works stockpiling food. When winter comes, Ant eats and Grasshopper starves. *As he should,* the fable always seemed to imply.

Still, I envy Eli's chill. "Seriously, dude—you're the least stressed-out person I've met in *years.*"

He grins. "Zero stress!"

"How does that . . . *feel?*" I ask. *Wow, what a sad question.*

"*Amazing!* I do shit that makes me *happy.* You don't need to worry about anything if you're happy. My nephews think I'm the coolest uncle on the planet—I'm heading there next, to spend Christmas with my sister and my nephews. I want to teach my nephews this lifestyle—that you don't need a lot of money to do amazing things. My brother and his wife make a hundred grand a year, and they can't make ends meet—they're thinking about canceling fucking *Netflix. Really?* People get stuck in their lives. They go to work to pay bills for houses they can't afford and cars they can't afford, and they hate their jobs and they hate their lives."

Zeb dashes through the rain into the tent for more Christmas cookies. I hand over the bag.

"Oh, my god, will you tell your mother these are *fucking kick-ass?*" he says, taking a blissed-out bite of a snowman. I promise to use those exact words. "What *are* they?"

"It's my grandpa's recipe. They're such a pain in the ass to make," I say. "He was a baker—like, he worked in an actual bakery—so the recipe makes about eight thousand cookies, and baking and frosting them takes all day. But they somehow don't taste the same when you cut the recipe down."

"My grandpa's sixty-five years old and just had his hip replaced a couple of months ago, and he's still out there building houses," says Zeb. "He's the biggest inspiration in my whole life. I love him, and I love the *idea* of him. He's been working his ass off forever, and he respects that I decided to hit the road. Because he's worked his ass off for fifty years and done what you're supposed to do, and he's still sixty-five years old and poor as *fuck*."

Zeb notices Eli reaching for a cookie out of the corner of his eye and slaps his hand away. "*No,* Eli!" he scolds. "You've got the di-a-*beet*-us! *No cookies!*" Eli scowls but retreats.

After Amazon, Zeb says, he's probably going to head back home to Texas, build some houses with his grandpa, settle down for a while. He's been traveling for six years, and his partner passed away last summer—that's how he ended up in Alaska, to get away from everything and get sober while he was mourning.

Building things with his dad and grandpa feels like the exact opposite of working at Amazon, Zeb says. "I really loved building and being outside—and leaving something *lasting,* you know? I get to work with my grandfather and learn his expertise; he knows everything about everything. I'm working for myself and my family instead of making someone else rich.

"And carpentry's so beautiful. Sometimes you get warped pieces of wood, and you have to think outside the box, abstractly, how you're going to put them together and make it all work. It's like a puzzle. You put your mental energy *and* your physical energy into it, and at the end you can sit back and look and people are going to *live* in there and enjoy it. It's, like—Yeah, I fucking *made* that. It's an amazing feeling, you know?"

One Day to Christmas

SDF8 feels deserted on Christmas Eve. The number of pickers at East Mod standup each morning has steadily dwindled to maybe fifty people—probably a quarter of what it was when I started. Standup is less businesslike than usual today; there's more smiles and conversation as we stretch. Peak's finally almost over.

Eli and Zeb and the gang are sitting on the stairs discussing what time we're likely to get out. Eli says last year there wasn't much work to do on Christmas Eve, so most of the day shift was sent home around 10:00 a.m. I very much hope this happens—I'd love to be home in time for the McPhersons' big family dinner and card-playing extravaganza.

As we stretch, a manager on a megaphone tells us few dozen temps still standing to stop by the Integrity office to fill out the paperwork that will begin our conversion to blue badges.* *I made it!* I think. I'm stupidly proud, despite having heard plenty of stories suggesting that this isn't as done a deal as it sounds. Still, I think, *I am a first-rate woman.*

I'm barely even grumpy to be assigned to the fourth floor, where I spend most of the morning singing Christmas carols to myself. When I catch a flash of red and white out of the corner of my eye, I wonder if SDF8 *has* finally driven me mad. But when I backtrack a few feet—*yes.* Bent over, rummaging in a drawer, is Santa Claus. Perfect natural beard, glasses, hat,

---

* Or I'm pretty sure that's what he said—I can still only *sort of* decipher anything said through the megaphone. I confirm it later.

red suit—though as a concession to the physicality of picking, the sleeves have been cut off. My scanner nags at me to move along, but it has no power over me anymore. I drop it into my tote and go talk to Santa.

He says he does this every year to lighten the mood. He's actually a professional Santa when he's not at SDF8. "In fact, I've got an appearance tomorrow—the Haven House Christmas party for the homeless. I've been their Santa for about three years," he says. It's a volunteer gig, he tells me. "But you know what? That's what it's all about. All this *stuff*"—he waves a hand at the shelves—"when there's so many people in this country that have *nothing*."

"I get that feeling in here a lot," I say, smiling at him.

"Stuff! That's all it is. It's *stuff*. And if we don't have people like you with a smile on your face, who know that they're blessed to be healthy enough to work here, even though it's hard work...why get upset?" He gestures at the cardboard labyrinth around us. "Some people get so angry with *this,* the bad things that happen here, and—it is what it is."

Before I can ask what that means, Santa notices his scan gun, which has been blinking at him for a while. Unlike me, he's still in its thrall. "Oops! I've got to keep going," he says apologetically, tossing a bagged shirt into his tote. "Have a blessed Christmas!" he says over his shoulder as he rounds a corner and vanishes.

After break, I'm assigned to TEK0, where all the small miscellaneous crap is stored. Since TEK0's yellow cubbies are tiny compared to the usual cardboard ones, there's always a much higher picker density in this area, and today we keep forming brief clusters to joke and exchange rumors about when we'll be sent home. Some, like me, are happy for the chance to get out of here; others would prefer to stay and get paid for the full scheduled shift. I'm pleased to have the novel piece of gossip that Santa's out in the mod somewhere. Nobody else has seen him.

During one of these little gatherings, we hear a far-off cheer, like a sports game over the hill. "That'll be inbound," a blue badge says. "If they're getting out now, we won't be much longer."

She's right. In another hour, my scan gun tells me that there's no more work to be done, so I drop off my last tote, park my cart, and head back to the standup area. There's no big group, just a slow trickle of pickers emerging from East Mod as they get the same message.

The shift manager barely looks up from his computer to say I can head home if I want. It's a bit of an anticlimax. I put away my scan gun, clock out, get my coat, and go to leave. I pause at the turnstile for one last look up at all the yellow totes, still flowing along. *Last chance for a joyride,* I think.

But instead, I walk through the turnstile, get in my car, and drive away.

363 Days to Christmas

On my last night in Louisville, I've arranged to meet up with Eli's friend Akasha and two of her friends for karaoke at the Levee, a small smoky bar on the Indiana bank of the Ohio River. All three women are blue badges, and all three like working at SDF8.

I drink a beer and watch the news on the TV behind the bar as I wait. I haven't really been following the election—keeping up with the news lately feels even more like work than my shame-pile of unread books. It's on mute, but Republican front-runner Donald Trump appears to have issued a Christmas tweet demanding credit for an Obama initiative to deport hundreds of families who'd fled violence in Central America. In other news, Bernie Sanders called Trump vulgar for saying Hillary Clinton "got schlonged" in the 2008 primaries.

God, 2016 is really going to suck, I think.

I recognize Akasha the instant she walks in. She sometimes led stretches at standup; I'd mentally nicknamed her Happy Goth. She looks much younger than her age, thirty-eight, and the best description I can come up with is that she almost certainly owns a Harley Quinn costume.

Today Akasha's wearing a black ruffled Victorian jacket that laces up the back like a corset. She's as cheerful as her wardrobe is somber—a proud self-proclaimed weirdo who loves to talk and is unrelentingly positive about Amazon. Throughout the night, I'm often unsure whether she's being aggressive or just aggressively friendly.

Akasha's been at Amazon for seven months, coming in as a temp but leveling up to a blue badge after a single week—an SDF8 record, she says with pride. Her husband's been at Amazon for three years. "I tried to get him to come out, but he doesn't stand for this kind of entertainment," she says with a giggle.

"I'm a country bumpkin—I only do country bumpkin songs," says Melody, leafing through the karaoke book. Melody is twenty-three and reminds me of Rhonda the Tank—big, young, strong, and athletic, a rugby coach's dreamgirl. Melody goes hard at life, which makes me like her immediately. She drinks Long Island iced teas, laughs loud, and somehow manages to hold down a second job on top of Amazon, which means she works seven days a week. "I'm kind of a workaholic," she says. She grew up doing manual labor on her family's farm, and she's held down two jobs for years—before starting at Amazon three or four months ago, she'd work an eight-hour shift at the gas station, wait half an hour, then work at a pizzeria until 10:00 p.m.

The third woman is Hailey, who's a stower most of the time. She's been at Amazon the longest, ten months. Hailey's twenty-seven, married, and the mother of two girls, ages seven and nine. Hailey's husband works the night shift as a school custodian.

"My dad worked a night shift for years when I was a kid," I say. "Looking back on it, that must have been really rough on both my parents."

"It is," Hailey says. Her husband gets home and goes to sleep an hour before she wakes up for work, so she hardly ever gets to see him. "We have Sunday if I'm not working mandatory overtime, and occasionally we have Monday morning—if I don't have to work Monday morning—to see each other, and that's pretty much it."

"Are you a socialist?" interrupts Akasha, leaning forward to look me in the eye suspiciously.

"A . . . socialist?" I repeat, confused. I can barely describe my own political beliefs to myself.

"Like, are you a communist?"

I decide to go with the least complicated answer that's also true, which is no.

"But you do support the unions?"

About one sentence into my rambling explanation of that one, Akasha loses interest and darts off to the bar. In hindsight, I realize she was probably asking if I was a union organizer—Amazon is hardcore antiunion and has historically made workers sit through a lot of propaganda to make them suspicious of unions.

Melody sips her drink, saying somewhat blissfully that this is her first day off in a month. I mention how I tried to pull off working two jobs seven days a week when *I* was twenty-three, and that it made me so tired, irritable, and depressed that friends staged a semi-intervention. How does *she* manage it?

"Well, peak's been tough. I think the part that helps me the most is that I have an amazing husband that completely understood," she says. Like Hailey, Melody works days while her husband works nights, and doesn't get to see him that much. It's a bummer, but it makes having dogs much easier—she doesn't have kids yet, either. "And I have a wonderful support system with my mother, who comes by every once in a while and lets her grandpuppies out. It's stressful, but the support system makes it possible.

"But yeah, my house has been a wreck the whole time. I don't have time to cook, and I'm a person who loves to cook. It's my stress reliever." She pauses. "Granted—I did break down a couple times. But it's okay. Because I have bills, and bills require *money*."

"Money's never been that important to me," says Akasha, popping back into the conversation holding a glass of something pink and potent-looking.

"It's not, except for the bills," says Melody. "The only part I like about money is that it keeps me in a car and it keeps the electric on in my house. I honestly don't spend money on anything but bills. Like, this—right here, right now—is a splurge for me."

Akasha hugs her. "I'm so glad you're splurging tonight!"

A waitress arrives with a tray of complicated-looking shots Akasha apparently ordered for the table, which taste like a root beer float mixed with a Jäger hangover. As we study the karaoke book, I mention my habit of singing around the warehouse and ask how they deal with the monotony.

"I volunteer to learn new things every chance," says Melody. "I'm a picker; I can stow; I can pack multiple items *and* single items. And I'm an ambassador, which is one of the people who trains newcomers. If you want to learn things, if you want to excel, they'll give you that opportunity. You just have to say yes."

Akasha also likes learning new jobs so it's not just the same thing every day, but she legitimately enjoys picking. "I love every single time I pick something out. Every bin is like a treasure chest, I open it up and—why are you laughing? It's so true!"

"No, it's just funny because a couple other people said that *exact* same thing—that it's like a treasure hunt," I say.

"I'm just laughing because I remember all the crazy things I pick," says Melody.

"Oh, my god, my first pick in TEK0 was a holy Bible, and my second pick was a set of three different size butt plugs!" Akasha giggles. "And I put it right on top of that Bible, thinking, 'They will *never know!*' "

"Honestly, what keeps me going is that I got people I can talk to for five seconds every once in a while, to just say hey," says Melody. "If I didn't have people to talk to—you can't go eleven hours without talking to people." She pokes Akasha. "Where were you that day I ran into the wall because I fell asleep?"

"Oh, my god—I came so close to falling asleep on the floor during my first week," I say. They know just what I'm talking about.

"You know that falling feeling you get right as you're falling asleep?" asks Akasha. "Sometimes it does happen at work! As I'm picking, I'll feel the falling, and I'll shake it off and go, 'How long was I gone?' And then I'll notice my scanner's doing that thing it does when you're inactive too long—'In so many seconds, you're going to be logged out.' "

"I had a stower come over and check on me once," says Melody. "She yelled and I didn't respond, so she came across the conveyor belt to check on me because I'd fallen asleep on top of my tote."

"As a stower, I have seen that happen *so many times,*" pipes up Hailey. "Someone will pull out a drawer and lean against it with their head down—"

"And next thing you know, you're signed out of your gun and the water spider* is shaking you, like—'Hey, man, are you all right?' " Melody laughs.

* "Water spider" is another odd Amazonian job title. From the few days I spent in packing, I gather that it involves running around keeping stationary workers supplied with materials.

"My main problem is when they've got us walking from one end of the mod to the other. I have a bad issue falling asleep while walking."

The karaoke DJ calls Akasha's name, and we cheer as she bounces up to the small stage.

"So you're in stow?" I ask Hailey. "That's one of the ones I never learned."

"Yeah! I fuckin' love my job!" Hailey says, but then Akasha's song starts, instantly derailing every conversation in the bar. Akasha seems to be profoundly tone-deaf, but makes up for it in volume, enthusiasm, and stage presence. Hailey, Melody, and I watch in rapt silence.

"What's that musical about the giant plant that eats people?" I finally say.

"*Little Shop of Horrors*!"

"I think this is from that."

I ask Melody what the best of her many jobs was. "Honestly? This one," she says. At previous jobs, she kept getting roped into doing managerial work for entry-level pay. "I've been told that I'm too damn nice. Whenever they ask me to go places at Amazon, I'm, like, 'Why do *I* have to go?' and they're, like, ''Cause you're nice. And you won't tell me no.' "

But picking is easy compared to farmwork, and it's the best-paying job Melody's ever had—or sees herself getting anytime soon. "I'm from a small town, so pretty much the only jobs you're gonna get are cashier, teller, manual labor—there's just not a whole lot of work opportunities," she says. "I have to drive an hour to get to Amazon, but my paycheck makes it worth it."

We again fall into silent awe as Akasha hits her big finish, and cheer as she bows. "Next is...Melody?" announces the DJ, to Melody's surprise. She goes to the stage, laughing and loudly protesting.

Quiet Hailey leans over. "I put in 'Like a Surgeon' by Weird Al Yankovic for her," she giggles. We die laughing at Melody's utter delight when the song title comes up. "So where do you ladies work? What do y'all do?" the DJ asks over the intro. *"Amazon!"* we yell. "Oh, yeah? I got a couple friends that work out there," he says.

"I think everyone does nowadays!" yells Akasha, staying onstage for a Weird Al duet.

"So can you tell me about stowing?" I ask Hailey. "As a picker, I mostly thought of y'all as those people who block the aisles."

Hailey gives me a long, detailed answer, but it's basically picking in reverse—she takes totes of items and distributes them in drawers around the mod. "I like it way more than it sounds," she says with a laugh. "I like to organize things. There's all these rectangles and squares and shit, and you put the rectangle in the rectangular place. I just love it. *Inventory!*" She punches the air with self-mocking enthusiasm.

Hailey started as a temp and converted to blue badge, and says working for Amazon directly is a lot less stressful than Integrity. "The job's the exact same thing, but with Amazon you don't have the people in the blue vests coming at you with, like—'You did this wrong; these are your errors for this week; you're working too slow; whatever.' If you're in the bottom 5 percent for something, they'll come talk to you and tell you to straighten up, though. And then you cry." She laughs. Blue badges also get more leeway with time off—some of it is even paid—and she says the insurance is great.

"I work really hard and just have a fuckin' positive attitude about shit, because that place is *oppressive.*" Hailey seems suddenly embarrassed. "Um. So." She returns to talking about what she likes about Amazon as Akasha and Melody return from the stage.

"The totes start flying down off the line, you throw 'em on the boats, and there's people standing around. It's your job to get that stuff onto the boats so they can take it and do *their* job," says Hailey. "You take this vast gray landscape, and you slowly fill it up with these nice, neat rows of yellow."

The constant monitoring I found so stressful doesn't bother these women. I felt like someone was always watching in case I screwed up; they feel like someone's taking note of the good work they do. All three have had to pick up slack from deadbeat coworkers at other jobs; when it's obvious who's working and who isn't, you never end up doing someone else's job on top of your own. They also say it's a relief to really know their place in the organization. Their job duties are clear, their hours are usually reliable, and when they clock out, they leave the job at SDF8. "I go home at six and don't have to worry," says Melody.

"Emily, take your jacket off and wear mine! I want you to feel what it's like to be me for a minute!" Akasha says suddenly. I shrug and swap my jacket for Akasha's ruffly Victorian waistcoat. She's a foot taller than I am, so it's much too big. "I just want to be able to see it!" she says, pleased. "When I wear it, I don't get to see it."

Seemingly empowered by wearing my clothes, Akasha assumes the role of interviewer, an antagonistic gleam in her eye. "So! Emily! How was *your* experience at Amazon? And if there was one thing you could do to change it, what would be the one thing?"

I think about this as a woman starts singing "Let It Go" from *Frozen.* "Well...there have been a few articles written about it, and I talked to a bunch of former workers beforehand, and the impression I got was that it was going to be hell on earth. And I didn't find it to be that way. Everyone was much nicer than I expected. It hurt way more than I'd expected, but it wasn't, like, a *hellhole.* The atmosphere and pick rate might be different from warehouse to warehouse, though, so—"

"Can I respond to what you just said?" Akasha breaks in. "The people that say negative things online are the people that were *not interested in working.* Of *course* they had negative things to say! They are not the hardworking Americans that they should be. They want handouts, even though Amazon gives so much leniency! Like, one girl I talked to had to come in late one day during peak, and they let her work over for the time that she was late so she could still get her gift card!"* She crosses her arms, smiling, as if to say *Argue with that!*

My insides twist up, only partially because of the latest round of shots. *But that's not what leniency is!* I want to shout. *If buying a few drinks at a dive karaoke joint is a splurge, your job does not actually pay well! If you describe your workplace as oppressive, you don't actually love your job!*

Akasha, Melody, and Hailey are ideal employees. Melody in particular reminds me of Schmidt—young and strong and hardworking. Schmidt, whose best quality in Taylor's eyes was that he didn't realize that he deserved more. *How can you not see that you deserve more?* I think.

But what am I going to say? Am I going to lecture these three women—who are, frankly, a lot further into adulthood than I am—about what they

* You got a $100 Amazon gift card for volunteering to work the maximum 59.5 hours during the final few weeks of peak.

should expect from a job? If they say Amazon is a hell of a lot better than their other options, who am I to doubt them?

"I dunno. I've read some of those articles about what it's like to work at Amazon," says Hailey, surprising me. "And, some of 'em, they kind of have merit. Well, I mean, they *do!*" She looks at Akasha defensively. "They're not *wrong* about the way that people are treated. But I think if you're working there to write something, you're observing it from the outside. So you might not necessarily feel that sense of community that I think a lot of us do."

"Because you're on the outside looking in," says Akasha. Melody nods.

"That's exactly why I wanted to talk to you—" I say, just as the woman singing "Let It Go" hits the song's big high note. She's got a good voice, but all four of us wince.

"I would applaud, but the song's ruined for me," says Melody.

"This song makes everyone I know with a kid want to die," I say.

"I have a fourteen-year-old. She loves this song!" says Akasha.

"I have a seven- and a nine-year-old, and the only way I've escaped it is that it's only on my laptop," says Hailey, which she has password-protected.

"But I think that's a big part of my experience not being as bad as I expected," I say. "I don't *have* kids. I don't even have dogs. Most people I talk to are taking care of kids or grandkids, and I just can't imagine how that works long-term."

"Well, during peak I was so tired I was really emotional—I wasn't dealing with things very well," says Hailey. "But now that peak's over and I'll be able to get more sleep again, I think I could stay with this job for an indefinite amount of time. It's really just about how long until they fire me for my negative UPT,"* she adds wryly.

"*What?* You have negative UPT?" Akasha looks up, deadly serious.

"Yeah, I have negative sixty-seven hours of UPT."

"Oh my god."

"I know. I'm gonna get fired," Hailey says with a sigh.

"What are some reasons you took UPT?" I ask, but Akasha holds up a "one second" finger, looking at Hailey in real distress.

"Are you coming back?"

---

* Unpaid time off.

"Yeah. Everyone ends up coming back."

"Okay, go ahead and answer her question. I'm so sorry...but—you're fine?"

"Yeah, everything's fine. We're good. We're good." Hailey turns to me.

"Reasons I've taken unpaid time? Well, we only have one car working, so if one of the kids is sick at school or having behavioral problems or whatever, I have to leave work to go get the kid, and then you can't clock back in after you've clocked out. I lost probably twenty hours that way over a month. Any time you're late clocking in or late clocking in from lunch, obviously. Then my uncle died—"

"But they have leave time for that!" says Akasha.

"Yeah, but I'm too scared to talk to them about it right now because I'm so negative," Hailey says. "I only missed one day for the funeral, but I went home early several days during the rest of the week."

"Because you *had* to! You couldn't help it!" says Akasha.

"I was going through my day super numb, I was just *crying*—it was terrible," says Hailey. "I went home early a bunch of days in a row. So that's about thirty hours there."

Hailey and Akasha retreat into an emotional conversation, their foreheads pressed together. To give them some privacy, Melody and I discuss the characteristics of a good karaoke song. After a few minutes, they share a long drunk hug and return to the conversation.

"So to get back to what you asked, that was my experience," I say. "With no kids, no deaths in the family, no emergencies—it was hard, but I could do it. But people are *humans* with *human lives!* That's the thing!" Some part of me notes my use of "That's the thing," a phrase I use in direct correlation with how drunk I am. "That's the *thing!* Humans aren't robots. They get sick, their kids get sick, their cars break down, shit happens—that's always *been* a factor in jobs, and it'll always *be* a factor in jobs. It's just that companies have made it so all the burden of that...that human lack of efficiency falls on you, and you, so that none falls back on them."

"But it's not the case here—they *were* able to give me some time off!" Akasha protests. "I even asked them right before peak; they were willing to give it *all* to me. But I said no."

"They do make an effort to make accommodations. But they have to mitigate the risk of people abusing the system," says Hailey. She understands why there have to be strict rules at a company as big as Amazon, she says, then pauses as if bracing herself to say something shocking. "But I'm of the mindset, myself—why should we have to work like this just to prove that we're worth shelter and food? So. So, like, the whole system is frustrating to me." She sighs. "You hear older people say stuff all the time—like, I'm a company man, you work for the company, and the company provides for you. But the company doesn't do that anymore, because it's not *company,* it's *corporation*."

"I'm with you," says Melody. "If you're a company man, the company is right where you are. They understand the situation where you live; they understand you're humans. If you're in a huge corporation—hell, I mean, all our questions go to Chicago."

"Chicago don't know what the hell we're going through," says Hailey. "The degrees of separation, the barriers, the hierarchy—"

Akasha squeals with delight as she's called up to sing again, kicking things off with an insane witch cackle. Her performance is just barely recognizable as "I Put a Spell on You" by Nina Simone. As advertised, we are spellbound.

"Is she even saying words?" Hailey eventually whispers.

"I think this is the entirely scat version," I whisper back, giggling, delighted at how much fun Akasha's clearly having.

"What I love about her is that she really *means* it," Hailey says. I agree.

"This is one of the songs I would just *belt* when I was pushing my cart around," I say. "I would sing every song I could remember to keep myself from going nuts."

"I sing constantly at my job," says Hailey.

"I heard this one dude belting out Celine Dion once," says Melody. "Sounded *just* like a chick. He turns the corner, and it's this guy with dreadlocks and a giant beard. And I'm, like, '*Dude.* You rock.'" We laugh, and I wonder if Matthias has a secret talent.

"Emily? Do we have an Emily still here?" asks the DJ. I look around, but nobody else stands up. I *love* karaoke, but I've been so in reporter mode all night I didn't put any songs in for myself. Melody and Hailey dissolve into laughter. "We put in a song for you!" says Melody. "Get up there!"

Fortunately, they picked "Sixteen Tons" by Tennessee Ernie Ford, a song I'd specifically mentioned I loved when we were discussing what makes a good karaoke song earlier. *Oh, man,* I think as I take the mic. *This is so on the nose.*

You load sixteen tons, what do you get
Another day older and deeper in debt...

That's the end of work talk for the night. We drink more, we sing more, we talk about our husbands and boyfriends and kids and pets and the new *Star Wars.* When we finally say good night, I sit in my car for an hour sobering up as a thunderstorm rolls in. The rain is crazy intense, and from where I'm parked I have a good view of the Ohio River as it begins to flood, the water climbing halfway up a lamppost down by the banks. *Oh,* I think muzzily. *That's why they call this place the Levee.*

The next morning, I wake up with a tremendous hangover, pack up my unread books, hug the McPhersons goodbye, and start the twelve-hour drive back home. *I get to leave,* I think as I pull onto the highway.

PART TWO

CONVERGYS

My phone pings. It's been twelve minutes since I logged out of my headset. I have a little under three minutes to finish my cigarette, get back upstairs to my desk, put on my headset, log in, and indicate that I'm available for a new call.

This tree-shaded cluster of picnic tables around the side of the call center is the only place on Convergys property where we're allowed to smoke. From a certain angle, the view is green and peaceful—you'd never guess all that lush overgrowth hides a sinkhole that swallowed a Buffalo Wild Wings franchise a few years back.* The heat wave that's plagued western North Carolina all summer has taken the day off, too, so it's actually pleasant to stare out at the trees, chain-smoking and trying to unfuck my nerves before I have to get back on the phones.

Usually I'd spend my break chatting with the ladies of the smoking crew—Kolbi, Jess, Kaitlyn, Destiny, Monae, Brianna, the Patties—but at this point, half of them have quit.† Or were fired. As with Amazon, it's often unclear.

I miss their company, but today I'm grateful for peace and quiet. I caught two nasty screamers in a row this morning, and I'm still jittery hours later. I could honestly use a few more minutes of dejittering, but can't afford any more points on my record for something as stupid as being a minute late coming back from break. So I stub out my half-smoked cigarette and start back toward the main entrance.

Rounding the corner, I almost run into Kolbi, a curvy black twenty-two-year-old from my class whose sense of humor aligns well with my weirdness. We both tend to finish classwork in half the time given, so we became early allies in the battle against solitary boredom.

---

* My low-key obsession with the Buffalo Wild Wings sinkhole, which I think is the single funniest detail in the entire book, continues to baffle my husband, friends, and editor.

† The call center, not smoking.

But I've hardly had a chance to talk with Kolbi since we got on the phones. They've stopped scheduling our group's breaks together, and it was made quite clear that chatting on the clock is time theft. Even if talking was allowed, it'd be hard. We sit in pods of high-walled cubicles, so you can't even make eye contact with your neighbor. And there's usually less than a minute between the end of one call and the beginning of the next.

I smile and walk over to say hey, wishing I had more than two minutes to take advantage of this bit of luck. But as I get closer, I spot an improbable number of other people from my class clustered nervously near the entrance. *Maybe not good luck,* I think.

When she sees me, Kolbi grabs my arm, wide-eyed, and says one of the Patties just had a heart attack or something.

"Holy *shit!*" I say. "Jesus, poor Patty! What happened?"

"She was sitting on my row," Kolbi says. "She was on a call, and then all of a sudden she said she couldn't breathe; then she said it again, louder, then she fell off her chair and was lying on the floor holding her chest, sort of rolling around. She looked *real bad*."

I mean, it was just a matter of time, thinks some unkind part of me. I squish the thought, feeling awful. I really like the Patties.

The pair of fiftysomething white women known as the Patties obviously already knew each other on the first day of class. When we went around introducing ourselves, our trainer Kimberly laughed at the silliness of two Patties sitting next to each other, saying we'd have to come up with nicknames.

"Well, you know I'm the good one, right?" said one Patty, grinning slyly. The other Patty punched her in the shoulder in mock outrage. "*Ow!* Yup, it's Good Patty and Evil Patty, remember that!" repeated the first as we laughed, rubbing her shoulder.

It was like watching a vaudeville team perform a routine they'd spent years perfecting. I didn't realize quite how many years until, as the smoking crew got to know one another better, the Patties mentioned living together and having grandkids.

The Patties are so inseparable that classmates and I often refer to them as a single unit. But you'd never mistake one for the other. We used their last initials to refer to them individually, but for clarity I'll call them Butch Patty and Aunt Patty.

Butch Patty—"Good Patty"—is short and sturdy, with graying, boyishly cut hair under a Carolina Panthers ball cap. She's a huge Panthers fan and often wears a matching shirt or basketball shorts in Panthers blue. I can't imagine her in a dress. Butch Patty isn't dumb, but often pretends to be for comic effect.

Aunt Patty—"Evil Patty"—is even more solidly built, but in a softer, more maternal way. Physically, she looks custom-built for snuggling grandchildren, but she's sharp as hell—her mouth included, if you piss her off. She and Butch Patty make an excellent comedy duo, and they've made the long weeks of training and memorization so much more fun than they could have been.

An ambulance pulls up the drive, sirens off. *That's good, right?* I hope it was a panic attack, not a heart attack—it's easy to mistake one for the other, and this wouldn't be the first panic attack that required an ambulance just in my twenty-person class.

I don't actually think to ask which Patty the ambulance is here for—it's that obvious. Aunt Patty's a natural on the phones; she's for sure in the top three of our class. Whenever I pass her cube, she sounds confident and in control.

Butch Patty is the opposite. Again, she's not *dumb*. But, like me, she's not great at talking on her feet, especially when someone's yelling at her. She's probably further handicapped by her Carolina accent, which stands out as thick in a class where most everyone pronounces "Hi" as "Ha."

Butch Patty just never seems to get a good call. Every time I walk past her cube, she's stammering and apologizing—clearly in the middle of being yelled at. Worse, she lets the screamers get in her head. During training, she spent breaks joking around. Since we started on the phones, every time I see her she's midmonologue, re-creating some terrible call for whoever will listen. She justifies herself over and over—she was just doing what she was *supposed* to do; she *couldn't* have done what the customer wanted, because... She does this even when nobody's really paying attention, as if the screamer's ghost came through the phone and followed her outside to continue the argument. It looks exhausting.

I feel awful for Butch Patty, and not just because I know *exactly* how bad it feels to fail and get screamed at. I've at least started developing an emotional callus, which Butch Patty seems unable to do. She's just so optimistic and hardworking and *earnest*—her work ethic reminds me a lot of my dad's, actually. Management's told us all along that all you have to do to succeed here is show up on time and work hard. Butch Patty is all in on the idea, and she's suffering for it.

"*Jesus,* poor Patty," I repeat, not knowing what else to say.

"Yeah—she gets so stressed out, you know?" says Kolbi.

I'm going to be late, so I say goodbye and head inside. I reach the main entrance just as the ambulance crew does, so I swipe my card and hold the door open as they wheel a stretcher into the lobby. They don't seem to be in a big hurry. *That's good, right?*

As I scan my card to let myself through the next set of doors, a paramedic approaches the front desk, greeting the security guard by her first name.

"Okay, who is it this time?" I hear him ask, wearily, before the door closes behind me.

I knew I wanted to work in a call center for the second part. Call-center jobs may be stereotypically outsourced to India or the Philippines, but the industry employs around five million US workers—that's around one out of every twenty-five American jobs. And, like Amazon, call centers are one of very few sectors of the economy that have been expanding through the recession. The sector is profitable and growing, and its labor practices are likely to spread.

Plus, when I started trying to figure out where I should get a job, the stuff I heard from call-center reps* was just as insane as what I'd heard from Amazon workers. An alarming number of reps responded with agreement and recognition rather than shock to online advice like "First day on the phones, don't eat breakfast. I've seen so many newbies puke it's no longer even funny."

* Customer service representatives tend to refer to themselves as *reps* or *agents.*

There were plenty of stories about horrible customers and bizarre calls,* but just as many about the difficulties of the job itself. Reps from across the industry expressed the same complaints about management's obsession with rigid, company-mandated scripts and metrics that punished taking extra time to actually resolve a complicated problem. A *lot* mentioned that it felt like they were expected to be a robot or a machine.

When you've read way too much about Frederick Taylor, it's easy to recognize the ghosts of his stopwatch and "one best way" in statements like this:

> *It's not that [we] don't care. . . . [Reps] are bounded by scripts and rules. They cannot say anything outside or they get the boot. They simply are told not to think.*

And:

> *We're so heavily scripted we might as well be robots.*

Another common complaint was, as one rep put it, "a system that reports what I'm doing every second of every shift I work," which sounded quite a bit like Amazon to me. Reps talked about constant monitoring and micromanagement, having as little job control as assembly-line workers, and metric-obsessed bosses counting not just how many seconds you spend on every stage of a call but also how many you spend in the bathroom.

A good rule of thumb: the more interest management takes in workers' use of the bathroom, the more that job is going to *suck*. And I could easily fill the next twenty pages with unbelievable stories *just* about call-center bathrooms. In at least one case, the Taylor connection was hilariously literal, with workers actually made to wear a stopwatch around their necks when using the bathroom.

"How dare you step away from the onslaught of angry callers flowing through one after the other with no break between them to go to the toilet?

---

* One Reddit thread title: "Woman literally gouged her own eye out while on the phone with me."

Here's a performance improvement plan; you're now allowed to go to the toilet no more than twice a month when on shift," wrote one rep.

"Imagine having to put a code into your phone when you go to the toilet, and then have a weekly meeting with your supervisor where you have to justify why you were 1.2 minutes above the average toilet break allocated to you last week," wrote another.

Lindsay, who worked as a rep on Walmart and Sam's Club accounts a few years back, told me the stress of her job caused her to develop digestive problems. "Even though I went to the doctor and brought a note explaining what was wrong, my supervisor still insisted on following me into the bathroom to 'make sure' I really did have diarrhea every single time," Lindsay said. "She would stand outside the stall door and listen to me shit."

Amazon workers complained about the physical stress of techno-Taylorism. But an alarming number of call-center reps mentioned experiencing its *mental* stress, citing their jobs as the direct cause of intense bouts of depression and anxiety as well as ulcers and other physical effects of stress. I could, unfortunately, fill yet another twenty pages with stories from reps who said their jobs had driven them to seriously consider self-harm or suicide.

"I considered driving into oncoming traffic every time I drove and thought of suicide constantly," said one former worker.

"Most mornings I contemplate how much throwing myself down my stairs would hurt, 'cause going to the hospital is the only way to have an absence that doesn't count against you," said a worker.

I asked Evan, a twenty-eight-year-old man who's held jobs in four call centers over the last seven years, how it's affected his health. He replied:

> I've had depressive episodes where I just lay in my bed because I can't be brought to be yelled at again. There have been days where I have literally attempted to kill myself because I don't want to be a human punching bag anymore. My first supervisory act was to talk down one of my agents from committing suicide *while he was on the phone.* You sit there for hours on end, eight to twelve hours a day, and are a human punching bag. The companies don't care. They say don't end the calls or your job is gone. The customers don't care.

> They just want what they want. We're getting abused on both ends, from the customers and the companies, and people wonder why agents have depression, anxiety, and other mental illnesses.

There's a huge body of research[1] directly linking repetitive, low-control, high-stress work with increased risk of mental-health issues—particularly depression and anxiety. Many of these studies were actually conducted *in* call centers because they're such a perfect model of a low-control, high-stress workplace. One recent study[2] concluded:

> Call center employees are expected to express positive emotions and suppress negative emotions like frustration, resentment and anger in their interactions with customers so as to create a desired state of mind in the customer. If not given a healthy expressive outlet, this emotional repression can profoundly affect a person psychologically.

A couple of days after the ambulance takes Butch Patty away, she's back on the phones. I hear through the grapevine that it was just a panic attack, not a heart attack, but our minutes of break time don't line up enough for me to actually get to talk to her. So I just write GLAD YOU'RE BACK!! on my whiteboard and hold it up for her to read across the aisle. She gives me a thumbs-up.

Week One: Twenty People

My very first day at Convergys, I wake up way before my alarm. It isn't just that it's light out—it's that the sunlight heats the interior of my 2010 Ford Fusion like a convection oven. I glare up at the ceiling, knowing I'm not going to get any more sleep and resenting the world for it.

Finally, I give up. I grope around the cluttered backseat of my car for my purse, shoes, and toothbrush, then poke my head up above the window like a prairie dog to see if anyone's around. The coast is clear, so I open the back-seat door and begin my morning walk across the enormous parking lot of the twenty-four-hour Walmart in Hickory, North Carolina.

Convergys is a huge company with dozens of sites in the United States—it's one of the largest call-center companies in the world, and the largest one with jobs stateside. I picked the Hickory site because the area has an interesting history as the furniture manufacturing capital of America, not because another miraculous Aunt Sue offered me a free bedroom there. So I don't exactly have a place to sleep. At the moment.

Again, I looked everywhere I could think of, but all the places I could find would either involve another forty-five-minute commute, a few thousand dollars I didn't have, or a male nudist roommate. So I figured I'd just go to Hickory and live the Car Life until I could find a reasonable place.

My family didn't like the Car Life idea *at all.* But it isn't as bad as it sounds. I'm a pretty small person who, given earplugs and a blackout mask, can fall asleep in nearly any setting—including, on occasion, the backseat of my car. I have rose-tinted memories of crashing at rest stops overnight when I was younger, then using the preposterous amount of money I would have spent on a hotel on things more valuable than a single night of sleep. It's been eight months since I've had a steady paycheck. My savings are gone, and Car Life seems like a mild inconvenience compared to jacking up my credit-card balance even further or having another miserable forty-five-minute commute every day.

The first step of Car Life is finding a good place to park. It should be out of the way enough for you to avoid being hassled by police or pedestrians but not so remote that there's nobody to hear you scream. You can reliably find this sweet spot at Walmart,[*] as evidenced by the omnipresent long-haul truck cabs camped out in their parking lots. I couldn't believe my luck when I found a twenty-four-hour[†] Walmart five minutes down the road from Convergys, across the street from a YMCA,[‡] *and* next to a Barnes & Noble.[§]

Like I do every morning, I use Walmart's bathroom, brush my teeth, buy a single-serving bottle of milk at the self-serve checkout, and fill my reusable cup with ice at the in-store McDonald's. Back at the car, I dig the giant jug of warm iced coffee out of the backseat clutter and pour some into my cup of ice. Then, slightly more awake, I drive across the street to shower.

The woman at the front desk of the YMCA is now used to seeing me, so she just waves me back to the locker room. The shower stalls here are claustrophobic, like coffins stood on end, but the showers are hot and have good water pressure. I walk out half an hour later looking clean and semi-professional; the front-desk woman smiles and says she likes my dress. *Seriously, bless her.*

Yesterday's dirty clothes go in the laundry bag in the trunk, next to my shower caddy and flip-flops. I mull over what to do with my damp

---

[*] Supposedly one of Sam Walton's sons complained about how much trouble he had finding places to park his RV overnight, so his dad declared that Walmart parking lots would thenceforth be a safe haven for long-haul truckers, RVers, and generally broke people across the United States.

[†] I.e., the bathroom's open all night.

[‡] I.e., a place to shower.

[§] I.e., a place with air-conditioning, free Wi-Fi, and two armchairs that's unlikely to kick me out for not buying anything.

towel—it won't dry in the trunk, but I don't want it to be obvious to coworkers that I'm living in my car.

Behind the wheel, I eat breakfast in a manner that would cause most people to take a hard look at their lives—taking a swig of milk, then tossing in a handful of Cheerios straight from the box. I am sorry to say that this is how I normally eat Cheerios if there's nobody around to make fun of me. At home, it's so the Cheerios don't get soggy and gross. Here, it's ideal because it creates zero dirty dishes.

After breakfast, I drive back past the Walmart, keeping my eyes peeled for the jungly overgrowth obscuring Convergys's driveway and the large billboard permanently advertising that they're hiring. I'm the first person from my training class to arrive, according to the front-desk guard, who then takes an unfortunate photo of me for my ID card. She buzzes me through the second set of doors, directing me in a heavy Carolina accent to go up the stairs and turn right. She warns me *not* to turn left—that'll take me out on the production floor, and I'm not allowed to be there yet.

I follow her directions past a display of AT&T merchandise to classroom 1. According to the sign on the door, this won't be unlocked until 6:55, twenty minutes from now. There's nowhere to sit and wait, so I wander around for a while, finding more locked classrooms and a small break room with vending machines.

In search of a bathroom, I retrace my steps and take the forbidden left, which takes me past the entryway to a huge room of cubicles. Every surface around this entryway is plastered with signs making it clear that NO CELL PHONES OR UNAUTHORIZED PERSONS ARE ALLOWED ON THE PRODUCTION FLOOR, and the room hums like a beehive with the sound of dozens of people talking at once, presumably to AT&T customers like me.

Convergys is a third-party for-profit call center, which means it handles calls outsourced by many different businesses, mostly very large ones. Down on the first floor, the reps take calls for a big health-insurance company—Aetna, I believe—and Convergys claims to handle calls from more than half the top fifty companies on the *Fortune* 500. I was able to verify some specific large-scale past and present clients, like Comcast, Dish Network, DirecTV, Verizon, and Walmart. Notably, most of the companies I could confirm as having outsourced to large third-party call centers like Convergys had at least one customer-service horror story go viral.

The job application didn't specify which account I'd be working on, so I was tickled to find it would be AT&T Mobility sales and service—my own cell-phone provider for more than a decade. The entire second floor is AT&T, and this is just one of a dozen Convergys AT&T sites.

Just past the production floor is the women's bathroom, which somehow has a line even at this early hour. Having nothing else to do, I get in line. As I wait for one of the three stalls, I overhear one woman say to another, "I've got two court dates and an ultrasound," a phrase that will pop into my head to the tune of "two turntables and a microphone" for weeks.

By the time I get back, it's almost 6:55. A bunch of people are now clustered around the classroom door—mostly women, mostly on the young side, roughly evenly split between black and white. I'm still not quite awake enough to make conversation, so it's a relief when our trainer, a cheery white woman in her midtwenties with ice-blond hair, appears to let us in.

She directs us to find a seat at either of the two long tables set up against opposite walls; each has ten workstations consisting of a computer and telephone. A table in the middle of the room holds a single enormous container of disinfectant wipes, and to my surprise a few people grab some to disinfect their areas before even sitting down. *OCD much?*

"My name is Kimberly," says our trainer, quieting us down. "I *am* bubbly and positive—the other trainers' name for me is Bubbles! You can call me Kim, Kimberly, whatever."

Kimberly has the vibe of a person who dots the *i* in her name with a heart or flower; her sweetness will prove to be genuine. Like most people I've met in Hickory so far, she has a western Carolina accent—short, flat vowels, verging on Appalachian. There's something else about the way she talks, too, but I can't quite put my finger on it. I try to figure it out as Kimberly tells us she's been at Convergys for four years.

"I started out on the phones, just like you guys," she says. "I *will* be honest: I was comfortable on the phones. I made a lot of money with sales on top of my base pay. My highest paycheck for sales was $3,500!" There's some oohs and aahs from around the classroom.

"So you *can* make a lot of money here! You just have to take in everything I give you over the next five weeks. Each and every day that I come in here, I am gonna train you 110 percent, with everything I got, and I ask that you give it back to me," Kimberly continues, smiling. "If you cannot understand something, you have to ask me. It *is* crucial that you ask questions—the only stupid question is the one you *do* not ask!"

Contractions! I think, pleased. *That's* what it is—she doesn't use contractions. And she tends to stress one of the words I'd usually, uh, contract—"you don't ask" becomes "you *do* not ask." "It's crucial" becomes "It *is* crucial." "I'll be honest" becomes "I *will* be honest." A lot of call-center veterans I'll meet share this odd cadence—formal, almost military. It makes Kimberly sound like a warm and fuzzy drill sergeant.

"Okay, now *I* have a question for *you,*" Kimberly continues. "What are some of the things *you* have heard about Convergys? Keep it clean, now! But—tell me! *What have you heard?*"

Convergys is one of the circles of hell.

Convergys turned me bald.

But I'm not falling for this one; I keep my hand down and my mouth shut. My classmates aren't falling for it, either. Kimberly raises her eyebrows and scans the room wryly, as if we're all in on the same joke.

"Nobody's heard *anything?*" she says. "I don't believe it."

A middle-aged black woman tentatively raises a hand and says she's heard it can be stressful. Sometimes.

I worked on AT&T for almost two years, and if I were to die and have a personalized hell made just for me, it would have been in my 2x2 cubicle answering AT&T calls. It was quite possibly the most stressful thing I have ever done.

I had a panic attack and literally fainted. They had to call 911 and I got wheeled off the floor in a stretcher.

"It *is* stressful at first," Kimberly agrees. "But if you do what you're supposed to, you're not gonna have to worry about it." A few people look relieved.

"But if you're one of those people who just do *not* try?" she continues. "Or you do *not* want to give it 110 percent? Or you just see the negative in stuff? It's *very* stressful. But call centers in *general* are stressful. You have customers calling in, they're mad, cussing you out; you have a team leader saying, 'Okay, guys, let's get *this many* TV sales today!' It *is* going to be stressful, because it's fast-paced, but you *will* get over that. You can't take it personal, because if you take it personal then your whole day's going to be messed up. 'Kay?" Kimberly looks around. "What else have you heard?"

"I heard the people who call in cuss at you," volunteers a pretty, timid-looking redhead I'd bet a million bucks can't legally drink.

> *You will deal with the worst of the worst. Only about 10% of your calls will be bad, but a hundred calls a day means ten assholes who will make you feel like crap.*
>
> *The job is very repetitive—mind-numbing, really. So it is hard to take that next call when you know the person has a high chance of being unhappy with you for something you have no control over.*
>
> *Your first day is gonna be fine. Your first four weeks are gonna be sweet. Then you hit the floor, and you realize you have no idea how to use Telegence, that Clarify is worthless, and the callers are overwhelmingly nuts.*

"Yes—you will have people who call in who are just downright rude, and they are nasty, and they *do* not care. 'Kay?" Kimberly looks around the room, making reassuring eye contact with each of us. "But—how many of you've worked in fast food?" Almost everybody raises a hand. "And how many of you have been cussed out face-to-face by a customer—they're upset, they're yelling at you, they throw something at you?" Every hand stays up.

"I've heard some horror stories about fast food—getting a burger thrown in your face? Nuh-*uh!*" says Kimberly, shaking her head emphatically. There's a *lot* of battle-weary nods. *Jesus,* I think, horrified. "Every job is stressful, to an extent. It's all about what you *do* with the stress."

The fiftysomething woman in a Panthers-blue ball cap whom I'll come to know as Butch Patty raises her hand. "You were talking about it's stressful?" she says in the thickest Carolina accent I've heard yet. She points a thumb at Aunt Patty, sitting beside her. "Well, when I was here for her interview, I sat in the lobby and watched the shift change. And I did not hear *one* person say, 'Oh, my god, I'm glad this day is over! Oh, my god, that *caller!* Oh, my god, I'm glad three o'clock is here!' They all came out with smiles! Did not hear *no* negativity. I really don't foresee it being a stressful job at all," she finishes confidently.

"People coming out smiling? That's because they're ready to *go!*" jokes Destiny, a black woman around my age whom I'd noticed disinfecting her area earlier. The class laughs, and I'm reassured that Kimberly laughs, too.

"I've heard good things and bad things," says Aunt Patty. "Different people who've worked here before, they're, like, 'It's a hard company to work for, they'll fire you for no reason!'" She shrugs. "But then you get to looking at that person, and you say, 'Okay, you're unemployed for a *reason*. You were probably mouthy or whatever or just didn't care.' My sister works here, and she loves it!"

"I agree with that 100 percent!" says Kimberly, beaming. "You just gotta make it every day. It's a job. At least you got money, you're putting food on the table, you're providing for your family. What else have you heard?" She looks around.

"Nothing at all? Okay, how many of you—don't laugh—have heard the rumor that you get fired if you don't make sales?"

Most of the room slowly raises a hand, including me.

> *Fucking Convergys. I worked there for two months, doing tech support for AT&T. Shit was awful because we didn't actually offer tech support, we just tried to sell things to people calling in for tech support. You had to get three nos before you stopped pitching, or you got written up. Three write-ups and you're fired. They tried to get me to sell to an old lady trying to cancel her dead husband's line.* Fuck AT&T, and fuck Convergys.*

---

* Thank god, the policy on trying to sell to bereaved spouses and children changed around the time I started.

"It's kind of funny how far from the truth that is!" says Kimberly. "The only reason you'd be fired for sales is if you don't *try*. It's what we call a *will* and a *skill* issue.... If you're trying, you'll be okay. We never fire you right off. We're going to coach you multiple times before we realize that you just don't *want* to do it. And *that's* a problem, because our contract says we have to sell. We don't have to sell every single time, but we've gotta make pitches, we've gotta make offers. If you make those offers, you'll sell. 'Kay? What else have you heard?"

I finally raise my hand. "I heard a lot of people don't last very long?"

Retention is up there with waterboarding. Every center I've worked in gets this black dust covering everything that my coworkers and I figured was the physical manifestation of human suffering.

Kimberly pauses. "I *will* be honest with you—the turnover that we have here is because of attendance. When you go out on the floor, you guys are allotted twelve points; I don't know any other company that gives you twelve points." It's true—I only had six attendance points at Amazon, but that was for peak. The twelve points here are supposed to last a full year.

"So when people are terminated for attendance, it's because they have, like, thirty or forty points, and we've tried to work with them multiple times and they just *could* not get it together," Kimberly continues.

"She's telling the truth! They let me go *way* beyond my twelve before they fired me," says Destiny, swiveling her office chair around to reassure me. "I got fired because I wasn't coming to work! I mean, over a year's time, I just overdone it." She laughs ruefully. "They do work with you, though."

Kimberly turns back to me. "So, yeah—we do have a high turnover rate, but it's not because we just *like* to get rid of people. We like to keep the ones we have and make sure they're happy. We'll try to work with you."

Butch Patty raises her hand again. "So you keep saying *when we go out on the floor*—when we do, you're going to be with us?" Despite her earlier speech, she sounds worried.

"Yes. You guys take your first calls weeks three and four, one at a time, but week five we go out and spend most of the day on the phones, and I *will* be there with you."

"Is that with, like—real people?" I ask.

"Uh-huh!" chirps Kimberly. "Then week six on you go to OTT* and you won't see much of me. Because I have a *problem*—I like to baby you guys. So my bosses challenge me with cutting the strings. It's hard to give you guys up! We really bond over five weeks, so I'm, like—*You can't have my babies!*" The class laughs. I decide I like Kimberly.

"Oh, and speaking of!" Kimberly gestures at the giant container of disinfectant wipes on the center table. "I have a lot of parents in here, so I *will* say that I am a *germophobe!* There's hand sanitizers around the site that I'll show you on your tour, but the wipes here in the middle are specifically for you. I'd suggest cleaning off your desk in the morning because there's a night class in here. So: always sanitize your desk! You never know who was there before." Kimberly looks around. "If I've grossed you out and you want to sanitize, that's cool! Go ahead, grab some." Half the class gets up to get some wipes, including Destiny and a couple of others who definitely already wiped things down.

"I'll just keep going while you sanitize," Kimberly says. "Anyway, I'm glad you're all here! You're gonna like Convergys. It's a good company—no matter what you've heard or what you've been told, it is a *good* company to work for. We'll have fun! At the end of this five weeks, we're gonna be one big family. Okay, I'm going to hit the lights..."

So begins the first of no fewer than five separate orientation slideshows that will be presented by five different managers over the next two weeks. Each has some unique information, but there's a lot of overlap—imagine a Venn diagram that looks like the Olympics symbol. As a benevolent narrator, I'll do my best to mash all five up into a more easily digestible format.

---

* Honestly, I don't remember what this stood for. There were a lot of acronyms.

Orientation: A Play in One Act

MANAGEMENT

FRED: Hickory's site leader, the big boss. White man, midforties, big guy. Loud, jovial, and genuinely friendly with low-level workers; prone to repeating himself. Southern accent, but not the local western Carolina one.

MARSHALL: Head of the AT&T project at the Hickory site, **FRED**'s second-in-command. White man, midforties, clean-shaven, former Marine. Texas accent, *very* into Texas. Kind of an odd bird who sometimes punctuates his speech with startlingly loud whoops. Can work the Marines into any conversation.

STEVE: Hickory's HR guy. Physically similar to Marshall but gentler, with glasses, a beard, and kind eyes. Somehow pulls off being a hugger without being creepy; genuinely cares about his job. Western Carolina accent.

JORDAN: Hickory's head of training for AT&T; the site's Bad Cop. White woman, blond, early thirties, intimidating in size and bearing. Often speaks with intense anger and frustration, as if her audience has personally spent weeks pushing her to the edge with misbehavior. Heavy western Carolina accent.

KIMBERLY: Our trainer. Midtwenties, iron-straight white-blond hair, solidly built, flawless eyebrows. Genuinely sweet and maternal about her students. Western Carolina accent.

CLASSMATES

Twenty recent hires that serve as a decent representation of the Hickory site—fifteen women and five men; eight black and twelve white; four teenagers, nine in their twenties, four in their thirties, three older than forty. Most of the women have at least one kid.

White students, unless otherwise noted, speak with some degree of the western Carolina accent, e.g., pronouncing "Hi!" as "Ha!" Black students, unless otherwise noted, have a similar but distinct Carolina accent blended with African American Vernacular English, e.g., soft or dropped final consonants.

DESTINY: Rehire, black woman, late twenties, long straight hair, no kids. The shoo-in winner of the class clown paper-plate award at our end-of-training potluck and the best person in the class on the phones by a long shot. She's a natural saleswoman, with charm, hustle, and a good grasp of the complicated systems left over from her previous year at Convergys. Most of the class will be incompetent, stuttering wrecks on our first real calls—**DESTINY** actually makes a sale. Rarely anything but good-humored and helpful, but you'd definitely want her on your side in a fight. Very into sanitizing.

BUTCH PATTY: New hire, white woman, fifties, grandkids, frequently wears Panthers blue from head to toe. Imagine a middle-aged butch lesbian from rural North Carolina—you're probably not too far off. Prior to Convergys, worked in a furniture factory for fifteen years. Mischievous and would win class clown in any group without **DESTINY.** Accent heavier than most. Tries extremely hard.

AUNT PATTY: New hire, white woman, fifties, grandkids. Previously worked at McDonald's and Walmart. Partner of **BUTCH PATTY.** Could be described as jolly, but I wouldn't try it within earshot of her. Much like **DESTINY,** she's a natural on the phones and someone you'd want on your side in a fight, despite being good-natured.

KOLBI: New hire, black woman, early twenties, no kids. Smart, good-humored, and nonjudgmental, she eventually wants to go to college to become a therapist. Short and thick, with a lovely face that's usually smiling. She can talk to anybody and tends to end up friends with everyone in a group. I'm outraged on her behalf when someone else gets the paper-plate award for Best Personality.

JESS: Rehire, white woman, midtwenties, wife, young baby at home. Round-faced with a curtain of straight dark hair. The younger sister of Bad Cop **JORDAN,** she can also be irritable at times. But she has a generous nature and often uses her prior year of experience at Convergys to help confused classmates, almost acting as a backup trainer. Her smoky voice and frank manner mean that male callers occasionally try to get her number, to her amusement. **JESS, DESTINY,** and **AUNT PATTY** are the top three sellers in the class.

KAITLYN: Rehire, white woman, late twenties, four kids. A wiry, tan brunette with a husband and blended family. Friendly. Obsessive about wiping down her workstation. Winner of paper-plate award for Most Professional.

EMILY: New hire, white woman, early thirties, glasses. General American accent. Unsuccessfully trying to hide that she's living in her car. Tends to brush off questions about her odd and possibly tragic personal life with "It's kind of a long story." Mediocre but not terrible on the phones. Told in performance review that she has a quirky personality but is making it work for her. Secretly a journalist.

ACT ONE

FRED: First of all, thanks for giving Convergys the opportunity to employ you. You say, "That's weird—it's usually supposed to be the other way around." *But!*

STEVE: What is there, twenty of you? That means you guys are the very tippy-top of the very tippy-top. So—yay! We're glad you're here! *[leads class in round of self-applause]*

MARSHALL: Have you met Steve? Steve handles all the HR issues and so forth. He and I are about the same height, same shape, we both wear glasses. But he usually has a beard, and he likes hugs. So remember: Steve—beard, hugs. Marshall—no beard, *no hugs. [laughter]*

FRED: You had other choices, I'm sure—you probably had six or seven or eight or ten or fifteen places you could go, but you gave *us* the shot. So: thank you.

MARSHALL: A little bit about Convergys for those of you that've never worked for us before. We're the second-largest call-center company in the world. We generate over $3 billion of revenue every year. We have 130,000 employees!

STEVE: We! Are! *Huge!* We are the biggest company in the US that does call-center customer service—the second biggest in the *whole world.*

MARSHALL: Forty-seven different languages and thirty-one different countries—*Nǐ huì shuō Zhōngwén ma? Sprechen sie Deutsch? Habla español? Parlez-vous français?* We have call centers literally from Dublin, Ireland, to Beijing, China, and everywhere in between.

STEVE: Right now, we have six hundred employees inside this building. That's a big company for little Hickory! The hospital's got more; the college might have more; a couple furniture factories—but we're probably one of the twenty biggest companies in the city of Hickory.

That's a nice thing! I worked in Conover in a little factory for fifteen years. If any of you guys have worked in furniture, you know it's kind of an up-and-down roller coaster. Working at a big company, you don't got that roller coaster like my little factory. When we get busy, we spread the calls out through other buildings—there's over eighty buildings just like this one.

MARSHALL: We've been around for a while. We were Transamerica back in 1998, changed our name to Convergys at that point in time. Back then, we had one call center in the state of Texas. You know how many call centers we had in the state of North Carolina? *Zero.* You know how many we got now? *Six.*

FRED: Here's the two things I tell everybody—it makes anybody successful here.

JORDAN: I've been a training manager for three years, and my main goal in taking this seat was to *[startlingly hostile] change* the *crap* that was allowed to happen back here, because it puts *crap* on the production floor.

MARSHALL: We're a *for-profit* center—bottom line is, we work for someone else. Most of your big companies—telecommunications, retail, manufacturing, and so forth—they all at some point in time had their *own* call centers. Those companies produce, sell, distribute, provide services—*that's* how they make their money. *Their* call centers are just a cost of doing business. They don't have to be profitable; they're there to take care of the customers. And so they don't have quite the same requirements that we have.

FRED: Only two things.

JORDAN: Before you become a distraction to this classroom, I *will* get rid of you. If you don't want the job, there's lots of people out there that do.

MARSHALL: Some of our clients, you might have heard of them? We've got a couple credit-card companies, some banks, some small computer companies like *[significant pause]* HP and Microsoft? You probably heard of SiriusXM radio? Everybody's heard of the country Brazil, down in South America? They have a national telephone service—we built their billing system. Oh, we also deal with another small computer company, might have heard of it—*Dell.*

STEVE: Actually, we do Verizon and Sprint, too! We just don't do it here.

FRED: This is the only two things you have to do.

JORDAN: Homeless folks out there, they need a job; single mothers, single fathers, people trying to make it on their own—I *will* open those seats for people that need it before I let someone entitled sit in here and act like that. We're not gonna argue about it, because I'm telling you now what's acceptable and what isn't.

MARSHALL: I'll let you in on a little secret: *[whispers]* y'all are the only ones who make money in this *entire building!* 'Cause you take phone calls, and that's how we make money.

FRED: This is it, just these two things. I will never ask anything else of you.

MARSHALL: So everybody else in this building? Their sole function is to take care of you, to help you do well, to see how much money we can help you make.

FRED: *Attitude*. And *attendance*.

JORDAN: *[pulling up slide that says* GROSS MISCONDUCT*]* Gross misconduct! Some of my favorites include things like work avoidance—like, trying to convince me that getting a break every two hours is not enough in an eight-hour day? That you still have to get up fourteen times a day and leave the room? You're gonna need to come see me and get a medical accommodation form and have a physician fill something out telling me that you need more bathroom breaks than every two hours.

FRED: *Attitude!*

MARSHALL: Now, if you're getting up and moving around and doing all sorts of other things where you're not where you can take phone calls, we have a problem. Not *we have a problem* like *Marshall's gonna take you out back and shoot you* kind of problem—because I *am* a trained Marine. But no—we have a problem because what we do is *take phone calls*. That's how we make our money.

JORDAN: Oh, another one of my favorites! How many of you smoke? *[a nervous pause]* It's okay, I smoke—you can tell me. *[half the class raises a hand]*

FRED: And *attendance!*

MARSHALL: If we're not here to take phone calls when those calls come in, guess what? We don't make any money.

JORDAN: Now, how many of you have made that judgment call on break—"Do I need to pee that bad, or do I want to smoke a cigarette?" *[every hand stays up; the smokers laugh, guilty]* So then you come back up, you clock back in, and you're immediately going to go to the bathroom? *Nuh-uh.* You just stole that time from me!

MARSHALL: You can't sell somebody U-verse if you're sitting in the bathroom. You can't sell someone a DirecTV if you're outside smoking a cigarette.

FRED: Your attitude—you control it. Nobody else controls it for you.

JORDAN: I need to know that you don't have a crappy attitude, a pissy attitude.

FRED: Everybody wants control nowadays, right? Control our destiny, control our future, control this and control that.

KIMBERLY: I sound like a grandma when I say this, but *sassafras,* or *sass*—I will tell you that sometimes if you have a little bit of a funk going on that day or you have a bit of an attitude. I'll look at you and be, like, *[quirks an immaculate eyebrow] "Sass?"*

FRED: But we can only control the things that we *can* control. Number one thing that you're going to have to control every day? Is your *attitude.*

KIMBERLY: I'm not trying to be mean. I'm just trying to get you in check before we have to go out and talk about something. I don't like doing that. Just act the right way. Keep it Convergable.

JORDAN: *This building.* I don't know *what* it is, but people forgot that you can have fun and still be *professional.* It's like someone dropped a bomb of disrespect in Hickory, North Carolina, and the surrounding areas.

KIMBERLY: We say "Convergable" around here—it pretty much means professionalism, in Convergys terms. If we hear cuss words, we say, "That's not Convergable." Or if we hear derogatory comments—which I should *never* hear—we also say, "That's not Convergable."

JORDAN: I don't know *when* it became okay for you to talk to other people the way people in this building talk. It's unprofessional; it's juvenile; it's *ignorant!*

KIMBERLY: I'm gonna need you guys to keep each other in check—if you hear somebody slip a word and I don't catch it, you look at each other like—*[muttering] "That's not Convergable."*

JORDAN: Other things, like vandalizing, breaking my chairs, writing on my tables, throwing my keyboards, stupidity, things you know you shouldn't be doing? We're *not gonna do*.

KIMBERLY: Yes, I want to hear what you did over the weekend, but make sure you aren't talking about inappropriate things that shouldn't be in a workplace. And make sure you keep your comments on political and religious stuff to yourself. You think what you think, and that's great! Everybody's entitled to their own opinion. But you can have that opinion *off* the property, not here.

JORDAN: If you have an opinion to share, go ahead and tell it to your car—inside your car, with the windows up and the doors locked. That's the only place where it's your property and you can tell it out loud when you're here!

KIMBERLY: Because we have clients on-site multiple different times a week, and they don't always wear suits and ties. Sometimes they come just to watch. If you're walking through the hallway cussing up a storm, they're gonna find who's responsible for you and make sure that we know about it.

JORDAN: You can make it through your day without seventy-five cuss words. You can make it through your day without demeaning someone else. It's not funny. It's not cute. It doesn't make you attractive. What*ever* it is you're trying to do, it is *not*. It is, quite frankly, juvenile and really stupid.

FRED: No stink faces. No nasty attitude. Have an attitude of *learning*.

KIMBERLY: I don't like excuses, I don't like bad attitudes, and I don't like it when you're not on your A game. I get that you can't always be on that, but I do ask that you try to give me 100 percent every day.

JORDAN: That *one* person that's dozing off, that *one* that's in the back corner talking, that *one* who can't focus and follow—Kimberly's not going to say anything to you, probably. Just go ahead and know that right now. She's gonna come right back to this thing *[gestures at slide showing a complicated form Kimberly apparently has to fill out for each of us every single* *day]* that afternoon and go ahead and flip you to red to let me know that I need to be watching for you.

KIMBERLY: You're gonna have days in here where it stresses you out, where you feel like you can't do this. But I'm gonna push you through it.

STEVE: You all started at $9.50 an hour. Once you graduate, we automatically add a dollar and make it $10.50. That's a 10 percent raise, automatic! I've been in human resources twenty years, and there ain't that many 10 percent raises. The chance to make more than that is up to you.

JORDAN: You become eligible for sales payout the minute you take your first call. We have people who've closed sales on their first call!

STEVE: If you do help a customer add something to their account, you get a commission—and you ought to! Just like somebody in the mall that gets commissions when they sell a pair of shoes.

MARSHALL: Second paycheck of every month is going to pay out incentives. And second paycheck of every month, if all you're seeing is your hourly rate? Something ain't right.

STEVE: People think furniture factories are the good-paying jobs? We got people out here making as much as they do. There *are* employees that do the minimum and just make that $10.50 an hour. But if I'm gonna be here forty hours a week, and I got bills to pay, why wouldn't I try to get that extra money?

FRED: I don't know if you've learned how you make bonuses here yet for selling, but some people here make an extra $1,600, $1,700, $1,800 a month.

DESTINY: *[as if responding to a fiery sermon] Yes.*

FRED: One guy—I want him to come off the phones and be a team leader? He won't, because he makes too much money on the phones!

DESTINY: Uh-*huh*.

FRED: You say, "What does that guy do? Like, has he got a degree from Harvard? Some six-year degree from MIT?"

DESTINY: *Nuh-uh.*

FRED: Nope! And you know you could say the same thing about me, right? I don't need no eight-year degree from MIT.

DESTINY: *Nope.*

FRED: Heck, our CEO, she started out on the phones, just like you.

STEVE: Sales? That's kind of the luck of the draw. You're going to let people know what's available, and 97 percent of them are going to say, "No, thank you."

JORDAN: We track sales—TV, broadband, add-a-line—*and* your cancel rate. We need to make sure you're selling clean, that you're not using devious language or dirty behavior, right?

STEVE: But every once in a while, they're gonna say, "Tell me more!" Every once in a while, you're gonna pick up the phone and say, "Thank you for calling AT&T," and the person on the other end's gonna say, "My neighbor just got DirecTV. Can I get that?" "Oh, yes, boy, you can! Let me tell you how!" Those are the golden tickets out of the Willy Wonka movies. *[laughter]*

STEVE: But sales is just a little tiny piece of how people make extra money! The other things you do in your normal job anyway, that's where the money is—the stuff up there on the bulletin board *[gestures at a bulletin board covered in indecipherable acronyms and numbers]*. Every one of these things that has an abbreviation? We track it, and we measure, and we get compared to all the other buildings that take care of AT&T.

FRED: Yes, there's people that come here for a beauty pageant. But nobody in here should be making less than $15 or $16 an hour.

EMILY: *[unable to help herself]* Do *most* people here make $15 or $16 an hour?

FRED: If you're willing to work hard, have a good attitude and great attendance? *Yes.* Let's say you work 160 hours a month. If you make a $440 bonus for the month, you just cut yourself two more dollars an hour. So now we're at $13, give or take, and with your NRS—

STEVE: NRS is "net rep stat"—that's where if the caller takes the thirty seconds to do that automatic survey after. Y'all probably already heard about *promoters, neutrals,* and *detractors?* When you start getting those promoters, depending on your scores, you get extra money. If you do your job well, you take care of customers, you can make between $750 and $800 extra every month—*before* sales.

JORDAN: To get good survey scores, you've gotta be able to come in and smile over the phone and have a *genuine* customer-service attitude. You fake it for a *second,* and they're gonna feel it, and you're probably gonna get cussed at.

STEVE: Or FCR—that's an abbreviation for "first-call resolution." If the customer calls in and you fix their problem and they don't call back for the next thirty days, that's considered a first-call resolution. We track that, and at the end of the month if we meet whatever the site goal is—looks like 68 percent right now—every employee that hit the goal, we go back to the month before and add a dollar an hour to their pay for the whole month.

JORDAN: Be sure you can talk while you're smiling and it doesn't sound fake. Test yourself by doing it around your family. If somebody looks at you and goes, "What is *wrong* with you?" *[laughter]* Congratulations! You have changed yourself, and now you can do this job!

STEVE: If you *beat* the goal, some months we go as high as four dollars an hour.

JORDAN: Your face should *hurt* from smiling. You should get cramps in your cheeks. If you don't, you're not doing the right thing.

STEVE: Anybody want that extra money?

CLASS: *[crosstalk] Yes! Hell, yeah! I want it!*

STEVE: Good! If you don't, you're probably not at the right job! So the number three way to make money: there's something called a referral bonus.

MARSHALL: I know Convergys kind of has a reputation that we fire a lot of people. Believe it or not, we really don't.

STEVE: If you tell somebody, "Hey, they're hiring!" and they mention your name at the interview, you get a $100 bonus when the new person starts. If the new person works ninety days, you get another $500 bonus on your next check.

MARSHALL: We don't want to see you walk out the door, because we have to start all over again, train somebody, do it again.

JORDAN: It costs me $7,500 to hire and train each person in this room *[looks around, making eye contact]*. $7,500 out of my budget, *per head*. I gotta pay a trainer; I have to pay facilities; I have to pay computer rights for your IDs; I gotta pay to have your IDs generated with AT&T. *And* what you get paid—that's a direct cost to the company, because you make us *no* money right now. You don't start making money for this business until sixty days after training, and we had to pay you that *whole time*.

MARSHALL: So whatever you heard... most of it is usually somebody, well, you know—they didn't really like their job anyway, so they looked for something to blame it on.

JORDAN: Do you know what my boss says to me when I say, "Oh, don't worry. I only fired two!" *[pause] "Where's my $15,000?"* That's right! It would be really stupid for me to go around firing people and having to explain why I costed this business $15,000, $30,000. *Right?*

FRED: So remember: *attitude!*

JORDAN: *Unless*... you give me a *reason*.

FRED: And *attendance!*

MARSHALL: Now, if you don't come to work, you *do* run out of attendance points—and guess what? There's a limit.

KIMBERLY: In the five weeks of classroom time you have with me, you can only get two and a half points—that is *it*.

MARSHALL: We're a little more generous than most employers—usually it's three strikes and you're out. But it's not an *infinite* attendance policy.

JORDAN: That's more than enough time. You really, really shouldn't miss that. Life happens, and I understand, but even that puts you at risk of us not being able to catch you up.

KIMBERLY: If you are tardy up to one hour, or you leave an hour early, it's .25. If you leave early up to two hours or you're late up to two hours, it's .5. Two hours to 50 percent of your shift, it's .75. Once you go over that four-hour mark, it's a full point. And no-call-no-show is *two full points.*

JORDAN: You can check your points out in your e-start. We note *everything.* You walk through that door a *minute* late? It's going to be noted in your e-start.

KIMBERLY: E-start's the little blue screen where you clock in, clock to break, clock to lunch, clock to go home. You *are* required to return from breaks and lunches *on time:* any tardiness, early outs, or absences *will* be recorded in your file and could result in termination of employment. So make sure that you're *on* time, *every* day.

JORDAN: At two points you'll turn red, and you'll have to come meet with me and sign your final warning so I can look you in the face and tell you I'm about to fire you if you go over this two and a half points. You'll sign, I'll sign, Kim'll sign, and that way *nobody* is *unclear* on where your points are and what I can do for you. Make sense?

KIMBERLY: Okay, let's talk about *escalations!* These are my favorite! I'm weird, I know. *[laughter]*

MARSHALL: The call-center environment, for those who haven't worked in it before—sometimes we make it harder than it really is. Sometimes people come in, like, "Good Lord, I gotta listen to customers *complain,* and they *whine,* and they're not *nice*—"

FRED: They're gonna call you up sometimes and they're gonna be *so mad!*

KIMBERLY: Your tone and demeanor should *never* change because of a negative customer. You have to treat that customer that's cussing your face off just like you'd treat that little old lady who was calling you sweetheart. It's the hardest thing you'll ever do, but you *have* to do it.

FRED: Somebody was in an elevator the other day saying, *[weepy voice]* "They were so *mean* to me!" I was, like, "Come *on*. Do you think they know you? Are they coming to your house?"

KIMBERLY: If they were face-to-face with you, they probably would not say half the stuff they say to you over the phone. Chances are they're just frustrated because somebody else has lied to them multiple times before they got to you. That's just the raw truth.

FRED: They're mad at AT&T! They ain't mad at *you!*

KIMBERLY: Most customers will even *tell* you, "I'm not mad at *you!* I'm just *mad!* I'm mad at your company!" And then they turn around and cuss *you* out again. *[laughter]* It's okay! *Breathe*. Don't let customers like that intimidate you. Empathize with them—you're human, too. If they've been lied to ten times, tell them that you're sorry. Apologize on behalf of the entire company. The best thing you can do is let them *get it out*. It's like a balloon—just let it deflate, let all the air come out of it, then jump in and resolve the issue.

KIMBERLY: But you gotta own it; you gotta take care of it. If you want to move up, if you want to make this a full-time career and stay here for a while, you have to show that you can take an escalation and de-escalate it. Take ownership! That is *your* call, not mine. 'Kay?

FRED: Now, there's gonna be *times* when you're like this—*[slumps over with a sad noise]*. You gotta keep your mojo. That's when you stand up and, I dunno—do jumping jacks or something.

KIMBERLY: Don't carry that phone call over to your next one, because then your phone calls are gonna be horrible for the rest of the day. Once that phone call's over, drop it, let it go, don't think about it anymore!

FRED: But listen—if you're scheduled forty hours a week, what are you trading for forty hours of pay?

CLASS: *[uncertain, murmurs various answers]*

FRED: Your *life*. Do you realize we never get that back? You can't hit the rewind button on life. It doesn't go backwards.

If you picture who you're working for every day, that little boy or that little girl, you're going to work harder. I promise you'll try harder.

But whatever that is, whoever you're working for—you're trading your *life* every day. Your *life!* I'd make sure you get the most out of it.

—FIN—

After orientation, Kimberly gives us another bad omen—several sets of randomly generated log-ins and passwords to memorize. None are the same; few are even related. We're not allowed to write them down in any way—paper, pens, and cell phones are forbidden anywhere but the break room—and they're not easy.* Kimberly will waste a lot of time over the next five weeks reading out half the class's log-ins and passwords for various systems when we need to use them. It's a good three weeks before I have mine completely down. I recognize the password situation, like highly scrutinized bathroom breaks, as a dead canary in a coal mine.

Psychologist George Miller published a famous paper in 1956 titled "The Magical Number Seven, Plus or Minus Two: Some Limits on Our Capacity for Processing Information." In it, he proposed that the human brain can juggle roughly seven separate bits of information in its "working memory" at a time: add more, and balls will start hitting the floor. Though our understanding of working memory has gotten much more complicated, this limit of seven balls, give or take a couple, is so well established that it's known as Miller's Law.

So if you actually want human beings to be able to remember something, you'll realistically keep it to seven digits or fewer.† Expecting average workers to be able to remember several randomly generated log-ins and passwords of between six and nine digits apiece is a red flag that whoever

* For example, my computer log-in was something like 101049967. Try to hold that number in your head as you read; I'll ask about it in a few pages.

† This is why, for example, phone numbers are the length they are.

designed this system doesn't understand—or isn't realistic about—the ways humans differ from robots and computer programs.

This proves to be a running theme over the course of training.

There's so many passwords because Convergys's computer system is actually about eight separate systems kludged together like Frankenstein's monster. Each system has its own log-in, password, and set of uses and rules, and they don't play particularly well together.

Kimberly's an excellent teacher and does her best to keep the weeks of memorization interesting, but the systems don't make it easy on her. Since Convergys is nominally paperless, our entire curriculum is online. But the computers are ancient, pages we need are frequently 404'd, and often half the passwords won't work. Everything feels really bootleg compared to the sleek efficiency of Amazon.

Slowly we learn how to use combinations of systems to handle the most common customer problems—the big two seem to be setting up payment arrangements for customers too broke to pay their bill right this second and explaining data-overage charges to customers who just received a huge bill out of nowhere. It's not intuitive, so we memorize which systems to use for what.

Technically we shouldn't have to rely so much on memorization. One of the systems we're learning is sort of the equivalent of Amazon's brain-work-removing scanners—"Just check CSP;* it has everything you need to know," says Kimberly. CSP is a searchable database of long, step-by-step scripts—sorry, *call flows*—and it supposedly contains the answer to every conceivable problem a customer could call in with. We're supposed to strictly stick to the text of these call flows because AT&T policies can change without notice.†

For example, we split into small groups one day to make and present posters on a given topic. My group is assigned the problem of what to do if someone calls in to cancel service for a loved one who's died. CSP specifically notes that this is one of the few situations where reps are *not* required to make a sales offer, so I write DO NOT TRY TO SELL THEM ANYTHING at the

* I also don't remember what this stands for.

† Hence the joke among some reps that AT&T stands for "At This Time."

top of the posterboard in big, bold letters. Then, because the fruit-scented markers take me straight back to elementary school, I surround the words with green stars and yellow lightning bolts for extra emphasis.

When Kimberly comes around to check on our progress, she frowns, picks up a marker, and crosses out my NOT. "I know it sounds weird, but you *always* make an offer on *every* call, regardless of why the person is calling," she says. Protesting, we pull up CSP and show her. "Oh, you're absolutely right. I *do* apologize," Kimberly says in that odd cadence, shrugging. She rewrites NOT above the one she crossed out. "They must have just changed the CSP—it was *not* like that the last class I had." I try not to imagine the situation that prompted the rule change.

Week Two: Sixteen People

"Now, *let me be clear,*" I say, doing my best Barack Obama impression, which is pretty bad. "I'm about to leave a job I've had for, ah... *many years.* I'm going to have a... *lot of free time.* I'm hoping for a little... ah, *change.*"

I hear Kolbi suppress a giggle in my headset.

"Well, sir, we have all sorts of DirecTV packages," she says, keeping her voice professional. "Let's figure out the one that best suits your needs! What are your... uh, your favorite shows?"

We've been doing endless sales role-plays, using our training phones to dial partners across the room and pretend to sell them DirecTV.* My classmates are a much easier sell than I suspect real customers will be—they'll be calling in for service, so they probably will be pissed off at AT&T. But we still have to try. It's mandatory.

To entertain myself and occasionally my partners, I've started role-playing various characters when it's my turn to be the customer—Batman,† Donald Trump, a woman who's obviously keeping someone prisoner in her basement, President Obama.

We spend at least half our classroom time on sales—doing memory drills on the many permutations of DirecTV packages, learning the systems

---

* AT&T bought DirecTV for $48.5 billion the previous summer—that is, in July of 2015.

† "The rates won't go up for a full year? *SWEAR TO ME!*"

that process sales, memorizing verbiage that will supposedly "overcome objections." It's emphasized that we *must* make a sales offer on every single call unless the caller formally invokes his or her right not to hear it,* and we must hear a clear "no" three times before we're allowed to stop making offers.

And it *will* be noticed if we don't, according to Kim. All our calls are recorded—that's why you hear those "this call may be recorded for quality assurance" messages on the customer end—and supervisors will be listening to our conversations.

Siempre va a te ver, I think—or, I guess, *Siempre va a te escuchar.*

Of course, that's not really possible—there's nowhere near enough people here to listen to every single call, and human conversations are way, way harder for computers to understand than GPS locations in a warehouse are. But we've been told that management screens calls randomly and that they listen to *every* call that trips an alarm suggesting customer dissatisfaction.

They're very vague about what gets a call flagged, which makes me suspect this "alarm" is as bullshit as SDF8's "high-tech security system." There's some low-hanging quantifiables, I guess—if the rep hangs up before the customer, which isn't allowed. If the customer gives negative feedback. If the customer calls back the next week. If the rep doesn't have all eight windows up and loaded. If the customer yells at you. If you don't say some specific keywords you're supposed to use.

I'm initially skeptical of rumors that some software scans every call for proper (or improper) verbiage and flags calls in which a customer swears or sounds irritated. As someone who transcribes a lot of interviews, I've followed the progress of speech-recognition technology pretty closely: last time I checked, the day I could trust a computer to do my transcription for me was still at least a decade away.

But later, I actually find a ton of companies claiming that their software will do exactly what the rumor mill says. One even can nag workers about tone in real time:

* Or, apparently, if the customer is trying to cancel a dead relative's plan.

> We all know how it feels to be low on energy at the end of a long work day. Some call-center agents at insurer MetLife are watched over by software that knows how it sounds.
>
> A program called Cogito presents a cheery notification when the toll of hours discussing maternity or bereavement benefits show in a worker's voice. "It's represented by a cute little coffee cup," says [manager] Emily Baker.... Her team reports that the cartoon cup is a helpful nudge to sit up straight and speak like the engaged helper MetLife wants them to be....
>
> In addition to nudging call agents to pep up their tone, or respond to distress in a caller's voice, Cogito's software listens to the pace and pattern of calls. Agents see a notification if they start speaking more quickly, a caller is silent for a long time, or the caller and agent talk over each other. Humans can notice all those things, but struggle to do so consistently, says [Cogito CEO Josh] Feast. "We're trying to help someone doing 60 calls a day, and who may be tired," he says.[3]

This form of "help" reminds me very much of Amazon's thinking-outside-the-box ambulances and pain-medicine vending machines.

Q: Your customer-service representatives handle roughly sixty calls in an eight-hour shift, with a half-hour lunch and two fifteen-minute breaks. By the end of the day, a problematic number of them are so exhausted by these interactions that their ability to focus, read basic conversational cues, and maintain a peppy demeanor is negatively affected. Do you:

A. Increase staffing so you can scale back the number of calls each rep takes per shift—clearly, workers are at their cognitive limits
B. Allow workers to take a few minutes to decompress after difficult calls
C. Increase the number or duration of breaks
D. Decrease the number of objectives workers have for each call so they aren't as mentally and emotionally taxing
E. Install a program that badgers workers with corrective pop-ups telling them that they sound tired

Seriously—what kind of fucking sociopath goes with E?

But it doesn't actually matter whether Convergys uses this kind of software. As with SDF8's security theater, what's important is that a lot of people *believe* it's being used and fear it.*

I used to live near Philly's Eastern State Penitentiary, a tourist destination that looks like a few square blocks of medieval castle plunked down into a residential neighborhood. From above, though, it looks a bit like a flower, or a windmill:

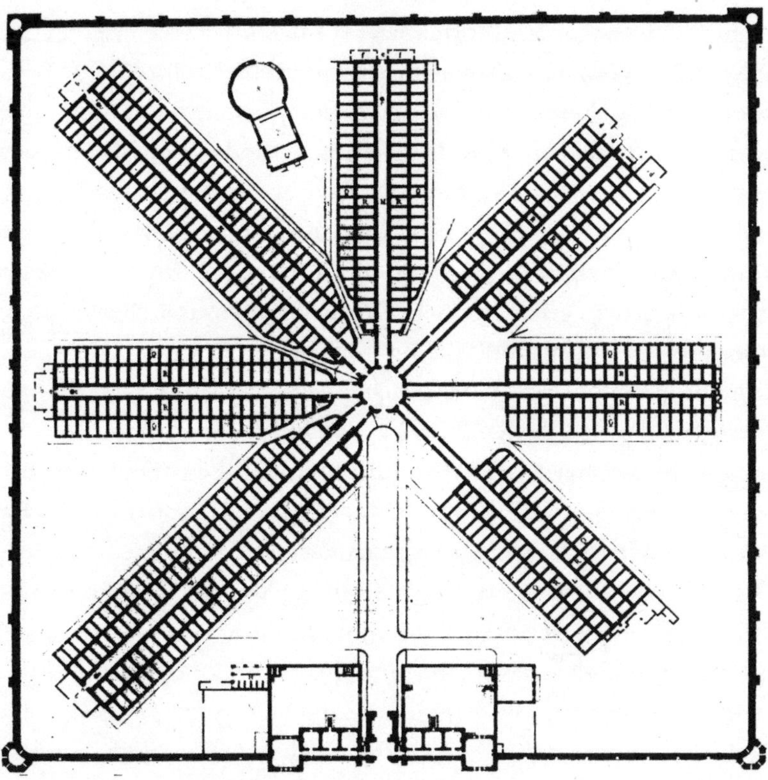

It's one of the first physical examples of a *panopticon,* a concept dreamed up by British philosopher Jeremy Bentham in the late eighteenth century. He imagined a circular prison built so every inch of every cell was visible from a central observation point—hence "pan-optic," meaning "all-seeing."

* Hey—how much of that nine-digit number can you remember?

A single jailer could watch over an entire prison from this central point, as in the diagram of Eastern State. Prisoners, however, would be able to see neither the jailer nor any other prisoners as they went about their daily labors.*

If prisoners could never know whether they were being watched at any particular moment—only that someone *could* be watching—Bentham thought they would behave as if they were *always* being watched. A prisoner would watch and police *himself,* as if his own personal jailer had been installed inside his head.

One benefit was efficiency—it's vastly cheaper to run a prison if you only need to pay one jailer. But Bentham seemed more interested in how the tiny jailer might permanently change the minds and behaviors of prisoners. The habit of self-policing could stick, making prisoners less likely to break the law again after their release. It was "a new mode of obtaining power of mind over mind, in a quantity hitherto without example," Bentham wrote.

I mean, an easy example of this power is red lights. Even in the middle of the night at a completely deserted intersection, I'll stop if the light's red and wait until it turns green to go. Even when I'm positive there's no camera and no other cars for miles and the light's been red so long I suspect it's broken, I *still* wait. It's not that I fear punishment: it's that I've internalized the rules of the road so much that I almost *can't* hit the gas. It just feels *wrong.*

French philosopher Michel Foucault revisited the panopticon in 1975's *Discipline and Punish,* a history of prisons. *Physical* panopticons like Eastern State went out of style long ago—prisoners tend to go insane from isolation, and closed-circuit cameras are much less of a pain. But Foucault was more interested in the everyday, nonprison implications of Bentham's tiny jailer in a world of increasingly unavoidable surveillance and monitoring.

Bentham's ideas for the panopticon didn't stop at prisons. He felt it would also be a beneficial model for insane asylums, hospitals, schools, and factories. Foucault saw increasingly subtle and normalized surveillance technology as a way for the leaders of a society to implant tiny bosses in the heads of workers, or tiny teachers in the heads of children.

---

* Bentham suggested that each cell be equipped with a sort of hamster wheel or treadmill so prisoners could walk on them all day, thus powering industrial looms or other equipment.

I wish Foucault were still alive: I'd love to hear his thoughts on social media and online culture,* the Patriot Act, Cogito, or "This call may be recorded for quality assurance." Because though I'm sure nobody listens to the vast majority of my calls, I can never be *really* sure that *this* one won't be picked for random screening or that there *isn't* some software that's listening for whether I say "DirecTV" or not. So I *do* always make sales offers to the many people calling in because they don't have forty bucks for this month's phone bill. The tiny boss in my head is always watching.

Though Convergys's haphazard web of rules sometimes makes me nostalgic for Amazon's perfectly integrated systems, it's always short-lived. Convergys can be frustrating, but SDF8 made me feel like I was actually going to go crazy. Here, the inefficiency of the training system manifests itself as time to talk and goof off with my classmates. Even if I were in as much physical pain as I was at SDF8, I'd still take this over Amazon every time.

Because I make *friends.* It's been a while since I've been part of a group of disparate women† thrown together to learn something, and I'd forgotten how nice that bond can be. I rolled my eyes when Kimberly said she wants us to become like a family, but we kind of *do;* people even consider making class shirts. I make friends, actual *friends,* people I can smoke and laugh and even go to the beach with, though I still feel I stick out.

The most obvious thing is the way I talk. Most of my classmates speak with the distinctly short, flat vowels of western Carolina. It's much more West Virginian–sounding than I expected—though, when I think about it, we aren't far from the state line, and the Appalachians *do* extend down into North Carolina.

This accent is central to my memories of Hickory, but I'm not about to write everything out in dialect. So here's a brief lesson on how to "talk southern" from my first-week seatmate, Misty:

"Okay, repeat after me," she says, waving a greeting. "Hi!"

---

* It's interesting to read Jon Ronson's *So You've Been Publicly Shamed* (New York: Riverhead Books, 2015) after reading Foucault.

† Only two of my male classmates are still around; by the time I leave, they'll all be gone.

I wave back, grinning manically, and do my best to match her vowels precisely. *"Ha!"*

Misty laughs and waves again. "Bye!"

"Bah!"

"Emily!"

"*Aim*-a-lay!"

"I like sweet tea."

"Ah'*locks wait tay*."

Misty giggles. "I need to pay my bills."

"Ah'*nade*—t'*pie*—m'*bails!*" I muster.

"I peed my pants!"

I'm laughing now. "Ah'*paid* m'*paints!*"

"You'll be talking like a real southern girl by the time I get done with you!" Misty says with pride.

Hard candy is the only food we're allowed to have in the classroom for fear of crumbs and ants, and, after the first week, classmates start bringing communal bags of peppermints and Jolly Ranchers to leave on the center table, next to the comically huge container of disinfectant wipes.

At first I tease the hardest-core sanitizers about being paranoid. I maybe should have paid more attention to *who* that was—Destiny, Jess, Kaitlyn, and Kimberly, i.e., everybody who'd worked here before.

"Seriously, just be glad they have wipes now!" says Kaitlyn when I poke fun at the eight wipes she uses every single morning. "It's so much better than before."

How so?

"It was really nasty the first time I worked here," which was a couple of years ago under the old managment, she says. "They didn't clean the desks, and they didn't have any of those wipes. You could bring hand sanitizer, and some people brought Lysol wipes even though you weren't supposed to. We were pretty much all constantly sick, though. I caught MRSA pretty bad, but it wasn't—"

"Wait, *what?*" I almost shriek. Half the room looks over, curious.

"Huh?" Kaitlyn looks confused.

My brain has stalled out. "*What?* Did you just say you got fucking *MRSA?*" *As in the "superbug" that doesn't respond to most antibiotics?* Like Ebola, it's something I'd read about, but never expected to encounter in real life.

"Well, the first time it was just a couple of sores. I was fine—it never got into my blood or anything," says Kaitlyn, looking at me oddly. "But I caught it again a couple of months later—there was a girl at work, I guess she was running a fever, she looked like she was just—clammy, sweaty, and covered in red open sores from head to toe."

"What?" My shriek is even higher-pitched this time. Most of the class seems to be listening in now; they mostly seem surprised that I'm being so weird about this.

"Yeah—so this girl looked really bad, but they let her come right on in and work," Kaitlyn says. "She was sitting at my desk the shift before me, and I couldn't find anywhere else to sit. I tried to clean it, but they didn't have the wipes then. Honestly, I was so grossed out I left halfway through the day because I felt like I just had to go shower."

I just stare at her with huge eyes.

"And I was *very* pregnant, too," Kaitlyn continues blithely. "That was two weeks before my C-section date. I went to the hospital early because I was so sick, and they put me on antibiotics and sent me home. But seriously, I was *so sick*—I couldn't get out of bed. I could hardly move to go to the bathroom by myself. My mom came over to help take care of me. I remember telling her if she did not take me to the hospital right then, I was absolutely going to die. She said, 'You're not going to die.' And I said, 'I am not kidding. I am going to *die*. I can feel it.' So she took me to the hospital, and they said that the MRSA had gotten into my bloodstream and my organs were starting to shut down and that in twenty-four hours I probably would have been dead."

I can't even say anything for a second. "Holy *shit,* girl!"

"Yeah, it was *crazy!*" Kaitlyn says. "After I had my C-section, the baby and I were both quarantined for two weeks, and I couldn't breast-feed, because he didn't have it but I did."

Kimberly comes back in, and we get back to memorizing DirecTV packages, but I can't get Kaitlyn's story out of my head. At the picnic tables later, I ask her if Convergys covered her medical bills.

"Well, I *tried* to get help with the bills from them, because I *know* that I got it from here," she says, grimacing. But at the time, she hadn't hit the three-month mark at Convergys yet. "So I was uninsured and paying everything out of pocket. My husband and I had saved up for the baby, so we were prepared for my C-section and maybe a little bit extra, but not something like this.

"So I went back and explained to them what happened, but they just refused." Kaitlyn sighs. "They said they were sorry, but that was that unless I had cold, hard proof of everything."

"Holy *shit,* that's awful!" I say. "Did you quit?"

"I stayed for a while—because, you know, *bills*—but I kept Lysol wipes in my bag whether they liked it or not. They didn't want me to use them, so I'd have to wipe everything down super fast and dry it and shove everything back in my pocket," says Kaitlyn. *Damn—I knew they were serious about the no-paper policy, but extending the ban to Lysol wipes?* I try to think of it from Taylor's mistrustful point of view—*I guess you could write someone's credit-card information on a Lysol wipe?*

"It was a little crazy," says Kaitlyn. "The only reason I came back was because I just...I couldn't find a job for a while." Before our current stint at Convergys, she'd had a job at a bank that she'd liked, but she had to take a leave of absence because she got sick and had to have surgery. Then she got sick again. "They told me I had to try to file for FMLA* because I couldn't do short-term leave again. And in the middle of the paperwork, my supervisors called me into the office and told me they had to let me go because it was a point system there, too, and I'd exceeded my points. I was gone from there for probably a year, and I worked at a couple of restaurants in between..." She trails off. "I really just got desperate, and Convergys agreed to hire me back. I thought if I could just go for the training and then if it was different, great. If not, then I'd try to find another job before I was out of training. And that didn't happen, so..." She shrugs. "But things aren't as bad as they used to be, really!"

* FMLA refers to the Family and Medical Leave Act of 1993, a federal law that lets employees of companies with more than fifty employees take up to twelve workweeks of unpaid leave a year without getting fired or getting kicked off health insurance, as long as it's to have a baby, adopt a child, care for a sick immediate family member, deal with a spouse's military deployment, or handle a serious health condition that interferes with their jobs.

After this, I join the ranks of the compulsive sanitizers.

Halfway through our second week, we go out on the production floor for the first time to listen in as real reps take real calls. I'm assigned to shadow Olivia, a young white woman who looks about eleven months pregnant and operates with a speed that leaves me breathless. As she speaks with customers in a sugar-sweet voice, Olivia's mouse is a blur of motion between windows, minimizing, maximizing, and typing so fast I can barely follow what she's doing. It isn't the most useful learning experience, but I sit and watch in awe, the way I'd marvel at someone dancing a high-speed hornpipe.

We've been doing timed drills in class, trying to shave down the time it takes for us to fully relaunch the eight-odd windows and programs for an individual customer—for short, I'm going to refer to this as "the launch sequence." The launch sequence involves maybe fifty or sixty steps and begins with the beep of a new customer in your headset. Most of the steps must be done in a specific order—some need information copied and pasted in from other programs; others you have to go start up something else and return multiple times because the pages load agonizingly slowly. Sometimes it's both.

I can actually do each part of the job individually just fine. But I'm *terrible* at doing them all simultaneously. Trying to remember everything without forgetting about any of the *other* stuff I'm supposed to remember *and* holding up my end of a conversation feels very, very similar to trying to hold a bunch of nine-digit numbers in my head* or trying to juggle with too many balls. I'm always either diving for a ball that's about to hit the floor or chasing after one that *did* hit the floor and is bouncing away. Even when I *do* manage to get everything going at the same time, it feels dangerous, as if the whole thing will come toppling down if I lose focus for even a *second.* And, judging by my partners for drills, it's pretty stressful for everyone, not just me.

Destiny's assured me that once you get the launch sequence down well enough to make good offers, sales are easy. But I haven't actually witnessed what "having it down" looks like in practice until I watch Olivia. Like Henry Noll with his forty-seven-ton days, she's living proof that it's, well, *possible.*

Olivia clicks around in a blur, looking up whether the caller has other services with AT&T, what his or her home address is, what services are

* Incidentally: how much of that nine-digit employee number can you remember *now?*

available there. And that's not even mentioning the subtle spycraft that's the real key to making sales—gathering even more intelligence via innocuous conversation* while you work through the caller's problem. Olivia pulls all this off with the grace of a swan gliding across a lake, not letting a hint of all the unseen frantic paddling into her voice.

At one point, during a brief break between calls, I ask Olivia how long it took for her to get so good at this. She says about six months. Seeing the expression on my face, she reassures me in her normal voice that I'll get the hang of it, really.

I've been learning things outside Convergys, too—like how to play Pokémon Go. My younger coworkers' brief obsession with the game when it comes out is so intense that management sends out an email specifically warning us not to play in the parking lot, for safety reasons. I make fun of the game at first, then quickly get obsessed after I'm goaded into downloading it myself.

A brutal heat wave has settled over Hickory, and finding a space with air-conditioning where I can spend the hours between 4:00 p.m. and 10:00 p.m. is now crucial. I'd never done Car Life for longer than a few days at a time before, so I hadn't really considered the long-term lack of somewhere to, well, *be* when I'm not at work or sleeping.

While the sun's out, I alternate between loitering at Barnes & Noble and loitering at the library. In the evenings, when it gets cool enough, I often eat my dinner by the lake in a public park or wander the few deliberately quaint blocks of small businesses that make up downtown Hickory. I'm almost always alone—my class friends mostly have kids and/or commute from forty-five minutes away, so they can't really hang out, and I literally don't know anybody else.

Since Pokémon Go came out, though, Hickory's downtown has been buzzing with life. Kids, adults, teenagers—it sometimes feels like the entire town is out catching Pokémon on summer evenings, like a Norman Rockwell

* "So, doing anything fun this weekend?" can tell you a lot about a caller's lifestyle—if she's taking the kids to the park, for example, she might be more interested in a DirecTV package that includes the Disney Channel.

painting with smartphones. Participating makes me feel a little silly, but also a little less alone.

Like on my previous trip, I had grand plans to read all my books and finish my stupid book proposal during these couple of months away—no distractions and lots of free time, right? But, also like before, every time I sit down after work to do *more* work, I get nowhere. Rote memorization leaves my brain fuzzy and easily irritated, so no matter how many times I sit myself down at Barnes & Noble to try to make myself finish a freelance magazine piece, I just can't seem to, even though this single thousand-word article will bring in more much-needed cash than a week and a half at Convergys.

Fuck it: I'm playing games on my phone, I think, again and again. *Fuck it: I'm getting Chinese takeout and eating it by the lake. Fuck it: I'm driving downtown to catch some Pokémon.*

Finally, desperate to make progress on my "real" work, I start giving myself reporting "assignments," like finding out more about the history of furniture in North Carolina. That *is* why I decided to come to Hickory, after all.

That's how I end up spending a Saturday wandering Hickory Furniture Mart, where the remnants of North Carolina's once-great furniture industry have banded together to present their products under one roof. It's a big, big roof—at a million square feet spread over four floors, the place is almost the size of SDF8. There's a hundred galleries, showrooms, and outlets as well as guides who speak Arabic, Farsi, French, and Spanish for international visitors. And it's just five minutes down the road from my Walmart.

Much of the furniture is a little formal for my taste, but some is absolutely gorgeous. The four- and five-digit price tags pull me up short pretty quickly, though. It isn't particularly busy, so I start chatting up salespeople, hunting for anyone who's been in the business long enough to have experienced its glory days. They're surprisingly easy to find.

"When I first started, you had customers from all over the States, all over the world, waiting in line for a salesperson. But it's taken a plunge," says Tonya, a saleswoman who's been in furniture twenty-nine years, more than half her life. She gestures to the mostly empty gallery around us. "The furniture industry has struggled; it's still struggling."

I ask if she remembers any specific turning point when things started going bad.

"Bill Clinton!" she blurts, then laughs. "I'm so sorry, that came out way too quick. But, honestly? I attribute it to the trade deals he made. I don't think it had to do with anything but."

Every single person I speak with at Hickory Furniture Mart will specifically mention Bill Clinton, NAFTA, outsourcing, or trade deals as the beginning of the decline of the US furniture industry.

"It took me a good several years to be able to sell these with pride, even though it's imported," Tonya says, patting a gorgeous inlaid dresser. "You can definitely tell the quality—the thickness of the woods, beautiful veneers, good heavy drawers. I hate to say it, but actually, there's a lot of solid woods being made in the import industry."

"Wait: are you saying some of this is imported?" I ask, taken aback—the whole ethos of Hickory Furniture Mart is "Made in America."

"Well, when you're looking at these upholstered items, you're still looking at eight-way hand-tied products, and *that's* done here," Tonya says. "But the solid-wood pieces—bedroom, dining room, tables?" She sweeps an arm to encompass the huge showroom. "Majority of this is imports."

Businesses have been moving jobs to take advantage of cheap labor since way before NAFTA. Actually, outsourcing is the reason the "furniture cluster" area of western North Carolina exists at all—because this used to be America's third world.

The first European settlers set foot in North Carolina at Roanoke Island in 1585. You may remember Roanoke as the "lost colony," the one whose governor returned from a supply run to find that all hundred of its settlers had disappeared, leaving the word *Croatoan* scratched into a fence post as the only clue to what happened. Even today, the only historical consensus is that whatever it was probably wasn't good.

Since those auspicious beginnings, North Carolina's been almost comically unlucky and poor, crippled by several factors—no large ports, a coastline nicknamed "graveyard of the Atlantic," pirates, hurricanes, unproductive soil, incompetent leadership, and active economic kneecapping from other colonies.

So as wealthier neighbors like Virginia and South Carolina developed Southern aristocracies based around huge slave plantations, North Carolina—especially this western area—remained mostly populated with subsistence-farming immigrants as likely to be from Germany or Scotland as from England. Supposedly, this is when North Carolina picked up the nickname "a vale of humility between two mountains of conceit."

After the American Revolution, North Carolina made so little economic and social progress that it acquired more nicknames poking fun at how backward it was, including "the Rip Van Winkle of the States" and "the Ireland of America." It was already the poorest and most desperate state in the South by the time it joined the Civil War, in which it lost more soldiers than any other Confederate state.

After the Civil War, Northern industrialists began looking at the wrecked Southern states as business opportunities, much the way the US looks at third-world countries today—places full of poor, desperate, non-unionized workers who'd be grateful to work harder and cheaper than unionized factory workers of the North. North Carolina, with the poorest and most desperate population of all, was a *very* appealing place to relocate your factory.

In particular, the furniture industry—previously based in Massachusetts, New York, and Michigan—began relocating plants to western North Carolina's paradise of cheap land, cheap timber, cheap labor, and no unions. By the turn of the century, North Carolina had forty-four furniture factories and soon led the country in furniture production.

At first, "Made in North Carolina" had a similar meaning to "Made in China"—cheap and potentially shoddy. But by the 1950s, companies like Lane and Henredon, based in the furniture cluster, had become known for high-quality craftsmanship.* Business here boomed in the 1970s and '80s—which is when my parents purchased the bedroom set that's been in their room my entire life.

Curious, I call my mom and ask where they'd bought it. "We had it shipped from North Carolina—that was just what you did back then," she

* The town of Hickory's motto is actually "Life. Well crafted."

says, going upstairs to check the maker's mark. It turns out to have been made in a factory half an hour away—one that's now closed.

Today, western North Carolina is cluttered with shuttered plants and factories. Soaking up the library's air-conditioning one day, I find the book *The Furniture Wars: How America Lost a Fifty Billion Dollar Industry,* a 2009 retrospective by Hickory's Michael K. Dugan about the industry's eventful years between 1987 and 2004, during which he served as president and CEO of Henredon Furniture Industries. Dugan writes:

> American furniture makers cannot compete with Asian workers happy to earn 32 cents an hour. And American furniture companies cannot match prices with Third World companies that operate with those lower worker costs and without the federal mandates of OSHA, EPA, FICA, MACT, ERISA, OFCCP, ADA, and COBRA.
>
> American workers who once earned decent livings producing furniture are scrambling for employment in lower-paying service jobs. The ones who view those jobs as inferior to making furniture go back to school to prepare for high-tech jobs that as yet do not exist in these counties. The community colleges are filled, thanks to government grants, but the unemployment numbers remain frighteningly high. Caldwell County, North Carolina, home of Broyhill and Bernhardt, two of the industry's biggest and best-known brands, has hit unemployment levels as high as 12 percent.

Numbers before and after NAFTA bear out salespeople's reasoning about the decline of their industry. In 1992, 19 percent of solid-wood furniture purchased in the United States was imported; in 2008, 64 percent was imported. In 1992, North Carolina had 80,403 furniture jobs; over twenty years, that fell by more than half, to 35,601. And that's not even considering the knock-on effects on related industries like timber and textiles.

I've seen so many ghost towns and shuttered factories in Kentucky, Indiana, and North Carolina—just drive twenty minutes in any direction, they're *everywhere*—and it gives me a better understanding of Trump's appeal. Politicians of both parties are almost universally positive about global trade—the concept was that free, efficient markets know best and that the loss of most of America's manufacturing jobs would be outweighed by how much cheaper prices would get for everyone.

The thing is, the *many* Americans whose jobs and communities were the collateral damage of globalization don't feel like anybody *asked* if they'd like to exchange their functional but inefficient local economy for a much more efficient Walmart. Nobody *asked* Butch Patty if she'd like to trade her $20-an-hour job making furniture for a $10-an-hour job at Convergys plus the ability to buy a T-shirt for five dollars. And I can't really blame them for feeling forgotten. Global trade would affect their lives the most and benefit them the least—at $10 an hour, you just don't have much money to spend.

Trump's the only major politician I've heard say plainly that global trade's benefits *weren't* worth it, actually calling NAFTA "the worst trade deal in the history of the world" on the campaign trail. It's not surprising to me that so many people who've spent twenty years watching their communities erode as a result of vast forces beyond their control were so desperately grateful when someone, *anyone,* finally said what they were thinking out loud.

"When you started, the actual parts were all manufactured here, too, correct?" I ask Douglas, a salesperson in another showroom who's been in furniture for more than a quarter century.

"Most of it," Douglas says. "When I first started, some of it began to go offshore, then more and more followed. So many of the wood plants here are vacant."

The shift overseas, he says, was attributable to "cost—strictly cost."

"The cost of paying American workers?"

"Yes," he says. "A lot of people will say, 'I want only American-made'—but when they see the price, it's not as important to 'em."

"What goes into the price?" I ask. "The furniture *is* gorgeous, but... yeah, I could never afford *any* of this."

"Well, it's how it's constructed," Douglas says. He indicates the sofa I'm sitting on. "This has a hardwood kiln-dried frame. The frame is corner-blocked, glued and screwed, eight-way hand-tied—that's a coil that drops down into the frame of your furniture and is literally hand-tied off to the frame eight different ways with a heavy nylon.

"The alternative is a sinuous coil, a continuous *s* that goes from front to back. It's a lot less expensive to manufacture. But this"—he pats the sofa's arm—"is how you get *longevity*. Eight-way hand-tied furniture is furniture you'll always have. My parents have had their sofa for twenty years, and it looks brand-new. Or—may I show you a piece?"

He shepherds me over to a wooden table whose surface is a complex inlaid mosaic. It's *breathtaking*. So is the sticker price—$7,899.

"Now, this is true furniture at its finest; you can *feel* it," says Douglas, running his fingers over the seamless inlay with pride. "This is an honest-to-goodness piece of *art*."

He's not wrong. But my last paycheck for two weeks of work at Convergys came to $525. If I saved every single penny—no food, no rent, no gas, no car payment—I'd have $7,899 in about four months.

Week Three: Thirteen People

The first call that makes me cry starts out so well.

At the halfway point of training, a third of the class is gone. The remaining thirteen of us start splitting our time between the classroom and the production floor. We spend all morning handling real customers on our own aside from four walkers, veteran reps who circulate answering our many questions. We trainees each have a set of colored flags; flipping the red one with a question mark on it so it sticks up over the cube wall signals "Someone please come help me!"

But it always takes forever to get help, because we are not remotely prepared to do this. Kimberly's been a wonderful teacher, but being on the phones alone feels like being tossed into the deep end of a pool after memorizing a book about swimming.

I do have my opening verbiage down, though—it's almost Pavlovian at this point. At the beep signaling that a new caller is now live in my headset, I confidently rattle off "Hello, and thanks for calling AT&T! This is Emily speaking. What can I help you with today?" as automatically as Woody from *Toy Story.*

The woman on the other end gives me a friendly hello, and says she's actually at a call center herself right now.

"Oh, no way!" I say, relaxing a little. "How's your day going?" She laughs and says fine, but she's on her lunch break and kind of in a hurry, so...

"Okay, I *definitely* get that. We'll get your issue taken care of as fast as possible. First thing, let's log you into your account...just one second..."

I've started imagining multitasking as splitting into several tiny robotic versions of myself, each simultaneously working on her own prime directive.

Helper Emily wants to figure out the caller's problem and find a solution.

Sales Emily wants to gather information about the customer and use it to formulate and deliver a personalized sales offer.

Protocol Emily remembers the details of Convergys's systems and preferred verbiage, including the launch sequence.

Scribe Emily types notes on the reasons for the call and actions taken in real time.

Conversation Emily is *supposed* to be in charge of listening and talking like a normal human being.

Short-Term Memory Emily can hold on to passwords, addresses, and other hard-to-remember things until they're needed.

Awareness Emily keeps an eye on the real world—whether a walker or manager is nearby, whether it's lunchtime, what's on the class group chat, how this call is affecting her metrics.

Journalist Emily notes when something might be relevant to the book and tries to remember it until her next break—though, frankly, Journalist Emily rarely breaks through the others, who are extremely busy.

And poor Boss Emily is stuck trying to keep everybody working in harmony. Her job *sucks*. It's a bit like managing a completely full clown car in which every passenger desperately wants to drive and sometimes tries to take the wheel by force.

Because, though "multitasking" is a common job requirement, the last half century of cognitive science has been very clear that it's just not something humans are any good at. We may *think* we can do two things at once—Lord knows I used to. But we're actually just switching back and forth between tasks really fast, never fully concentrating on either and losing energy with every switch. We end up slower and less competent at both tasks than if we'd just focused on each one at a time.

The most obvious example is texting and driving, because the consequences can be fatal. But it's even harder when the two tasks use similar areas of the brain. I've personally *never* mastered the Reporting 101 skill of scribbling down notes while also holding up one end of a conversation, or even writing while music with English lyrics plays in the background.

So it's no surprise that I have a *lot* of trouble keeping all these Emilys working together instead of fighting each other. The more of them there are, the smaller, dumber, and more distractible each one is. Information, time, and focus get lost every time a new Emily grabs the wheel. And each one adds another voice to the chorus vying for attention. It feels as mentally stressful as SDF8 was physically stressful.

And it actually kind of is. At least, studies have linked attempts to multitask to a short-term increase in levels of cortisol and adrenaline—the "stress hormones"—and long-term increases in depression and anxiety.

Unfortunately, whatever Dr. Frankenstein awkwardly kludged the jobs and systems of sales and service together didn't know any more about multitasking than he did about Miller's Law of seven—or didn't care.

But he wouldn't have had much incentive to care. What are customers going to do—*switch providers?* They almost certainly signed a multiyear contract, and why go through the huge annoyance of switching to a new company and a new phone number when the customer service there will inevitably be just as bad? Hell, there's a decent chance they'll just end up talking to a rep from a different Convergys site.

And what are the reps going to do—*quit?* They know all too well that it's just as stressful at Chick-fil-A.

I get the caller's PIN and log in to her account in Clarify but have barely started the launch sequence when she starts describing her problem, which—*shit*—sounds complicated. *Crap—I think this is a Telegence one.* Handling anything involving Telegence feels like being tossed into the deep end *without* having memorized a book about swimming. I'd seen the mysterious word in forum posts:

> *They took our Telegence a while back. It's actually driven a lot of people to quit because the customers become so agitated waiting on System X or Zone* to load, so agents get bad scores.*
>
> *They said that they were dropping Telegence and never taught us how to use it in training. But apparently they've been telling everyone that for the past*

* Like Telegence, System X and Zone are systems in the launch sequence.

year or so. If they take it away, I'll for sure be looking for another job. Telegence runs everything.

Very true. I hear that people are told "You'll learn it on the floor."

That is *exactly* what we were told—*Telegence is being phased out soon; you don't need it; you'll learn it on the floor.* As far as I can tell, it used to be the main way to do things and is still the *only* way to do a bunch of things. Four out of five times I flip my red flag, my walker ends up using Telegence.

Thank god I had Destiny and Jess for partnered calls last week and was able to pick up a little from them. On my own, though, most of the time the only thing I can do is flip my red flag and stall. Walkers are in such high demand that it usually takes at least ten minutes for one to get to you, and *that* usually means "customers become agitated."

I frequently fantasize about MBAs from the F. Kafka School of Management cackling as they designed this system for maximum alienation, frustration, and existential anxiety. I'm sure the reality is mundane, though—I'm guessing some rep figured out how to use Telegence to steal customer information,* so upper management isn't willing to risk letting *any* reps officially use it despite the lack of a functional replacement. It's *infuriating* for both reps and customers, but seems to be an acceptable status quo for the company—some of the they-took-our-Telegence posts are more than a year old.

I flip my red flag as my customer continues describing her problem, and I try to continue feeding Conversation Emily exactly enough attention to make understanding noises at the correct moments. Behind the scenes, Protocol Emily racks her brain for the launch sequence.†

---

* The only thing I'm able to find out about why they're getting rid of one of their key systems is "security." Around a year before I started training, the FCC fined AT&T $25 million over a big data breach at one of its vendor call centers, and posts mentioning getting rid of Telegence started showing up shortly afterward.

† I couldn't really take notes on this, so I'm reconstructing it from memory. The actual sequence is probably different, but I assure you that I am not exaggerating how long and complicated it is.

Okay, Clarify's loading. Over to Internet Explorer. Reload Zone from the last customer. You have to click through three separate pages to do this, and each one takes a minute and a fucking half to load, so if you don't remember to start it off at the beginning *and* check back in twice, you're boned.

Back to Clarify—now fully loaded. Launch Telegence from the drop-down menu. We may not know how to use it, but we still need to have its window up and ready for each customer.

Back to Clarify; launch the notes on the woman's account. We're supposed to type in our own notes on why the customer's calling and what actions we took in real time, but half the time I end up either saying what I'm typing or typing what I'm saying.

Uh-oh, thinks Helper Emily, scanning the notes from the previous reps the woman's spoken with. It isn't the first time she's called about this issue. Helper Emily scrolls back through the notes and—

I belatedly notice that the woman has stopped talking and is apparently waiting for me to say something. *Dammit, Conversation Emily, keep it together.*

"I'm so sorry that happened; that's not the experience we want you to have with AT&T," I say. *Remember to verbalize.* This lets the customer know I'm still there, I'm paying attention, and I empathize with her problem. *Empathy is important*—one of the million acronyms here, though I can't remember which one, exactly, involves an *E* for *Empathy.*

The caller returns to her monologue as if I hadn't said anything. Helper Emily takes the helm again but eventually concludes that she *definitely* does not know how to fix the caller's problem. I half stand and poke my head up over the cube edge, but there's no walkers in sight.

I sit back down, shove Awareness Emily to the back of the bus, and try to refocus. *Shit, where was I? Who was up?* The caller's account notes are still open, and Helper Emily really wants to finish reading them, but she's muscled aside by the tag team of Protocol Emily and Sales Emily. *You don't know what to do—what else do you need to know? Get the other systems up and running, right now, or you're not going to be prepared to make an offer.*

Okay, I've done Clarify, Zone, Telegence, notes, and now...I blank for a second, and Protocol Emily hisses *System X.* After starting the first page of System X loading, I go back to Clarify and call up the woman's personal information so Sales Emily can start checking which AT&T services are available at her home address and whether she has them already.

Infuriatingly, the systems are so poorly integrated that not only do you have to copy and paste addresses by hand, you can also only do it one line at a time. It takes way less time if you manage to hold the caller's city, state, and zip code in your head long enough to type them in, so Short-Term Memory Emily takes the wheel, chanting, *Missouri City Texas 77035, Missouri City Texas 77035, Missouri City Texas 77035, Missouri*—

"Hey, are you paying attention?" The woman's voice is sharp, setting my nerves jangling and—*dammit*—waking up Fight-or-Flight Emily, the dreaded tenth passenger of the clown car. She spends almost all her time napping in the backseat, but it's game over if she ever gets control of the wheel. *She's getting pissed,* Conversation Emily notes as Boss Emily tries to coax Fight-or-Flight Emily back to sleep. *Say something!*

"Yes, ma'am, I *am* listening, promise! I'm just pulling up some programs that'll let me help you," I say, trying to make the lie convincing. I'm not, really—half the stuff I'm fumbling with is for sales, not for fixing her problem.

I really do wish I could just give this woman my full attention. We'd both be so much happier. Because though it's tough, I can competently juggle the four balls having to do with the customer's actual problem. But when I try to add another four sales balls to that, all eight usually end up on the floor. At the end of a bad call, it's incredibly frustrating to know that I probably could have done a good job if I hadn't been so distracted.

But supposedly the panopticon can track what windows are open on our computer at any given time, so after poking my head up again to look for walkers, I continue trying to get all my windows up while paying better attention.

Okay, I don't know what to do, but maybe CSP does, says Helper Emily. I click over to CSP, reload it, think for a second, then type in a keyword I hope will bring up the correct call flow. CSP's also a slow loader, though it's not as bad as Zone or System X, and—

Shit. Forgot about System X. To get System X ready for a potential sale, you have to get through three unbearably slow windows, and I'm only on the first. I click over to start the next page loading, and—

She's stopped talking again, notes Conversation Emily.

"Okay, I'm so sorry that happened. I know it's important to be able to trust your phone company, and I am going to make that happen for you again," I say. *Use reassuring verbs.* Helper Emily grabs the wheel back, and I click over and scroll the list of CSP call flows for something that sounds like the woman's problem. *No dice.* I try another keyword.

Restate the problem. "Okay, now, just so I'm sure I got all that correctly..." I continue. *Still no dice on CSP.* As I summarize, I type in yet another keyword to search, which makes me stutter.

"No," the woman says, the anger in her voice making Fight-or-Flight Emily stir again. *Shitshitshitshitshit.* "That's not what I said *at all.* My problem is..." She again goes into a monologue.

Helper Emily tries one more keyword in CSP before giving up. The company line is that CSP is omniscient, and it's useful for simple problems, but—

Ah, fuck, gotta get back to System X, which... yes, it's finally loaded! Now ctrl-V the address, and the rest of it was... I look to Short-Term Memory Emily, but she's long since dropped her balls. She can only shrug and hazard, *Uh, New Texas, Missouri? New Missouri, Texas?*

I click back to Clarify to get the address again, because either way, I need to get the zip code. Okay—*Missouri City Texas 77035, Missouri City Texas 77035, Missouri City Texas 77053, Missouri...*

I leave Short-Term Memory Emily reciting this in the backseat as I go to pull the System X window back up. But the bar at the bottom of the screen is now so crowded with minimized windows that the tabs have scrunched up and only show around three letters of identifying information.

I finally locate the proper System X window, and this time Short-Term Memory Emily comes through. *Missouri City Texas 77053, Missouri City Texas 77053...*

I type the rest of the address in and set the next page loading, then half stand again to look for walkers. They're all still busy with other people. One's over with Destiny, who has her green flag up. *Goddammit, Destiny, why do you have to be so good at this?* The green flag of a sale takes precedence over all others, and processing one will take a walker out of the rotation for at least half an hour.

I pull up the class group chat and type *Hey can anybody help me?* with a quick description of her problem.

All the Emilys are talking at once now.

You haven't even started your notes, says Scribe.

Go load the last page of System X, says Sales. *Jesus, how hard is this?*

Maybe try this keyword? says Helper.

She's going to go screamer in about two minutes, says Conversation.

Graaaah, says Fight-or-Flight, groggy.

Boss Emily, under duress, decides to preemptively drop all the sales balls and let Helper Emily drive unimpeded for a bit. I pull CSP back up, try the new keyword, and, desperate, pick a call flow that sounds *sort of* right. I start reading the script's first question aloud—

"The *fuck* are you *talking* about?" the woman says, angry.

Make that one minute, says Conversation Emily.

Graaah! says Fight-or-Flight Emily, almost fully awake now. As she wakes up, she starts to get bigger, like the Hulk. The clown car starts feeling even more cramped. *Fuckfuckfuckfuck*—

"I'm sorry—" I say, pulling up chat again. Nobody's responded. I type *Please somebody help she's getting really mad.*

It's a self-fulfilling prophecy, because saying one thing while typing another makes me stammer, and callers lock on to signs that you're flustered like sharks lock on to blood in the water. The phones can be weirdly primal like that sometimes—if customers sense weakness or fear, they *will* turn on you.

"I'm really sorry, ma'am, I, uh, I—"

"*Look,* you incompetent—" says the woman.

Make that five sec— says Conversation Emily, but she's cut off as Fight-or-Flight Emily's growth spurt pins every other Emily in the car against the walls. Boss Emily desperately tries to regain control, but she's wedged into the backseat so firmly she can barely breathe, let alone talk.

"—bitch, I've already called about this twice and..."

The woman completes her werewolflike transformation into a screamer, and Fight-or-Flight Emily slams her foot down on the gas pedal.

GRAAAAAAAH!

An electric jolt runs through my body. My heart starts racing, my face gets hot, my muscles tense, my throat chokes up, and I'm suddenly flooded with unpleasant, jittery, *violent* energy. It's way, way too much; it feels like

I'm going to burst. Time seems to slow down, which might be helpful if I could focus. But I can't even seem to *think.*

Any ability I had to even simulate multitasking is gone. I know I was around halfway through the launch sequence, but have no idea where I left off. In this state, I can't even keep four balls in the air. I manage to search CSP a couple more times but barely register the words; Boss Emily is desperately preoccupied with *not fucking crying at work.*

A few minutes later, the screamer has barely stopped to breathe, the walkers are still busy, and the clown car is totally out of control. I get a second of relief as a flashing box pops up on my screen, but it isn't help from the group chat—it's just the familiar yellow window that pops up when a call hits six hundred seconds. The box reminds me that my target average call time is around seven hundred seconds and reminds me to ask for help if I need it. *Yeah, yeah,* I think, dismissing the pop-up.

Hold! Put her on hold, you idiot! croaks Boss Emily from where she's crushed against the backseat.

"Ma'am, if it's all right with you, I'd like to put you on a short hold—"

"Don't you fucking dare put me on hold! How the fuck do you even have a job, you stupid fucking bitch?"

Our training was very clear: there are *no* circumstances in which we can hang up on a customer. Sending a customer to hold without explicit permission is also forbidden. I'm not allowed to escape.* I type another desperate *Please please help she's yelling at me* into group chat.

There's still no sign of help when the second automatic warning pops up at 750 seconds. This one is red and more strongly worded. I bury my head in my hands.

By the time a walker finally gets to me, I'm a trembling, red-faced mess. The screamer's kept up a steady high-volume torrent of abuse for ten straight minutes. I might be impressed by her stamina if it wasn't causing me to melt down right along with her. It just makes her angrier when I try to speak, so

* If any readers are under the impression that screaming at service workers is an effective motivational tool, (A) *be a better person,* and (B) *it's the exact opposite.* Flipping out will almost always stretch things out longer, because Fight-or-Flight is very bad at driving.

I've given up in the hope that her balloon will eventually deflate. But it keeps coming and coming and coming.

Awareness Emily has been squished into unconsciousness, so I jump a mile when walker Mara reaches from behind to flip my red flag down. She takes in my red, contorted face. "What's up?"

I try to explain, but the screaming in my ear is so distracting that I can't seem to form coherent sentences. My throat's so constricted that my words come out in an indecipherable croak, and I keep having to take long pauses to avoid starting to cry.

"What's the *problem?*" Mara says.

Can't talk... can't put her on hold...

"I, uh, I, she—"

"Wait—can she hear you right now?" says Mara, alarmed.

Huh—yeah, I guess she can hear me, Awareness Emily thinks, dreamily. *That's no good. Put her on hold.*

But I can't put her on hold unless she agrees to it, objects Protocol Emily. *Can't talk while the screamer can hear me... but can't put her on hold...* I'm so out of sorts that I get stuck in this two-step logic loop for a couple of cycles. I can't figure my way out of it, so I eventually try to pull a Kobayashi Maru and start to remove my headset.

"No no no, *never* take your headset off!" says Mara, quickly stopping me. "What are you *doing? Put her on short hold.*"

Of course—put her on short hold. I shakily hit the button. There's no change on my end—"short hold" just mutes my mic. I can still hear the screamer in my ear.

"Spit it out! What's the problem?" Mara repeats, impatient.

"She, uh, the tablet deal—"

You fucking incompetent bitch I can't believe

"—uh, you know, the two-for-one thing with the, uh, data plan contract—"

can't fucking believe how stupid you are

"—and the, the, the, uh, bill—"

I mean Jesus Christ I don't

"—uh, you know, she, uh, got the, uh—"

you dumb bitch you fucking idiot just fix my

"—the, uh, the data plan was—"

should be fired I swear I'm going to

"—it was more than, than she—uh—she's, uh, screaming—"

what the fuck are you

With an exasperated sigh, Mara reaches over me and expertly hits the combination of buttons to send the screamer to a long hold—a *real* hold, with Muzak, during which neither of us can hear the other. Her ranting cuts off midobscenity, to my incredible relief.

"Okay, take some deep breaths, calm down," Mara says, not unkindly. "What happened?" A wave of deep, desperate affection for Mara washes over me. I'm a little shocked; what she just did is supposedly a zero-tolerance fireable offense. I could *marry* her.

I'm still a stammering, shaking, frog-voiced, teary mess, but without the constant screaming in my ear, Fight-or-Flight Emily slowly shrinks down to a size that allows me to haltingly explain the situation. Mara walks me through using Telegence—*fucking Telegence*—then finally shrugs.

"Tell her she signed a contract," Mara says.

"I, uh, I, she—"

"Tell her she can cancel service if she wants, but there's going to be a big penalty. That's all there is to it," says Mara, then she briskly walks off to defuse the next in our never-ending stream of red flags.

I watch her go, then slowly pull my gaze back to my phone, where the Hold button blinks a malevolent green. I start moving a shaking finger toward it, then stop. I reach out again, then stop again. *Come on, you pussy,* I think. *Suck it up. What is she going to do, hurt your feelings? Do it. Do it. Do it do it do it do it do it doitdoitdoitdoitdoit!*

But I just *can't.* I can't make myself do it.

I've thought a lot about the phrase "I made myself do it" since those first weeks at SDF8, when my bone-tired body mutinied on my brain. The phrase suggests two halves of a person in conflict. There's *You*—the brain, the diligent, responsible taskmaster. And there's *Yourself*—the body, trying to avoid stress and pain and other things that aren't good for either one of the halves.*

---

* Or you could call them ego and id—whatever.

You can whip *Yourself* into doing a lot of things. But *Yourself* gets veto power in certain situations—if you try to hold your hand over a flame, for example. As I continue trying to make myself hit the button that will take the screamer off hold, it strikes me that there's a finite number of times *You* can force *Yourself* to do something before *Yourself* decides *You* don't understand your best interests and mutinies.

Feeling almost hypnotized, I just stare at the blinking Hold light for about five minutes, unable to force myself to pick up the phone. Finally, it stops blinking. The call's lasted almost half an hour; presumably the woman's lunch break ended.

The instant the light goes dark, I log out of my phone, speed-walk to the bathroom, and just barely keep it together for the few minutes I have to wait in line. In the privacy of a stall, though, I just try to keep my sobs at an unintrusive volume as I try to coax my heart rate and breathing back to normal. It takes a while. *I guess this is why there's always a line,* I think. Nobody knocks or tries to hurry me up. I resolve to never think uncharitable thoughts about the bathroom line again.

I hate, hate, *hate* that I'm crying at work. It makes me feel like an utter failure. But screaming at myself about it only makes things worse, so I just try to focus on regulating my ragged breathing. After a few minutes, the panicky, jittery wave of energy I've been riding since the woman began screaming starts to subside, as if it's being drained through my tear ducts. But I don't feel any better—just hollow, empty, and exhausted. I rest my head on the stall wall, suddenly and desperately homesick.

What the fuck are you even doing here? I think. *You idiot.*

I check my phone to see how long I've been away from my desk, and, thank god, there's only a couple of minutes until lunch now.

Fuck it, I think. *I'm going to Chick-fil-A.*

The only time I've attempted to go out for lunch so far was a total failure. We'd been rewarded with an extra four minutes for our lunch break, which by then had felt like a real reward and not the joke it would have been in any newsroom. I figured thirty-four minutes was enough time to hit up the Five Guys a quarter mile down the road.

It wasn't. I didn't even get to eat the damn food—my lunch was a sad fistful of fries, eaten while white-knuckle-driving back. With two minutes left until the system marked me late, I got stuck behind a cautious minivan in a left-turn lane and found myself uncharacteristically leaning on the horn and yelling "Come *on,* motherfucker!"—totally consumed by road rage.

The only fast food I ever see around Convergys is Chick-fil-A, but I'd assumed it was because their chicken sandwich is so good. After Five Guys, though, I started wondering if it was just somehow possible to get takeout from there without being late. After my apocalyptic screamer, I can't handle the idea of eating yet another goddamn peanut butter sandwich, so I resolve to find out for myself, even if it makes me late. *Who fucking cares, anyway?*

I emerge from my stall, splash water on my face, and pull my hoodie up, trying to make it less obvious that I've been crying. I walk back to my computer, log out for lunch, start a timer on my phone, jog to my car, and book it past Five Guys to the Chick-fil-A.

It *is* different here. This Chick-fil-A has a three-lane drive-through, each lane manned by a worker walking from car to car taking orders on a tablet. It's a brutally cloudless ninety-five degrees out today, and there's no shade. The workers all wear black uniform pants, and their shirts are drenched with sweat. I feel like passing out just looking at them.

But the efficiency is *amazing.* I'm back at the picnic tables with ten minutes left to eat my food. The smoking crew is even still outside.

"Oh, hey, did you go to the Chick-fil-A on 70?" asks Kolbi as I plunk my beautiful greasy bag on the table. "I worked there for, like, four years before I came here!"

"Yeah!" I say, granting tablewide requests to steal a couple of fries. "God, I felt so bad for those kids standing out in the sun—it's *so hot.* Did you do that?"

Kolbi shrugs—only between ten and two, and it was worse in the winter, in her opinion. "Your body starts to go numb—like, you can't feel your fingers. We had girls cry before just because they're so cold, or they're so hot and they're about to pass out." There's a reason she isn't working there anymore, she says.

People ask about my increasingly frantic group chat messages earlier, and I tell them about my terrible call between chicken nuggets.

"It sucks that we can't express, like, 'I'm sorry, I'm still learning how to help you,'" says Savannah.

"Ooooh, they do *not* want to hear that!" says Kolbi.

They really don't. A few days earlier, I made the mistake of telling a caller the truth—that I didn't know how to fix his very complicated problem, but that I was doing everything I could to find someone who did as soon as possible.

I'd known not to do this hypothetically—we'd talked about it in class—but I felt so genuinely bad for the caller that I figured I owed him the truth. After that, I *knew* not to be honest with customers in the same visceral way I *know* not to stick my hand in a fire.

"Yeah, they don't care!" says Savannah. "They're just, like, 'Well, *why* do they have you on the phone if you're new?'"

"And what are you gonna say to that—like, 'Take it up with the CEO'? It's not like you can transfer them so they can yell at anybody who's in charge of any of this shit, although I'd *love* to listen to *that* call." I sigh. "Was it this crazy at Chick-fil-A?"

"Sometimes customers could be too much? Like how we get on the phones here and customers are kind of wacky, like—'Oh, how do I turn off my phone?'" Kolbi rolls her eyes. "It's the same way with food. It just makes you go *crazy* after a while.

"Oh, *or!*" She holds up a finger for emphasis. "What *really* irritated me was when I'd be outside on iPad—that's when you walk up to the car—and they'd be on the phone and refuse to roll down the window, and they make you wait because you can't skip a car 'cause then everything gets out of order."

"Like, they don't even acknowledge, 'Hey, there's a human being standing here'?" I say.

"Yup. One time I lost it and I knocked on the window. They looked at me, they *seen* me—and they kept the window up and kept talking!" Kolbi shakes her head. "It's, like—*I'm* sorry, are you not a person like me?"

"I feel like that's *exactly* the same kind of person who calls us up to scream, though!" I say. "Like—they don't see other people as the same as themselves, as human beings?" I put my head in my hands, still feeling that post-jitters hollowness. "Seriously, what is *wrong* with people?"

"I feel like they think they're better than you," says Kolbi, affecting a snooty voice. "'Oh, it's just a *fast-food* job, they're lower than me, they're lower income, they don't make as much as me. If I'm on the phone, they can wait a minute because they're on *my* time. They're here to serve *me*."

I laugh. "I sometimes wish every person in America had to work fast food for a year," I say. "Like the Mormons, you know? I bet the world would be a nicer place."

"Right?" says Kolbi. "I mean, fast food is *intense!* And it's *stressful!* You're always feeling rushed; you're on a time crunch for literally eight hours straight; you're never allowed to have one moment just to *chill*. If you wanted to get away, you had to sneak away and go in the cooler just to breathe. We had people have panic attacks in there, we had people break down and cry, we had people pass out..." She laughs. "*So much* was going on in those coolers! Like the bathrooms here—I swear, I've heard people just *crying* in there."

The end-of-lunch migration back inside is beginning, so I cram the last two chicken nuggets into my mouth and check my timer—three minutes. No time for a cigarette. *Dammit.*

"I said before that I haven't had a job that's been timed, like, *by the minute* for a while, yeah?" I mumble, mouth full. I've been open about my previous career in journalism, even citing it as relevant work experience at my interview—any reporter could tell you that three-quarters of the job is wrangling difficult people over the phone. "Like, at the newspaper, I could do pretty much whatever I wanted as long as I got my work done on time."

"Man, I've *never* had a job like that," Kolbi says wistfully as we start heading back inside. I continue eating fries as we walk.

"Never?"

"Pretty much," she says. "I've only worked at Chick-fil-A—that was for four years. While I was working there, I worked at T.J. Maxx and Bed Bath & Beyond on the side, too. It's pretty much the same way everywhere—I haven't had a job where they *don't* time you like that yet. When you get off from break, you better be clocked in, like, *at that time*."

I make a face, stuffing another few fries in my mouth.

"I think it's crazy—like, Chick-fil-A, if you go over two minutes of your break, you're gonna get wrote up," Kolbi continues. "If you're more than five minutes late, then you get wrote up, and, depending on how they feel, they're gonna send you home."

"That sucks. Because, seriously, I get *so much more pissed off* than I used to." I describe my fit of road rage trying to get back from Five Guys on time. "Like, it never used to even *occur* to me to honk! My husband makes fun of me about it! I thought all the people who honked like maniacs were, like, almost a different *species*—crazy, angry people! But now that I think about it, I'm sure some of them were just trying not to get attendance points."

Kolbi laughs. "Right? It makes you think! Like, 'Is *this* why that person behind me last week was so angry?' "

"That was the shittiest thing about that shitty call, though!" The woman wasn't even close to my first screamer, and though she had above-average stamina, she didn't say anything I haven't heard before. But she really got under my skin.

"I think I've been making myself feel better by thinking all the screamers are just ignorant, you know? Like, I imagine some trash-ass lawyer on the other end, thinking my job is *so easy* compared to his, and that I must be lazy or stupid or whatever." I toss the empty Chick-fil-A bag in the trash can at the front entrance. "I can at least think, like, 'Bitch, you wouldn't last a *second* here,' and feel a little better. Because I'm *better* than him, I don't treat people like shit."

"For real—I'd *never* yell at a rep," says Kolbi.

"Yeah, right? But that call-center lady *does* get it, and, I mean—she wasn't *wrong.* I *am* incompetent. I wasted her *whole entire lunch,* and she for sure has exactly thirty minutes just like us. She had every fucking right to be pissed! I would have been furious!" I sigh.

"I mean—*I* treat people right, and *I've* always had the clock running," says Kolbi.

"That's different, though—you're a good person!" I say, laughing.

But Kolbi looks at me very seriously as she scans her ID and holds the door for me. "Well, the Kolbi that you see now is usually how I was—I'm always happy, I'm always, like, 'Hey, what's up?' I can talk to anybody," she says. "That last year at Chick-fil-A, though? I had *never* seen myself so irritated and mad and unhappy. This new owner came, and the whole atmosphere, even the customers, went from happy, joyful, 'I wanna be here!' to *everybody's* miserable. Everybody mopes around, everybody is just, like—'*Fuck,* I'm *here.*' It sucked, it really did. I just *hated* my job. And I had *never* hated a job a day in my life."

"I can't imagine you grumpy, to be honest," I say, scanning my ID at the second door and holding it for her.

"I actually *loved* working at Chick-fil-A before we got a new owner, believe it or not. I knew I was gonna leave eventually, because I didn't want to work fast food for the rest of my life. But I just loved working there. I loved the customers, I got along with them; I loved my employees, we vibed really well; I got along with everybody. And I could be myself—be happy, smile and joke around, show the customers that they could have fun *with* us while we're having fun."

"So what happened?" I ask. A change in management, she says.

"We weren't ignoring customers, but they made it seem that way. Corporate came in all, 'Don't laugh and don't smile if there's a car at the window; only focus on *that car.*' We can't joke around, we have to stay strict, we have to stay focused 100 percent, there is no leaning on it, we can't just be ourselves." Kolbi looks at me as if making an appeal. "But I feel like when you're yourself, the customer likes you *more!* Not being fake, know what I'm saying?"

"For sure," I say.

"We weren't allowed to be who we really were anymore—we had to be what they wanted us to be. That's why they had a lot of problems out of me! I wouldn't give in." Kolbi shoots me an evil grin I haven't seen before. "I just don't see a point in being what you want me to be when I'm *me.* You can't make me someone other than who I am. And I couldn't take it no more."

"How would they try to make you not you?"

"The new guy put cameras legit *everywhere.* We called him Big Brother for the longest, 'cause he's *always watching.* He can even access it from his phone, so he can watch us, like, while he's at home in bed—and if he sees something he doesn't like, he'll rush in from forty minutes away to say, 'I seen you do this, and you *better* not do it again!'"

"Holy *shit!*" I say, curious. "Like, what sort of stuff?"

"Like..." Kolbi thinks, then laughs. "Oh, I got a good one—we weren't allowed to use cups. We can give customers free waters of any size cup, but us, ourselves, we weren't allowed to use cups—not even for water, not for anything. We had to bring our own cups. So if he'd see someone with a cup, he'll come, and he'll *get* you for it. He fired a person over that."

"*What?* That's *insane!*"

"You have *no idea,*" says Kolbi as we reach our pod. "So, yeah—that place brings you down as a *person.* You're always afraid, every day. And even when you're not there, you're still irritated and mad from earlier. It stays *with* you. It's really weird, and I hate it. I felt so much better when I quit."

"I'm really glad you did!" I say.

Kolbi nods sagely, putting on her headset. "You can only deal with so much before it's *too* much."

The rest of the day sucks the way it always does after a bad screamer. It's such a relief to just *leave* at the end of the day that I skip smoking with the squad and head straight to my car, which is practically an oven. The steering wheel's too hot to touch, and my granola bars have gone as liquid as Dalí clocks. Also, at least one appears to have leaked molten chocolate all over the inside of the box. I sigh, staring at my sticky hand like it's a puzzle or something. *God, I need a nap.* But I'd probably cook myself trying to take one in here.

The heat wave has made Car Life very hard. Even at night, it's often so hot I can't fall asleep, and I can't just sleep in my underwear or leave the windows open like I would in a hot apartment. I tried leaving the car and AC running overnight once, but the engine kept switching on and off all night and waking me up, and it used up a surprising amount of gas.

At my Barnes & Noble, *both* comfy chairs are occupied *and* the internet's out *and* the goddamn *Hamilton* soundtrack* is playing for the millionth goddamn time, and I can't take it. I head back to the car, intending to drive to the library, but the blast-furnace wave of heat when I open the doors is the last straw.

Fuck it, I think. *I'm sleeping in a bed tonight.*

---

* My first and only experience with *Hamilton* was the Hickory Barnes & Noble playing the soundtrack from beginning to end nearly every afternoon I spent there. It will forever be corny and irritating to me.

I'm able to find a room at the Baymont Suites discounted from $80 to $50 a night—about half the price of the second-cheapest hotel. Baymont's practically around the corner from Convergys, too. I'm enormously pleased with myself until the actual total comes back up to $85 after taxes and fees. I hesitate. *It's only for tonight—and hey, maybe you can get some writing done,* I tell myself as I put it on my credit card.

I can't really afford this. But—*oh.* The Baymont Suites. Every mundane thing in my discount motel room feels like a celestial revelation, bathed in golden light and soundtracked by a choir of angels. *A minifridge! My own personal armchair! A real bed! Curtains, blessed curtains!*

After cranking the AC and closing the curtains, I strip to my underwear and starfish on the queen-size bed, luxuriating in every inch of skin in contact with the cool, clean sheets. *This is mine,* I think. Nobody can sit in my chair or look in at me lying around in my underwear. Looking over at *my* beautiful desk, I weakly will myself to get up and write. Instead, I fall asleep as if shot with a tranquilizer dart.

When I open my eyes fourteen hours later, I feel better than I have in what feels like years. The bathroom contains my own private shower, and it's larger than a coffin. I could even take a bath if I wanted. I shower, get dressed, and step outside feeling bright-eyed and bushy-tailed just as four guys in construction gear exit the room next door. As we exchange yawning good mornings, I can't help taking a peek into their room, which is identical to mine. *Are they seriously splitting it four ways?* I think.

But then a delicious smell short-circuits my brain. I follow my neighbors and nose downstairs to discover something even better than privacy or sleep: *a complimentary waffle maker.*

My desperate gratitude for chairs and curtains will eventually start to fade. But, my god, I could still write *poetry* about the waffle maker at the dingy continental breakfast of the Baymont Suites. I make and eat three waffles in a row, daring the four construction guys to look at me funny. But they don't care. We all sleepily half watch CNN on the TV above the vending machine. *Everything* is about the upcoming elections.

I haven't been following the day-to-day details of the 2016 campaigns the way I did when I was a reporter. I kind of hate it, to be honest. It stresses me out, and I already have more than enough stress to deal with. I miss everyone back home, but the only thing people seem to post about on social media is politics—specifically, the Democratic National Convention, which will be held in Philly in a couple of weeks. But it all seems like it exists in another world, far from Car Life and Hickory and Convergys.

The waffles tip me over the edge—I just can't bear the thought of packing back up and sleeping at Walmart again tonight. *Just one more night,* I think, using my phone to rebook my room. To somewhat justify the cost, I squirrel away a truly shameless quantity of free bagels and fruit.

Eating them at the picnic tables later, I cannot shut up about the waffle maker. The smoking crew is extremely tolerant of how annoying I'm being; I think they're mostly just pleased I'm not sleeping in my car anymore.

Everybody knows about Car Life at this point. Misty figured it out after we ran into each other at Walmart before work. She was very concerned about my safety, in part because my Walmart is minorly famous from one of the many internet urban legends* about legions of white slavers supposedly kidnapping women from small-town parking lots. So when I failed to show up for class one morning, Misty was worried enough to let Kimberly in on my living situation—along with, I'm pretty sure, the rest of the class.

But of course I hadn't been abducted by white slavers—I'd just overslept after another sweaty, near-sleepless night. Ever since, Kimberly and a few classmates have started acting distinctly maternal, checking in on how I'm doing, asking friends about rooms to rent, texting to make sure I'm okay during a crazy summer hailstorm. It's sweet.

Jess is one of the most maternal. She's the little sister of management Bad

* I'm sometimes surprised by how unskeptical a lot of my classmates are about stuff they read online. I'm a weirdo who reads Snopes on the regular, so I actually recognize several of the stories presented as facts in conversation around the picnic tables—that a guy caused a huge pileup by stopping on the highway to catch a Pokémon, that a teenager was shot and killed while trespassing to catch a rare Pokémon, that a guy got stabbed while playing Pokémon Go and turned down medical treatment to keep playing, that robbers were using the game to lure players and steal their phones. I grandly cite my journalism experience in dismissing these stories, then end up embarrassed when the second two turn out to actually be true. It's kind of hard to tell what's real sometimes, especially when it's all so far away.

Cop Jordan. Though Jordan's tall and blond and Jess is short and dark-haired, they have the same tough aura and low, smoky Carolina voice.

Jess worked here for a year before having a baby girl several months ago, and her knowledge of Convergys's sorcery and black magic has helped me out of a few sticky calls when no walkers were around. I've tried to make it up to her during down time by braiding her long hair and listening when she's having a bad day.

Jess is open about being in recovery from opiate addiction. Though she's only in her midtwenties, she's been clean for years. She rents a two-bedroom with her wife,* Anthone, and their baby girl, McKenna.

Eventually—I presume to get me to shut up about waffles—Jess asks how much my room at the Baymont Suites is.

Only $50 a night, I say proudly, with my natural tendency to exaggerate a good deal. Well, what I *thought* was a good deal.

"Are you *crazy,* girl?" Jess says, appalled. "There is *no waffle* worth $50 a night. That's what we make in a *day!*"

My bubble bursts. I'm glad I didn't say it's technically $85 a night. Because Jess is absolutely right: even the cheapest, most discounted motel is

---

* Nearly half my female classmates were gay or bi, which seemed to be true of the building overall. North Carolina's HB2—one of those trans bathroom bans in vogue during the summer of 2016—was all over the national news when I applied for the job at Convergys, so I was pleasantly surprised to find the Hickory site to be quite chill about sexuality.

For example, we had a trans substitute trainer one morning—I'll call the person Pat, as the name could have swung either male or female. When Kim got back and asked what we'd covered with Pat, there was a bit of fumbling over pronouns.

"He? She? *It?*" asked the far-and-away dumbest guy in the class, raising his eyebrows meaningfully.

I winced, but Jess put up her hand.

"Ooh, I know this! I know him, he's a *he,* so you wanna say *him,*" she said, matter of fact. Everyone nodded, and that was that. It was nowhere near the big deal I'd expected it to be. At the picnic tables later, I asked the veterans if there was a reason so many LGBTQ people seemed to work there; the consensus was that management came down hard on people who were dicks about stuff like that. Whatever else I may think about Convergys, I give the Hickory outpost full credit for that.

completely unsustainable for a single person making $9.50 an hour. Even before doing the math, my quartet of next-door neighbors is evidence of that. *A week at the Baymont Suites would cost... $595. Your last paycheck for two weeks of work was $525. You're supposed to spend an absolute max of 30 percent of your gross income on rent. The Baymont Suites is... 225 percent.*

"I know, I *know!*" I say, making a face. "It just got so *hot!* I couldn't fall asleep!"

Jess looks exasperated at my continued inability to take care of myself. "Look—why don't you just move in with us?" she says. McKenna's been sleeping in bed with her and Anthone every night, she says, so her room is pretty much unused. If I don't mind a little pink and sleeping in a twin bed, Jess says, I can move right in. "And we could carpool to work, too!" she says, brightening.

"How much would it be?" I ask, tempted.

Jess mulls it over and says she'll discuss it with Anthone. That night, I'm luxuriating in my glorious queen bed at the Baymont Suites when she texts that I should just come up with a number I think is fair.

The cheapest rooms on Craigslist had been around $200 a week—much less than Baymont, but more than I could afford. I tentatively text back asking if $150 a week would work.

Jess replies *lol that's way too much!! $75 a week is fine.*

And that's the end of Car Life, thank god. Jess brings a spare key the next day, and I move most of my stuff from my trunk to their one-story two-bedroom about twenty minutes from Convergys. I meet Anthone, a light-skinned butch black woman in her late twenties whom I've seen around the production floor, and McKenna, a very cute biracial toddler. As advertised, the bedroom is very pink indeed. But, for the moment, it's *mine.*

Moving in with Jess reminds me yet again how few responsibilities I have compared to most of my coworkers—I'm a bit of an oddity for having no kids at my age. I have fewer responsibilities than a lot of people a decade younger than I am, really—Brianna's only nineteen, and she's a single mother of two small kids. And if my math is right, most of my classmates started having kids in their teens and early twenties. One gushes about her nine-year-old daughter, then wears a tiara to class a couple of weeks later in celebration of her twenty-first birthday.

But now I get to see what it really *means* to be a poorly paid working parent. I'm exhausted just watching Jess and Anthone navigate work, child care, family, and health care, and they're actually in a better situation than many—a two-parent household with a car and only one kid.

The cost of living in Hickory is pretty cheap, but a breadwinner here still has to make a *minimum* of $20 an hour[4] to support a stay-at-home partner and one child. Anthone is good at sales, but Convergys only guarantees her the same $10.50 base pay as the rest of us—and it's not as easy to get those bonuses as orientation(s) implied. Welfare made up some of the difference for a few months after McKenna was born, but Jess hated feeling like she was sitting around taking handouts. So she decided to go back to work—a decision that makes no logistical or financial sense.

When both parents in a household work, the added cost of child care raises the combined amount they need to stay afloat to about $25 an hour. Jess and Anthone could *hypothetically* net that much together if they sell a lot of DirecTV packages, but it's a risky bet. And day cares are hard to deal with, anyway, Jess says—they require stability, and workers at Convergys just can't promise that. The start time of your shift can change by up to two hours from week to week, and it isn't like you can just hang up on a caller because day care is closing soon—you're there until the call's done, however long that is.

So you've got a young kid, and without welfare, you can't afford to stay home with her yourself *or* put her in day care. What can you do?

I think of what Convergys big boss Fred said at the end of orientation—about what we're exchanging for our paychecks. "You're trading your *life* every day," he said. "Your *life!* I'd make sure you get the most out of it."

Readers with decent jobs may be familiar with the other side of the life market, where you can trade money for extra minutes of sleep or free time. You could also call this the happiness market. The gist of the vast scientific literature on money, free time, and happiness is that you can't exactly *buy* happiness—millionaires report feeling just as much stress about money as hundred-thousandaires. What money *can* buy is free time and sleep, which are so closely correlated with self-reported happiness that they're almost the same thing.

So if you have the means, hire a house cleaner, a night nurse, a gardener, an au pair, a general contractor, a handyman. Life-hack. Drop your laundry off. Take an Uber instead of waiting for the bus. Live alone instead of with roommates. Pay higher rent for a shorter commute. Get a meal-delivery service instead of buying groceries and chopping vegetables. Take a job that pays less but allows more time with your family. Buy yourself out of the weeds. It's honestly pretty cheap.

But you only have access to that side of the market if you're paid well enough to have money to spare—the sweet spot seems to be between $75,000 and $100,000 annual income for a household, with diminishing happiness returns after that. If your life and time are valued so little that forty hours a week doesn't keep your kids fed and diapered, you end up on the *other* side of the market, exchanging your remaining pieces of life* for whatever it takes to fill the gap. And the exchange rate there isn't any less lopsided.

Take Jess. Until we're out of training, our schedule is a blessedly straightforward 7:30 to 3:30, Monday through Friday. So every morning, Jess wakes up before 5:00 a.m., drives forty-five minutes to drop McKenna off with her parents, drives forty-five minutes back, passes the car off to Anthone, who works the early shift at Convergys, then gets a ride to work with me around 7:00. On Tuesdays and Thursdays, when Jess has to stop at the methadone clinic on the way back from her parents' house, she wakes up at 4:00 a.m.

It takes me a week to realize how much work they're doing before I even wake up. I think of Miguel's weird moment at SDF8 orientation: "Where I come from, they talk about this country as the American Dream. Then we come here and we find out we cannot sleep! *Right?*" Awkward silence.

It's less obvious that Jess and Anthone are monetizing their spare time than if they'd, say, taken second jobs or driven for Uber after work. But they absolutely are—they're just trading *life,* which is assigned a value of zero in most economic equations.

Let's look at everything Jess and Anthone trade away every week *in addition* to their eighty combined hours at Convergys:

---

* Sometimes that can get pretty literal, as with the new-in-town classmate who went around the picnic tables on our first lunch break asking, "Where can you donate plasma around here?"

Jess trades around seventeen hours of sleep in the mornings.

Anthone trades five hours of leisure time after work waiting for Jess's shift to end.

Both trade a combined ten hours of leisure time after work driving to pick up McKenna.

Both trade their privacy, renting out McKenna's room to a fairly pleasant but random stranger from work for $75 a week.

Jess's parents contribute nearly forty hours of labor looking after McKenna.

Jess in particular trades some of her long-term health, as long-term stress and lack of sleep are terrible for you.

Both trade the cost of the wear and tear accumulating on their car from all those miles of driving.

And, I think most importantly, both women trade a big piece of their relationship with each other.

As we drive to work one day, I ask Jess if she's looking forward to the shift bid next month—she's almost as good as Destiny at sales, and top performers are likelier to get the shifts of their choice. I figure she must be looking forward to getting on the same shift as Anthone, because they don't get much time together. But of course it's the opposite—they want schedules that overlap as *little* as possible so one of them can be home with McKenna as much as possible.

There's a lot of talk about the decline of the American family in certain circles, and I don't think it's unfounded. Family is powerful: it motivates us, and it ties us down. It's the strongest force in most people's lives.

But a lot of this talk blames the decline of the family on weird stuff—gay marriage, women in the workplace, video games, *Frozen,* sluts, lizard people, Miley Cyrus. After my experiences in the low-wage sector, I have no doubt whatsoever: *the way we work in America* is what's crippling family life.

So, *so* many working parents I met in the course of writing this book sacrificed their relationships with each other for the sake of their kids. Like Hailey from SDF8 and her husband, working opposite shifts so one can always be at home: "We have Sunday if I'm not working mandatory overtime, and occasionally we have Monday morning—if I don't have to work Monday morning—to see each other, and that's pretty much it."

Could *you* maintain a marriage living like that? A sex life? Could you be a good and loving partner if both of you were constantly stressed and irritable?

Jess and I talk a lot when we carpool. We discuss her mixed feelings about McKenna's father—her high school boyfriend—Convergys gossip, her wonderful niece, the long story of how she and her sister ended up marrying Anthone and *her* sister, the car crash that left her dad a quadriplegic.

On the way home from work one day, she confides that someone in our class had asked if she was holding. It had really bothered her—she's proud of having gotten clean and worries about people seeing her as the person she used to be. I'm surprised when she tells me who it was—I'd never have guessed. Jess says a lot of people will surprise you like that around here—opiates are just *everywhere*.

Thinking of the time I spent in Kentucky, I ask what she means by *around here*.

"Is that, like, specific to Hickory?" I ask. "Or is it this part of North Carolina, or the state, or the South, or what?"

"Nah, man," Jess says dismissively. "That's just *everywhere*."

The words of the addiction expert I spoke with while working at SDF8 ring in my ears: "The human mind is designed to *not feel bad*. It does not *like* to feel bad. And it will tend to do things that it can to correct for feeling bad."

Week Four: Twelve People

I have exactly one photo from inside Convergys; the place just isn't photogenic like SDF8. It's a drab, two-story office building with cubicles, a drop ceiling, and that gray carpet that instantly integrates new stains into its pattern. And, frankly, Jordan scares the *shit* out of me. Though Jess swears her sister's Bad Cop act is just an act, I do *not* want to end up explaining myself to her if I get caught breaking the strict no-photos rule.

I did risk the one, though, taking it through the narrow window on the door of an empty conference room. Someone had left a personal-size whiteboard propped up so the message would be visible to anyone walking by:

GET THAT CASH WAVE 337!!!!
OR WHAT'S LEFT OF IT
:(

The sad little message and its frowny face were the only things that felt visually representative of Convergys, because the turnover here is *madness*. My class of twenty—we were Wave 339, I think—is down to twelve after a week on the phones with real customers.

Convergys doesn't make its internal numbers public, though it does vaguely discuss high turnover as an industrywide problem,* so I try stitching

---

* The call-center industry as a whole has roughly a 70 percent annual turnover rate, based on what I can glean from industry publications.

together stray numbers from all the orientations. Jordan said she trains forty-eight classes a year, *minimum;* at twenty people per class, that's at least 960 new hires a year just for AT&T. Steve said there's six hundred people at the site total, and Marshall said AT&T takes up twice as much space as the insurance company downstairs—that's a base staffing of four hundred AT&T reps. So the annual turnover on the second floor would be... *240 percent.*

That's *crazy.* That's like replacing every single AT&T rep in the building every five months.

The only official Convergys numbers I manage to get my hands on are from an abandoned presentation on SlideShare titled "Turnover Reduction Model for Business Units," created by regional HR director Kelly Wadsworth and dated December 11, 2014. In it, Wadsworth writes:

> Turnover continues to be a major business issue for all CMG [Convergys Customer Management Group] groups and divisions.... The costs associated with our current turnover trends are enormous. On average, across CMG, we turn our employee base over 1.8 times per year.

That's slightly lower than my estimate, but it's still *wild*—like replacing all Convergys's 125,000 employees worldwide every six or seven months. It's pretty obvious why the billboard partially obscured by the Buffalo Wild Wings sinkhole constantly advertises that Convergys is hiring and why management pushes stacks of referral cards on us to give to our friends and family, promising bonuses as big as an entire week of pay per successful referral.

I had to laugh at the slideshow's pages and pages of in-depth hypotheses about potential reasons for the high turnover—I could have saved them a lot of time and money with a single slide reading THIS PLACE SUCKS DONKEY BALLS. *Maybe try making this job less awful—or at least paying enough to make up for how awful it is,* I think. *I mean, it worked for Henry Ford. Kind of.*

Henry Ford and Frederick Winslow Taylor have a lot in common. Both became machinists' apprentices instead of going to college, to their families' dismay. Both were obsessed with efficiency and productivity as cures for poverty: "It is possible to increase the well-being of the workingman—not by having him do less work, but by aiding him to do more," Ford wrote in his 1922 autobiography, *My Life and Work.*

Both Ford and Taylor were deeply, deeply weird workaholics.* Reading *My Life and Work,* you get the idea that the title is redundant—Ford's life was his work, and his work was his life. "The day's work is a great thing—a very great thing! It is at the very foundation of the world; it is the basis of our self-respect," he wrote. "Work is our sanity, our self-respect, our salvation. So far from being a curse, work is the greatest blessing. Exact social justice flows only out of honest work."

Both men pioneered methods of factory management that doubled or tripled production rates—more, sometimes—and became the new standard. In 1913, when Ford debuted the assembly line at his Highland Park plant in Detroit—a.k.a. the Crystal Palace†—it revolutionized American manufacturing.

And, as they did under Taylor, workers *hated* this new kind of work. They hated it so much that Ford initially couldn't keep the assembly lines of the Crystal Palace staffed. He had even worse turnover than Amazon *or* Convergys that first year.

Ford was much more of an engineering savant than Taylor, though. He built his first engine at age twelve and kludged together a working car as a young man:

> My "gasoline buggy" was the first and for a long time the only automobile in Detroit. It was considered to be something of a nuisance, for it made a racket and it scared horses. Also it blocked traffic. For if I stopped my machine anywhere in town a crowd was around it before I could start up again. If I left it alone even for a minute some

* Henry Ford's obsessions were a lot less harmless than Taylor's—Ford was a devoted anti-Semite who published pamphlets like *The International Jew: The World's Foremost Problem,* accepted the Grand Cross of the German Eagle from the Nazis, and got an approving blurb from Hitler himself: "You can tell Herr Ford that I am a great admirer of his.... I shall do my best to put his theories into practice in Germany.... I regard Henry Ford as my inspiration."

† So nicknamed because Albert Kahn was hired to design it, and he put in a *lot* of windows and skylights.

> inquisitive person always tried to run it. Finally, I had to carry a chain and chain it to a lamp post whenever I left it anywhere. And then there was trouble with the police. I do not know quite why, for my impression is that there were no speed-limit laws in those days. Anyway, I had to get a special permit from the mayor.

My Life and Work can feel surprisingly modern for a book written almost a century ago. Ford reads like an old-timey Travis Kalanick, invoking a lot of the same mythology as Silicon Valley startups—disruption, government red tape holding back progress, the greedy fat cats of organized labor, a pathological devotion to work.

Ford's biggest contribution to the history of industry was not the car, but the assembly line. He didn't exactly *invent* it, but he was the first person to really demonstrate how insanely profitable standardized large-scale mass production could be.

The assembly line was a drastic change in the way work was done. Even scientifically managed tasks generally required several motions and the supervision of human managers. But Ford took Taylor's principles and did him one better.

A workman under Taylor would have drilled each of the forty-five holes in a Model T engine one by one, carrying a set of craftsman's tools around the workshop as he walked from engine to engine. Even after being Taylorized, the process of drilling a bunch of variously sized holes still involved some autonomy and at least a little skill.

Ford designed his own standardized tools that were perfect for making Model Ts and useless for any other purpose, stripping away the skill Taylor had missed. A workman at the Crystal Palace didn't have to know how to use a drill: he made those same forty-five holes by pulling a single lever that, Ford wrote, "might be attended to by a child of three." And, unlike the Taylorized workman, who at least could put "knows how to use a drill" on his résumé, any skills a workman developed at the Crystal Palace were as useless anywhere else as an encyclopedic knowledge of DirecTV packages.

Ford got still more efficiency by stripping the remaining autonomy Taylor had overlooked, particularly via the most recognizable trait of the assembly line—that it's, you know, a *line*. Ford writes:

> The undirected worker spends more of his time walking about for materials and tools than he does in working; he gets small pay because pedestrianism is not a highly paid line [of work]. The first step forward in assembly came when we began taking the work to the men instead of the men to the work.... The principles of assembly are these:
>
> (1) Place the tools and the men in the sequence of the operation so that each component part shall travel the least possible distance while in the process of finishing.
>
> (2) Use work slides or some other form of carrier so that when a workman completes his operation, he drops the part always in the same place—which place must always be the most convenient place to his hand—and if possible have gravity carry the part to the next workman for his operation.
>
> (3) Use sliding assembling lines by which the parts to be assembled are delivered at convenient distances.
>
> The net result of the application of these principles is the reduction of the necessity for thought on the part of the worker and the reduction of his movements to a minimum. He does as nearly as possible only one thing with only one movement.

By suspending the auto parts to be worked on from a chain that moved the parts down a line of stationary workers, there was no need for the constant individual managerial oversight of Taylorism. It was visually obvious when someone wasn't keeping up, because unfinished pieces started building up at his station. It was impossible to hide any deviation from the pace of work. And since management controlled the speed of the chain, workers lost any remaining control they had over that pace.

Productivity skyrocketed. In seven months, the time it took to produce a Model T fell from twelve and a half hours to an astonishing ninety-three minutes. That year, Ford made more Model Ts than all its competitors put together. By its high point, in 1925, the Crystal Palace churned out nine thousand Model Ts a day.

But workers *hated* it there.

One former Highland Park worker described his time there as "a form of hell on earth that turned human beings into driven robots." Another: "[Ford] attempts to standardize the machines, and so he does with labor." The wife of another worker was so concerned she actually wrote Ford a letter: "The chain system you have is a slave driver! My God! Mr. Ford. My husband has come home & thrown himself down & won't eat his supper—so done out! Can't it be remedied?"

Workers hated the assembly line for more than just the physical demands, though. It's tough to take pride in a job that "a child of three" might do. And tasks were broken down so minutely that, as Ford wrote, "the man who puts in a bolt does not put on the nut; the man who puts on the nut does not tighten it." Workmen found tightening the same kind of nut a thousand times a day brutally boring.

But Ford didn't take their complaints very seriously. Despite all evidence to the contrary, he appeared to believe that workers didn't actually mind jobs that were monotonous, unrewarding, and physically exhausting. He wouldn't want that sort of thing *himself,* of course, but he saw himself as practically a different species than the oxlike laborers on his lines:

> Repetitive labour—the doing of one thing over and over again and always in the same way—is a terrifying prospect to a certain kind of mind. It is terrifying to me. I could not possibly do the same thing day in and day out, but to other minds, perhaps I might say to the majority of minds, repetitive operations hold no terrors.

Ford goes on to write that, anyway, the repetitive nature of work on his assembly lines wasn't so different from the repetitive work done by bankers and businessmen. "Here he veers off into fantasy," writes Richard Snow in his excellent biography of Ford, *I Invented the Modern Age:*

> Bankers and businessmen rarely walked off their jobs in disgust after five days. Just when the efficiencies of the moving assembly line had proved themselves at the end of 1913, the Ford managers discovered that they were having to hire 963 workers to be assured 100 of them would stay with their jobs long enough to learn them.

You read that right: during the first year of Ford's assembly line, turnover at the Crystal Palace was *378 percent.* That's *unbelievable,* even compared to Convergys and Amazon—that would be the same as if every three months, every single worker in the factory walked out and never came back. Though Ford paid slightly better than most factories in Detroit and was willing to hire non-English-speaking immigrants, workers decided by the tens of thousands that it just wasn't worth it.

Because, obviously, it's not just delicate hothouse-flower geniuses who hate exhausting, repetitive work. *Everyone* does. Don't you? Ford's horror at the prospect of working one of the jobs in his factories didn't make him unique. It made him *human.*

When you're very invested in an idea, though, it's easy to ignore the evidence in front of your face. Ford writes in *My Life and Work:*

> I have not been able to discover that repetitive labour injures a man in any way. I have been told by parlour experts that repetitive labour is soul- as well as body-destroying, but that has not been the result of our investigations.... It would seem reasonable to imagine that going through the same set of motions daily for eight hours would produce an abnormal body, but we have never had a case of it.... [And] the most thorough research has not brought out a single case of a man's mind being twisted or deadened by the work.*

Science was notably not so great back then, though—particularly when it came to treating the lower classes as full human beings.† For just one example, this was around the time eugenics came into scientific vogue and the government started forcibly sterilizing tens of thousands of "inferior"

* This is what's known as *sample bias,* like deciding that all Uber drivers love their jobs because that's what every Uber driver you've talked to told you. Well, yeah—if he didn't, he wouldn't be driving anymore, so you would have never spoken. Ford's workers who decided it wasn't worth it or got too injured to continue were by definition no longer around to contribute to internal investigations and research.

† Ford was pretty into eugenics, as you might expect.

and "undesirable" US citizens because they were poor, disabled, immigrants, or nonwhite.

In the century since, science has gotten much, much better, and tons of research has found that dull, repetitive work is in fact *very bad* for humans.

There's the obvious physical side in repetitive stress injuries like the tendinitis in my right elbow—a souvenir from SDF8—and the much more serious injuries common in preregulation factory work.*

But an even bigger problem is that monotonous work *does* kind of twist and deaden the mind—or the soul, to use Ford's word. The mind and the body have a much closer connection than scientists suspected in the 1920s. And it turns out that an overload of mental stress will screw up your body just as much as ten-hour days lifting pig iron will.

To really get how bad stress is for you, you have to understand what the stress response does, why it exists, and how it helped our ancestors survive.† Because the stress response, sometimes called the fight-or-flight response, was crucial to human survival until *very* recently on the evolutionary timeline—"recently" as in practically a few seconds ago. But in those few seconds, humanity's stress response has changed from a lifesaver to the source of an epidemic.

Okay, let me explain the evolutionary timeline thing.

Picture a hypothetical fast-evolving human who lives in your backyard. Her name is Wanda, and she'll be going through the entire three-million-odd years of humanity's evolution in exactly one week.

Say the *homo* genus emerges at midnight on a Sunday night. And say that right now, as you're reading this, it's midnight on the following Sunday. Each half hour of Wanda's week represents roughly ten thousand years, and roughly five years pass for her every second.

When you first noticed Wanda in your backyard, she looked...human*ish*.

---

* A union organizer once said that Detroit was "full of cripples who had stamped on their backs: 'Made by Ford.'"

† If this section interests you, I suggest picking up Robert Sapolsky's *Why Zebras Don't Get Ulcers,* 3rd ed. (New York: Henry Holt, 2004), a readable and much more in-depth look at these ideas.

She was walking around upright but still looked very simian, with a sloped forehead, a *lot* of hair, and no tools or clothes. She's rarely fast enough to catch most birds or rodents and not strong enough to kill larger animals. Even if she *could* catch them, it wouldn't make much sense to—when she's lucky enough to catch something a step above insects on the food chain, she eats it raw and has no way of storing leftovers. Anything bigger than what she can eat in a single sitting will rot or be taken by bigger animals.

So, for most of the week, Wanda will be far from the top of the food chain—much, much likelier to be prey than predator. Without the capacity to build shelter, she's never truly safe from the many giant tigers, giant snakes, giant crocodiles, and various other giant predators that stalk your backyard.

When you first spotted Wanda, at midnight on Sunday, she was digging up your lawn for roots and grubs. *Hey, quit that!* You banged on the window, and she jumped a mile and a half. Wanda is jumpy as *hell,* which is exactly why she's survived this long in a world where so many things want to eat her.

But she's not any jumpier than you. The reaction inside Wanda's body when you knocked on the window is nearly identical to what happens in yours when something scares you. The stress response is much older than me, or you, or even Wanda. Even on Wanda's vastly sped-up timeline, the same fight-or-flight response was present in her monkey, lizard, and fish ancestors two and a half *years* before this week began. It exists in all vertebrates in one form or another, suggesting that it's older than wings, scales, and live birth. And when an evolutionary trait's that old, it's been *really, really helpful* to survival.

So let's look at how Wanda's stress response helps her survive the cruel and unforgiving wasteland of your backyard.

Vertebrates usually exist in one of two modes, which I'll call *chill* (homeostasis) and *overdrive* (fight or flight). You spend almost all your time chilling, with your body prioritizing dull, long-term projects—keeping your temperature stable, digesting food, storing extra calories as fat, breathing, pumping enough blood to your muscles to move around, patrolling for foreign bacteria, growing, making the stuff you need to reproduce.

When you knocked on the window, Wanda's autonomic nervous system shrieked *TIGER TIGER TIGER* before she even realized she'd heard anything. The signal actually cuts her conscious brain out of the loop—if Wanda had to take the time to consciously decide whether every noise was a real threat or a false alarm, she'd be much slower to react and more likely to get dragged out of the gene pool by a giant tiger. Having a nervous system that's trigger-happy verging on paranoid is exactly how Wanda—and you—have survived this long.

So it doesn't matter that what scared Wanda isn't actually a tiger. What matters is that her nervous system's alarm triggered overdrive mode, which primed Wanda's body to either run for her life or fight to the death. Various glands flooded her bloodstream with the hormones adrenaline, cortisol, and norepinephrine, which pauses the everyday chores of chill mode and reroutes that energy so it's more helpful *right now*—mostly turbocharging the muscles and brain.

Going into overdrive often feels like a physical jolt coming from the torso, because that's where the adrenal gland is; people sometimes describe their stomachs dropping or feeling like they've been punched in the gut. Other physical effects of overdrive may sound familiar, too:

- **Her mouth went dry; she felt sick.** When digestion shuts down so that energy can be redirected to your muscles, your salivary glands stop making spit and your stomach may feel weird or nauseated. All the sphincters between the various stages of your digestive tract clamp down like airlocks so no partially digested food gets anywhere it's not supposed to in the upcoming commotion.
- **She mopped her forehead.** If things are about to get seriously physical, pre-sweating is a good way to avoid overheating.
- **Her breath was short and shallow.** Breathing faster saturates your blood with the extra oxygen you'll need for a big burst of muscular energy—sort of like how you can hold your breath much longer underwater if you make yourself hyperventilate beforehand.
- **Her hands began to shake.** Your liver dumps a ton of stored-up glucose into your bloodstream as backup fuel in case all that oxygen isn't enough. And if you've got rocket fuel running through your

veins and don't do anything with it, it'll often manifest as shakes or trembling.

- **Her heart hammered in her chest.** Heart rate and blood pressure spike as arteries narrow and tighten, sending blood shooting around the body crazy fast.* The superspeedy blood gives your brain and muscles (particularly your legs) faster access to all that oxygen-and-sugar rocket fuel.
- **The hair on the back of her neck stood up.** This is a leftover from our furry days; it's the same principle as an angry or scared cat poofing up to make itself look bigger.
- **She tensed.** This gets you ready to move—and when your shoulders draw upward toward your ears, they're like armor to protect your neck.
- **She paid her paints.** Despite what movies might have you believe, peeing yourself isn't a sign of cowardice. It just means your body seriously thinks you might die in the next few minutes and is trying to help by ditching excess weight from your bladder so you can run a tiny bit faster.

There's a lot of other things happening that aren't as easy to feel. You actually *stop growing* until you feel safe again. Your blood gets thicker and more clot-prone so that you're less likely to immediately bleed out if something gets a bite of you. Your kidneys stop making urine. Your immune and reproductive systems go into power-saving mode, just like digestion does—your body will go back to seeking and destroying cancerous cells and obsessing about sex after the immediate threat is gone.

Your perception of the world changes. It may seem like someone's turned the dial on everything up to 11—everything seems brighter and louder as your pupils dilate and your ears become more sensitive to sound. Time seems to slow down as your brain, hypercharged with all that oxygen and sugar, starts processing information differently. You feel very afraid or

---

* It's the same reason water shoots out of a garden hose faster when you put two fingers over the mouth.

very angry—either way, you urgently want to do *something, right fucking now.*

Look down at your freaked-out ancestor—puffed up, teeth bared, looking around frantically. It may not seem like you have much in common. You own a blender, and she doesn't even have stone tools yet. She's naked and probably intermittently malnourished. An unthinkable number of her children won't make it past infancy.

Your stress responses, however, are identical.

There's a perception that life before modern civilization was, as philosopher Thomas Hobbes famously put it, "solitary, poor, nasty, brutish, and short"—an idea stemming from his personal observations of the brutal poverty of London's underclasses in the mid-1600s.

But since the 1960s, the perception of what life was like for early humans has been shifted by a lot of evidence that they spent most of their time straight chilling.

Wanda's life isn't exactly Eden—she *could* be dragged off by tigers at any moment. But it isn't exactly *stressful,* either— literally, her stress response goes off *occasionally,* not constantly. It probably only takes Wanda about five hours a day to find enough bugs, roots, and berries to survive. She spends the rest of her time socializing, napping, having sex, and wrangling her tribe's children.

When you check back in on Wanda on Monday morning, you're delighted to see she's figured out how to use simple stone tools to catch and eat a smallish lizard.

Tuesday night, you notice a faint glow from the backyard; Wanda appears to have preserved some fire from a lightning strike or something and made a campfire to keep warm.

On Wednesday, you witness the invention of cooking when Wanda accidentally drops a rodent she caught into the campfire. Cooking is going to be a *very* big deal for Wanda. It's way, way easier for her body to chew and digest cooked food than raw food, so she uses up less of her energy on digestion *and* doesn't have to spend as much of her time finding and chewing*

---

* Picture the scene from *Game of Thrones* in which Dany eats a raw horse's heart.

food. Wanda suddenly has a lot of spare time and energy on her hands. Her body wisely begins to invest that extra energy in a bigger brain.

Thursday morning, Wanda's head has already grown a *lot* to make room for her new, bigger brain. She looks noticeably more human, and her stone tools are looking less rudimentary.

You're a little irritated when you wake up Saturday morning to find that Wanda's used a stone ax to chop down some trees and used vines to tie them into a raft.

But Sunday—today—is when things start getting really nuts. When you check the window this morning, your yard is littered with weird animal totems that suggest Wanda's discovered religion. You squint, looking around for her with no luck until a spear flies out of the rhododendrons to impale a passing wild pig. Wanda emerges and drags the carcass off to a hearth she's built to cook bigger game. She's still naked, and looks much more human, especially in the face—her forehead's gotten *huge* to make room for her extravagant brain.

You have to leave to go to church and end up stopping at the grocery on the way home, so you don't see Wanda again until 1:00 p.m. She's now anatomically the same as a modern woman, which you can tell because she won't invent even rudimentary clothes until 2:30. That's also when you notice the grave markers in the flowerbed where she's started burying her relatives.

You're a little embarrassed about this, but you get caught up in a marathon of *So You Think You Can Dance* and forget all about Wanda for a while. You finally come out of your binge at 10:00 p.m.—that's around 30,000 BCE, if you're counting—because you hear a weird, off-key tootling and intermittent *thunk*s coming from the backyard. Outside, Wanda appears to have carved herself a crappy flute, covered your house with cave paintings, and turned your back door into target practice for a crude bow and arrow. Irritated, you bang on the glass, but this time *you* jump a mile as an arrow *thunk*s into the window frame.

But you can't tear yourself away now, because Wanda's getting *crazy* busy. The Neolithic era begins around 11:00 p.m., when Wanda manages to make crappy flour out of some grasses. You leave for, like, a *second* to go to the bathroom, and by the time you get back, she's somehow acquired a herd of sheep and is planting your yard with crops. She also starts weaving cloth, making pots and baskets for storing dry food, and building rudimentary houses—trading her nomadic lifestyle for something more permanent.

Around 11:30, Wanda invents the wheel. There's clusters of houses around the crops and sheep now, marking the first time Wanda's lived in a group of more than 150 or 200 other people—the biggest that nomadic tribes tend to get, historically.

By 11:45, Wanda's invented writing and equipped her raft with a sail. She's also somehow built a forge and is using it to make glass, bronze, coins, a sundial, and an iron sword. Empires rise and fall with startling speed, leaving your backyard strewn with the ruins of pyramids, ziggurats, and aqueducts.

By 11:55, loud bangs suggest that Wanda's invented gunpowder. Your backyard is now getting crowded with windmills, churches, synagogues, temples, mosques, algebra, spinning wheels, paper money, soap, and rudimentary democracy.

By 11:58, things get even louder with the booms of cannons and rifles, the clacking of a printing press, and the ticking of pendulum clocks.

By 11:59, Wanda's got steel, a steam engine, a piano, and the smallpox vaccine. She's also begun amassing large-scale industrial equipment—power looms, threshing machines, automatic flour mills, foundries, etc.—in small factories.

Thirty seconds before midnight, Wanda invents the stopwatch, the diesel engine, dynamite, genetics, concrete, and photography. Your backyard is suddenly crisscrossed with railroad tracks. The factories have gotten much bigger, and their smokestacks are starting to make things hazy.

Twenty seconds before midnight, Wanda invents the Model T, airplanes, antibiotics, television, the assembly line, penicillin, the quartz clock, the latex condom, and the transistor. A small mushroom cloud takes out your birdbath.

Ten seconds before midnight, Wanda walks on the moon. She then invents birth control pills, the microprocessor, personal computers, cell phones, the Big Mac, and the internet.

Five seconds to midnight, Wanda's gotten herself a laptop, wireless internet, a smartphone, Google, Facebook, YouTube, and Amazon.

At one second to midnight, Wanda's made self-driving cars, Tinder, and commercial space flight. The society Wanda's built in your backyard is, for this single second, identical to the one you live in right now.

By the time the clock finishes striking midnight, Wanda will have technology you can't even imagine.

Wanda spent almost the entire week evolving to better fit her environment with what seemed like agonizing slowness. Wanda's actually fantastic at adaptation, though—her skill and comparative speed at it are exactly why she's done so well for herself in your backyard. For example, an hour ago, when she first domesticated animals, drinking their milk made her sick. Twenty minutes later, her guts had already rejiggered themselves to digest lactose.

But around half an hour ago, Wanda's brain size reached a tipping point. She no longer was content to wait thousands of years for her body to change to suit her environment. Instead, she began adapting her environment to suit *her* needs. This brief period when Wanda's gotten proactive is what we generally think of as human civilization.

But the *really* monumental changes Wanda's made to her environment—what we think of as the modern world—have mostly been in the past minute. Houses! Cities! Laws! Hygiene! Refrigerators! Internet! Cars! Medicine! Her inventions have defused nearly all the major threats of the previous six days, twenty-three hours, and fifty-nine minutes—there's no tigers in a city. In a single minute, Wanda's become, by an enormous margin, the dominant species of your backyard.

But Wanda's *body*—now only cosmetically different from yours or mine—hasn't had anywhere near enough time to adapt to the insane, sparkling, deafening, terrifying, all-singing, all-dancing modern world. Wanda's body and nervous system still think that tigers are everywhere, and she's just as likely to jump out of her skin if you knock on the window now as she was a week ago.

And the very thing that's saved Wanda's life millions and millions of times has suddenly become deadlier to her than all the tigers in history. Wanda's stress response flails around in the mostly tigerless modern world. It's occasionally useful, helping a panicked mother lift a car off her child or a soldier survive an ambush, but those situations are the exceptions, not the rule. And the flailings of humanity's uprooted stress response are deeply involved with the "diseases of civilization"—heart disease, obesity, cancer, depression, anxiety, diabetes, etc.—that afflict first-world countries.

When's the last time you felt your stomach drop, or the blood rush to your head, or your hands tighten into fists? Was it because of a tiger? Someone trying to kill you?

Or were you being screamed at by a customer? Getting cut off in traffic? Waking up and realizing you were supposed to be at work half an hour ago?

It doesn't matter at all that these things aren't *physically* dangerous. We evolved to be trigger-happy, remember—overreacting to potential threats. As our giant, imaginative brains got bigger, we got smarter—and at some point, we made the leap to being able to throw ourselves into overdrive just by *thinking really hard** about the time a tiger almost got us.

You may have wondered—if overdrive makes Wanda so strong and fast, why doesn't she just stay in that mode all the time? It's because overdrive, while very useful in the short term, is extremely toxic when you're constantly marinating in it. Living like a car-lifting, tiger-wrestling superhero is *terrible* for you, in a couple of different ways.

First, the fight-or-flight response is a bit like doing burnouts with your body—if you peel out in a cloud of smoke every single time a traffic light turns green, you're going to wear out your car pretty quickly. If you keep flipping your overdrive switch back and forth like you're hosting a light-switch rave, you'll quickly wear out the systems in your body affected by fight or flight.

A racing heart and high blood pressure are very helpful for running and fighting. But if you activate them several times a day for years, your heart and circulatory system will start wearing out, which means a high likelihood of cardiovascular disease.

---

* I could write an entire other book on embodied cognition and its relationship to language and learning and art and empathy—I highly recommend Arnie Cox's *Music and Embodied Cognition: Listening, Moving, Feeling, and Thinking* (Bloomington: Indiana University Press, 2016) if that interests you. But for a fun demonstration of how your brain can trick your body, try imagining what it feels and tastes like to bite into a lemon, using as much vivid sensory detail as possible, and notice what the salivary glands under your tongue do in response.

Thick, clot-forming blood is very helpful if a tiger gets a bite of your arm. But if you're *constantly* making your blood go all thick and sticky, it's more likely to clump up into a plug and cause a heart attack or stroke.

All that extra sugar-fuel in your blood is exactly what you need for a desperate burst of muscular energy. But regularly flooding your blood with sugar-fuel—particularly if you don't make a point of exercising it away afterward—makes you more likely to develop diabetes.

The extra energy from shutting down your digestive system can mean the difference between life and death in the short term. Shutting it on and off all the time, though, will give you ulcers, acid reflux, and all sorts of other digestive troubles.

And, believe it or not, burning out your organs isn't even the worst effect of chronic stress.

In Wanda's first six days, twenty-three hours, and fifty-five minutes, there were very few circumstances in which she was flipping into overdrive dozens of times a day for months or years on end. Tigers weren't *that* common, and food was pretty abundant if you didn't mind eating bugs. Plus, Wanda and her tribe were nomads, so if an area got full of tigers or short on food, they'd just walk a few days to another area.

There also weren't many humans to fight with over territory or food. There really weren't very many of us for most of human history because we reproduce so slowly. And there still would have been enough bugs to go around if territories overlapped. Our unique evolutionary niche made the world our oyster—kind of literally, in that we're very good at finding ways to pry open and eat weird squirmy things that other animals can't figure out.

Wanda's default set of social behaviors is useful for navigating the abundant world of your backyard, where resources are plentiful and stresses are life-threatening, but temporary. Her lifestyle in a world of abundance reminds me a little of Eli, the least stressed man I've ever met, traveling from temporary job to temporary job in his van.

But now say a volcano erupts in the middle of Wanda's tribe's territory. Her fight-or-flight reaction helps her escape the initial danger of falling rocks and lava, but afterward, ash gets into the water and soil and kills most plant life in a fifty-mile radius. It's apocalyptic.

With their food gone, the herbivores start dying off. Carnivores get desperate and start going after humans more as the food chain dries up. Finding enough food to survive was never *easy,* but during the years of famine after the volcano, Wanda will have to physically fight someone or something over nearly every meal. In this world of scarcity, Wanda has to be constantly on guard if she wants to survive. So Wanda's body, trying to protect her, goes into apocalypse mode.

My interest in stress began with my own PTSD diagnosis. Over the last decade, I've had a few violent encounters with groups of teenage boys in Philly,* and my body eventually started trying to protect me in ways that were less than helpful in the modern world.

For *years* afterward, I'd get jerked into overdrive every time I saw a group of kids who reminded me of the ones who hurt me. And that happened pretty much every day I left the house, multiple times a day, because loud, rowdy teenagers are a normal part of city life, even if you *don't* live within two blocks of three high schools. Which I did.

It didn't matter how many times I tried to pound into myself that THOSE ARE CHILDREN: THEY ARE NOT GOING TO HURT YOU. My body had been so overwhelmed by the trauma it experienced that it came out the other end utterly positive that loud groups of teenage boys were *tigers*. In hoodies or in polos, riding those baffling tiny bikes or swaggering around in packs, on the subway or in my neighborhood—something deep and primal inside me had decided loud teenage boys were dangerous and refused to consider any evidence to the contrary.

I wish PTSD wasn't associated so closely with military service, because it would have taken me way less time to figure out what was going on. PTSD *is* more common in soldiers than in the general population—14 percent of veterans of the post-9/11 wars report symptoms, but about 8 percent of Americans total do, too.

That's because even though soldiers are way more *likely* to experience some traumatic shit, their reactions aren't any different from *any* human who's experienced some traumatic shit. Loud noises become tigers. Teenagers become

---

* You may have read back in 2011 that an *Onion* editor got hospitalized by a flash mob in Philly? That was me.

tigers. People speaking Arabic become tigers. Your ex-husband's cologne becomes tigers. And once your body classifies something as a tiger, it's really hard to convince it otherwise. Feelings don't care about your facts, so to speak.

So for years, my nervous system would scream TIGER TIGER TIGER several times a day, even as my conscious mind screamed STOP IT YOU'RE BEING RIDICULOUS. And after a while, something in my body concluded that this many tigers meant the volcano had gone off and tried to prepare me for life in the apocalypse. That's when things got really bad.

I started having trouble getting to sleep, and would wake up in the middle of the night to stare at the ceiling for hours. I found it almost impossible to relax my back, neck, and shoulders. I was incredibly jumpy and distractible and had a hard time concentrating on anything for long. I couldn't stay focused on writing, or on anything that required my full attention, for more than ten or fifteen minutes at a time. I became much more angry, irritable, and negative; I lost my temper much more. I didn't want to go out with friends, and had a lot of trouble even getting myself out of bed in the morning. When I wasn't angry, I felt strange and empty, as if my emotions had dried up. Everything seemed stupid and pointless.

It took me a few years to finally go to a doctor about the way I was feeling, because Henry Ford's not the only one with a talent for overlooking the obvious.* But I finally made a doctor's appointment, got diagnosed with depression and PTSD, got treatment, and finally started feeling better.

Since then, I've done a lot of research trying to make sense of those gray years. The most frustrating part of the whole thing had been how irrational it all felt—as if this were all happening out of nowhere, because of nothing. Objectively, my life was great, which only made me feel worse—what kind of ingrate couldn't appreciate this much good fortune?†

So even as I started getting better, I'd stare up at the ceiling at night and wonder what the *point* of all this was. It actually made me *angry*. What possible evolutionary benefit could there be to something as fucking stupid and counterproductive as depression?

---

* Honest to god, I once titled a blog post "*Onion* piece on Sen. Toomey would be funnier if life weren't so goddamn bleak" without realizing I needed to see a doctor.

† I *did* grow up Catholic, why do you ask?

But when I started thinking about my gray years in the context of Wanda and the volcano, it didn't seem pointless at all.

- During an apocalypse, it's helpful to have your senses on high alert for possible threats twenty-four hours a day—that's why I was jumpy and distractible, couldn't lose myself in writing for long stretches anymore, and had been sleeping badly.
- The apocalypse is a violent place, and the guy who throws the first punch often wins the fight—that's the reason I got so aggressive, irritable, and bad-tempered. Being optimistic in the apocalypse is a good way to end up dead.
- In the apocalypse, it makes sense to be constantly tense, with your shoulders up protecting your neck. Violence could happen at any moment.
- During the apocalypse, if you've found a nice safe place with enough food to last awhile, why put yourself in danger by venturing out? There's nothing good out there—better to stay hidden. In fact, you should physically exert yourself as little as possible—stay warm in bed all day and conserve your energy.
- In the apocalypse, you should gorge yourself on anything you find that's rich in calories. You're going to need them later, and if you store extra ice cream *inside* your body as fat, nobody can steal it. And the most efficient place to store all those compulsively eaten calories is the beer-gut area; that's the easiest place for the body to remobilize fat as fight-or-flight fuel.
- In the apocalypse, sex and reproduction are a huge waste of energy—it's a terrible idea to invest the enormous amount of resources it takes to grow and birth a baby when that baby isn't likely to survive. It's understandable, then, that my vagina had decided to essentially sew itself shut—a unilateral move that deeply bothered and confused me.
- In the apocalypse, it's best not to feel your feelings too much: they're mostly going to be overwhelming grief, fear, and sadness, and those will just slow you down.
- In the apocalypse, the future is a distant runner-up to the all-important *now*—which could explain why I had even more trouble than usual forcing myself to work on long-term projects, or eat healthy food, or quit smoking.

- But most of all, you take care of *yourself* during the apocalypse. Maybe your family, too. But everyone else? They can take care of their own damn selves. *Fuck Darryl—I want McDonald's.*

Until I began researching this book, I'd always assumed Wanda's world *was* kind of apocalyptic. Like many people, I just took the Hobbesian "nasty, brutish, and short" view of prehistory as fact. Anthropologist Marshall Sahlins begins his famous 1966 essay "The Original Affluent Society" by outlining the common view at the time:

> "Mere subsistence economy," "limited leisure save in exceptional circumstances," "incessant quest for food," "meagre and relatively unreliable" natural resources, "absence of an economic surplus," "maximum energy from a maximum number of people"—so runs the fair average anthropological opinion of hunting and gathering.

Sahlins had a new theory—that Wanda's world was actually one where "all the people's wants are easily satisfied."

> A good case can be made that hunters and gatherers work less than we do; and, rather than a continuous travail, the food quest is intermittent, leisure abundant, and there is a greater amount of sleep in the daytime per capita per year than in any other condition of society.... The food quest is so successful that half the time the people do not seem to know what to do with themselves.

Sahlins makes his case with a ton of fascinating evidence from the few remaining societies that most resemble Wanda's life during her first six days—nomadic hunter-gatherers with few possessions or hangups about food—and historical records of the very first interactions* between European explorers and similar tribes.

These accounts tend to be just as telling about the Europeans as the

* By this, I mean *true* first encounters, before Europeans drastically changed these tribes' way of life by attacking them, colonizing them, enslaving them, giving

people they describe. One of the funnier things is how much of the idea that Wanda lived in terrible scarcity is based on European explorers being totally grossed out by the locals' eating habits. You'd obviously have to be *starving* to eat bugs, and they don't even have private property—therefore, they live in crippling poverty.

But that's kind of a silly assumption, especially if you're okay with eating crabs and lobsters. If you're ever caught in an *actual* apocalypse, you should start eating bugs *immediately*. They're surprisingly nutritious.

In the 1980s, archaeologist David Madsen was excavating a site in Utah when he noticed that all the ancient poop in the latrine area was full of grasshopper bits. Curious about the energy efficiency of catching and eating bugs, he set his team to catching the area's omnipresent Mormon crickets, a traditional food of native people in the area. After an hour of picking crickets off bushes and from the grass, each person had collected an average of two and one-third pounds of bugs—nearly three thousand calories.* In areas where the crickets clustered, such as the cave Madsen was excavating, you could do much, much better. "One person collecting crickets from the water margin for one hour, yielding eighteen and one-half pounds, accomplishes as much as one collecting 87 chili dogs, 49 slices of pizza, or 43 Big Macs," Madsen wrote.

Today, most anthropologists do think Wanda probably lived in an abundant world, and technology has taken it beyond speculation—you can see it in her bones. When kids don't get enough food for as little as a week, their bodies switch to short-term mode and stop putting so much energy into getting bigger. When kids start eating enough again, they resume growing. By looking at X-rays of a human's long arm and leg bones, then, you can actually tell whether she went hungry for longer than a week or two as a child. Ditto her teeth—when you starve, they tend to develop a particular pattern of pits and spots.

And for the vast majority of the week that Wanda spent as a hunter-gatherer—remember, she only started farming maybe an hour ago—her

---

them smallpox, or selling guns to the tribe in the next valley. (Looking at you, Pinker.)

* A physically active modern man is supposed to eat around 2,500 calories a day; you generally find 3,000-calorie diets in the context of bodybuilding and getting swoll.

bones and teeth show way fewer signs of long periods of scarcity than the bones and teeth of most people since the dawn of agriculture. Nomad Wanda often went to bed hungry, but she rarely starved for long periods. That's when the apocalypse mode set of behaviors is useful—for those rare periods when things get really bad.

As a rule, you can predict the behavioral effects of chronic stress by imagining what would help Wanda stay alive in an unpredictable, brutal Mad Max world. She becomes less generous. She gets extra jumpy and paranoid, and is easily distracted. She's more impulsive. Her temper has a lower threshold. She's more afraid of and hostile toward people outside her "tribe," that circle of empathy that encompasses "people like me," and that circle shrinks as things get worse. She's less likely to care about nuance. She's more likely to see patterns in static and conspiracies in unrelated events. And she's more likely to put her trust in a strongman leader.

You'd think some of these adaptations could help Wanda in times of abundance, too. But constant vigilance doesn't come cheap, just as overdrive is very biologically expensive. Remember why telephone numbers are seven digits long—our brains can only juggle so many balls at a time. In a world of scarcity,* it makes sense for Wanda to keep two or three balls in the air looking for threats. But that means she has two or three fewer slots left for other useful things—logic, patience, paying attention, resisting temptation, long-term thinking, remembering things, empathy. It's an exhausting way to live.

I can personally attest to that. Not every customer's a screamer, obviously, but I'm still tense and nervous every time I take a new call—every one of them is a potential tiger, according to my body. The more time we spend on the phones, the more noticeably tired I am by the end of a shift. By graduation day, my shoulders and neck ache all the time.

On graduation day we spend the morning on the phones as usual, then get two hours off after lunch for a potluck and awards ceremony. Kimberly, beaming, presents the remaining eleven of us with certificates, and we hand out paper-plate awards. We cheer when Butch Patty wins most improved.

---

* If this interests you, check out *Scarcity: Why Having Too Little Means So Much* by psychologists Sendhil Mullainathan and Eldar Shafir (New York: Times Books, 2013).

Our new schedule will be Tuesday through Saturday, which means we have a three-day weekend. Kolbi, Brianna, Savannah, and I hit the road for Myrtle Beach after work. Being around people whose average age isn't old enough to get into a bar can make me feel ancient, but I have a fantastic time. I feel like I'm back in my early twenties—splitting a single hotel room four ways, lolling around on the beach all day, playing Skee-Ball, ogling boys and cars, laughing until we can barely breathe at the woman in a Confederate flag crop top whose legs suggest some sort of unspeakable self-tanner disaster. The last thing we do before heading back to Hickory is get sand from the beach and balloons from Dollar General to make souvenir stress balls.

I get back late Monday night and tiptoe past Jess and Anthone's bedroom in the dark. When I wake up for work the next morning, the house is weirdly silent. I call out a pointless "Hello? Anybody home?" though the house is small enough to make its emptiness obvious.

When I go to shower, the bathroom reeks of the sharp, surgical smell of rubbing alcohol. A bottle of it is sitting out on the sink, next to a straightened-out safety pin. It's the most ominous tableau I've seen in my life.

I see Jess at Convergys, but we aren't seated next to each other today and our breaks don't line up, so I don't get a chance to talk to her. She doesn't appear at the picnic tables at the end of our shift, so I run some errands and eat Chinese takeout by the lake.

When I get home, the atmosphere is tense. Jess is on the phone, looking worried. Anthone is laid out on the couch, holding McKenna with one arm and looking like *hell.* The left side of her face is swollen, as if she's holding a golf ball in her cheek, and she looks like she's in a lot of pain. I take the baby off her hands and tell her not to try to talk as Jess discusses something called Fish Mox.

When she's off the phone, Jess fills me in—while I was gone, Anthone's abscessed tooth got so bad that it actually gave her a black eye. They'd gotten up early this morning to try to fix it, but it was harder to get at than the last one Anthone had.

I wince. Abscessed teeth happen when bacteria get inside a tooth via an untreated cavity or crack and infect the supersensitive pulp and root, which is *incredibly* painful. As the tooth rots from the inside, a pocket of pus forms, putting more and more pressure on the dental nerves as it swells. An emergency root canal is a common treatment, because the infection can spread down into the jawbone, then into the blood and organs. An untreated abscess can *kill* you.

"Wait, go back a second—are you saying..." I think of the straightened safety pin with mounting horror. "You mean you—you tried to fix it *yourselves?*"

Yeah, says Jess. They'd managed to DIY the last one Anthone had, and it wasn't *that* hard. "There's the white thing—you know, the white swollen thing?—and you just stick it with a needle, and then she just spat the stuff all out, and then you have antibiotics so it doesn't get infected."

This time they'd had more trouble getting to the abscess, though—the pocket of pus is higher up and farther back. After many failed attempts to drain it this morning, they'd had to give up. Jess drove them both to Convergys early instead of getting a ride with me because Anthone had a fever.

"Holy fuck, you *went to work* like this?" I ask, horrified. Anthone nods, mumbling that she made a sale, too.

Jess has spent the past couple of hours calling friends and relatives who might have some spare antibiotics lying around. Someone in West Virginia has penicillin, but even if they met up at a rest stop halfway between here and there, it's a four-hour round-trip. So she's also looking into other options—her grandpa always told her that, in a pinch, you could go to an aquarium-supply store and get something called Fish Mox, which he said was just the same as amoxicillin.

"Dude, you *have* to go to the emergency room," I say. But they can't—if they go to the ER, they won't have enough money to fill the prescription.

"Hang on. I'll be right back," I say, taking my laptop into my room. I don't know what the hell else to do. I don't have antibiotics or emergency root-canal money. *I'm good at research—maybe I can find a low-cost emergency dentist? Or some sort of fund that gives people money for emergency dental work? Or make sure this Fish Mox stuff won't kill Anthone?*

I find very quickly that sliding-scale emergency dentists don't exist, at least not anywhere near Hickory. There also aren't scholarships for emergency dental work. *Of course there aren't, you idiot.* I call Rajiv, who says amoxicillin *should* be the same fungus regardless of what it's used for, but that antibiotics intended for fish might have all sorts of crazy additives. He refers me to his dad, who's a medical doctor. Rajiv says he vaguely remembers his dad writing a prescription for human antibiotics for their golden retriever once when he was a kid—it was cheaper than veterinary antibiotics and basically the same thing.

My father-in-law's with a patient but says he'll call me back in a few minutes. Waiting, I scour the internet and learn that survivalists often stockpile Fish Mox along with canned food and bottled water. It doesn't have to be approved by the FDA, so it *could* basically have anything in it, but I don't find convincing evidence that it *will* kill you. Antibiotics for mammals are better regulated, though, so I fall down another rabbit hole of farm-supply stores and horse pills until my father-in-law calls back.

He doesn't know what the deal with Fish Mox is but very strongly recommends that Anthone go to the emergency room. I tell him what they told me, and he says to put him on the phone with Jess.

"Hey, my—" I say, poking my head into the living room, but they're on their way out the door.

"Hey, wait, my father-in-law's a doctor—" I say.

"It's okay! We gotta go pick up antibiotics," Jess says.

"No, he wants to talk to you—" I say.

"Don't worry about it! We got this," Jess says, waving as she closes the door.

As their car pulls out, I thank my father-in-law, who's now a little alarmed, and hang up. I go back to my pink bedroom and sit on my pink bed, feeling heavy all over. My laptop is still open to the prices of horse antibiotics at a nearby farm store.

You idiot.

I slap my laptop closed, hard, as if *it's* responsible for how fucking shitty everything is. Then I have an ugly cry, because otherwise I think I'll scream.

Week Five: Nine People

"You've got to be fucking kidding me."

"I'm really sorry, sir—I'm not allowed to open your account without your passcode. It's a government-mandated thing. If you don't remember it, you can try guessing. It's numerical, and most people—"

"Are you fucking kidding me?" The guy cuts me off. We've been speaking for—I check my call timer—thirty seconds. "I have no idea what it is, okay? Just let me into my fucking account!"

"I'm sorry, sir," I say. "I know this must be frustrating, but I'm really not allowed to—it's a legal thing. I can't tell you what your PIN is or access your account without it. If you don't want to try guessing, I can reset your PIN for you. It'll take just a few minutes—"

"No, I'm not fucking doing that! It's *my account!* Can't you see what number I'm calling from? Jesus *Christ*—"

I roll my eyes and flip off the phone with both hands. *Fuck you, fuckface.*

Though my class is still technically in training, we're out on the floor taking solo calls pretty much full-time now, usually spending an hour or less in the classroom at the end of the day. And the more time we spend on the phone with customers, the worse this job gets.

I've gotten slightly better at controlling the *TIGER TIGER TIGER* reaction I have to screamers, especially with customers like this one, who frankly has no valid reason to be screaming. I'm 100 percent sure of the rule on this, which makes sense to anyone who thinks about it twice. I absolutely *could* be fired for giving him access to an account he doesn't have the passcode for—otherwise it would be trivial for someone to steal his identity.

Also, understanding *why* it's happening makes it a little easier to...sort of *bodysurf* the waves of *TIGER TIGER TIGER* instead of trying to win a fistfight with the ocean. And I'm out of sympathy for people who'd rather scream than let me help them. So, *fuck this guy.*

I've finally gotten semicompetent at the launch sequence and the most common problems people call in with, and I've had nothing but positive performance reviews so far. I made good personalized sales offers on the three of my calls that were randomly selected for coachings with Kimberly. She says I'm doing well and passed me and my remaining eight classmates on to the next phase of training.

I'm still totally clueless about how to fix more complicated problems, but I've stopped feeling bad about it. This shit is *ridiculous.*

I sometimes imagine myself in the Crystal Palace, stationed at the lever of that specialized tool that drills forty-five holes in a Model T engine. The job would suck even if I were just pulling the same lever all day. But here, it's as if half the time the engine needs thirty-eight holes—or fifty-five, or seven—and I have no clue where any other levers are, or if they exist at all. And when you ask around about where the thirty-eight-hole lever is, every single person has a different answer.

One will patiently show you where it is.

Another will less patiently show you a *different* thirty-eight-hole lever on the other side of the building.

Another will continue to ignore you, making you wonder what about you makes her dislike you so much.

Another will show you where the sixteen-hole and twenty-two-hole levers are and how to jerry-rig them together to make thirty-eight holes.

Another will roll his eyes and just do it himself.

Another, who always seems like he just got back from blowing lines in the bathroom, will treat you to an excited monologue on how that's *bullshit:* engines don't really need thirty-eight holes, and *this engine is probably trying to scam the company.*

Sometimes there *is* no thirty-eight-hole lever.

Sometimes the engine calls you a stupid bitch.

"Why don't you explain to me why I can't get into my own fucking account? *Huh?* The account that *I pay for* every fucking month?"

I pounce on this brief opening.

"Well, sir, your credit-card and Social Security information are in your account, and scammers can spoof what number they're calling from, so we're actually required by federal law to get additional verification—"

"Jesus Christ, will you *shut!* The *fuck! Up!*"

For some reason, "shut the fuck up" is what trips my overdrive switch. *Goddammit.*

My body goes rigid. Blood roars in my ears as rage and adrenaline shoot through my body. *Oh, FUCK this fucking guy.* I'm shaking with anger. *This fucking asshole, this fucking guy, this stupid motherfucker who can't remember a fucking four-digit code that's for sure just his birthday or his debit card PIN, which he would know if he'd shut the fuck up for a second and let me tell him but he's too much of a self-centered dipshit to see I'm just trying to fucking help him—*

It's easier to control myself because I don't have Fuckface's passcode. Without it, I *can't* start the launch sequence, and therefore don't have to—and it's *so* much easier to maintain control of the clown car in my head when it's not moving. So I allow my brain to wallow in violent, primal fantasies, which always seems to help burn off some of Fight-or-Flight Emily's towering rage.

I'd tackle his bitch ass to the ground and demonstrate that I am an actual real human being just like him by punching in his fucking face with my actual real human fists—

Okay, settle down, says a distant voice, faint as a birthday candle in a burning building. *Breathe. Breathe. Breathe. Slower. Breathe.*

I've been developing a sort of callus over the earnest part of myself that genuinely cares about the customers and wants to do a good job for them. It thickens every time someone says something terrible to me. As it gets tougher, I've become increasingly numb to my customer interactions, good *and* bad. It's harder for angry people to upset me, but I get much less pleasure from making people happy. This dead, muted feeling reminds me a *lot* of depression, and it worries me.

I don't know why this particular guy's "shut the fuck up" is what ripped the callus off, but it's *raw* underneath. Over the last month, I've swallowed my pride dozens and dozens of times. I've been unfailingly polite to screamers. I haven't responded in kind, or hung up, or even defended myself. But in this moment, I've never been surer of anything: if I force myself to be nice to Fuckface for even *one more second,* some small, irretrievable piece of my soul will crumble into ash.

"Fine," I say, trying to make the syllable communicate my desire to knee him in his stupid fucking face. He wants me to shut the fuck up? I'll shut the fuck up. I flip my headset's mic up and away from my mouth and try to tune Fuckface out as I work on calming my body down. *In . . . out . . . in . . . out . . .* I figure if the eye of the panopticon happens to fall on me, I can maybe get away with arguing that I was just doing what he asked.

Fuckface rants on for at least half a minute more before realizing I'm no longer speaking to him. When it becomes clear that I'm either gone or not responding, he hangs up with a final *"Fuck you!"* just in case I'm there to hear it.

Click: he's gone. I exhale and continue trying to settle my nerves. I could really use a cigarette, but break's an hour away. Instead I close my eyes and picture a slideshow of calming, happy things: *Rajiv. My family. My cats. David Attenborough's voice. Objects Rajiv has glued googly eyes to.* I will my hands to stop shaking and count my breaths.

One.
Two.
Three.
Four.
Five.
Six.
Seven.
Eight.
Nine.
Te—
BEEP!

My eyes pop open, and my body roars back into full overdrive as a new caller pops into my headset. I can actually *feel* the pulse of panic radiating outward from my adrenal glands. We're never supposed to have less than thirty seconds between calls; I've never timed it, but I'm pretty sure that's not actually the case.

I stammer out a greeting while clicking over to the notes I forgot to make on Fuckface's account as the new customer begins describing her problem. Thank god, it sounds like something easy. I listen to her with half my brain as I add *cx is cuntface bitch** to the previous customer's notes and hover my mouse over the Save button. Foucault's tiny boss in my head glares. Even in our own notes, which the customer will never see, reps are supposed to use blameless adjectives like "upset" and "frustrated" instead of "screamer," "jerk," "abusive," or, obviously, "cuntface bitch."

I delete my assessment and replace it with *cx can't remember PIN, is upset,* save, then frantically start the launch sequence for the new customer. *Shit shit shit shit shit oh no she's stopped talking and I have no idea what she just said shit shit shit shit shit—*

"I'm so sorry, ma'am, you...uh, broke up for a second there—would you mind saying that one more time?" I hazard as I click and type at top speed, feeling a bit guilty for scapegoating the cell service I'm representing.

"I said I have some charges on my bill that I don't understand," says the woman, already sounding irritated at having to repeat herself.

"Great, I can...ah, totally help you with that today! First thing, let me get you logged in to your account—could I get your passcode, please?"

"Passcode? What are you talking about?"

I gently thunk my head against the cubicle wall that, today, I share with Jess. She looks over, raising an eyebrow and mouthing "You okay?" without even a blip in her own conversation. *Man, I wish I could do that.* I mime shooting myself in the temple. It's not even lunch.

Not all AT&T customers are screamers, of course. Most are perfectly nice. One man even insists on waiting on hold to personally tell my manager what a good job I did with his complicated problem. It really does make my day, just like a terrible call can ruin my day. But the glowing commendation makes no difference jobwise—it doesn't factor into my metrics

---

* *CX* is shorthand for "customer."

at all. If anything, the extra six hundred seconds the guy spent on hold probably wrecked my average call-handle time for the week.

I'm still appreciative, but underneath, there's a strange mix of resentment, envy, and contempt for the guy. *What kind of half-assed job does this guy have that he can just waste six hundred seconds in the middle of the workday?* I think. *He wouldn't last a second at this job.*

Same with an older couple from Texas* whose grim determination to understand *exactly* why their bill went up by three dollars keeps me handcuffed to the phone for more than an hour, wrecking my stats and keeping me half an hour past the end of my shift. *Jesus Christ, it's the middle of the afternoon,* I think, almost weeping with frustration and a painfully full bladder as the wife reiterates that "it's the *principle* of the thing!" *What world do you live in that you have five thousand seconds to waste on the fucking principle of the thing?* I think. *You wouldn't last a second at this job.*

My resentment of callers with free time during the workday is ridiculous, pretentious. Until recently, I had *exactly* that kind of freedom, and I took it for granted. When I imagine telling Kolbi or Jess that I made twice as much money working thirty laid-back hours a week at my first newspaper job as we make answering phones forty hours a week at Convergys, I cringe.

Because it's so, so, *so* unfair. It's embarrassingly unfair. It's hideously unfair. It's obviously, blatantly, criminally, unforgivably unfair.

Though we have our certificates and we're out on the phones full-time, what remains of my class is technically still in training for two more weeks. Kimberly's assigned a fresh batch of newbies, and we've gone to a new trainer—Vicki, a tall, heavy, intimidating blond woman with none of Kimberly's warmth.

Work has gotten *way* more stressful, and not just because I'm positive Vicki already dislikes me. There's a surprisingly big quality-of-life difference between spending *most of the day* on the phones and *the entire day.* We have even fewer walkers now, too, and we don't get breaks or lunches together anymore. Two more people quit this week—I thought we'd lose

* Others' experiences may vary, but so many of my calls with Texans went south that I developed a Pavlovian dread of the accent.

Butch Patty after her panic attack for sure, but she's back on the phones a couple days later, still never seeming to get a good call.

An hour before the end of our shift on Saturday—right before our Sunday-Monday "weekend"—Vicki tells the remaining nine of us to log out and head back to the classroom after we finish our calls. I *just* finished one, and jump to punch in the log-out code before another caller beeps into my headset.

I'm the first to start heading back, and I step on something weird by Savannah's cube. Looking down, there's a decent-size pyramid of sand on the carpet. I stare for a second, then point at the sand, mime squeezing a stress ball that then explodes, and make a sad face. Still on the phone, Savannah nods, giving me an exaggerated pout.

It takes fifteen beautiful minutes for the last person to get to the classroom. It's the first time we've been back since the potluck, and the room feels noticeably empty.

"Y'all have *got!* To *stop! Toggling!*" says Vicki, punctuating with hand claps. Her young assistant, Kendall, stands behind her, nodding emphatically at every point like a hypewoman.

"Toggling" means briefly logging out of your phone, then logging back in again. There's no Pause button—we have as much power over our next call coming in as a Ford worker would have over the next auto part rolling down the assembly line. If you need to do something between calls that will take more than thirty seconds—finish up something complicated from the previous call, use the bathroom, yoga-breathe yourself back from the brink of tears—you have to completely log out. This is extremely forbidden, but I still do it a lot. I don't really have any other option—I just can't keep up with the pace yet, no matter how hard I try.

Toggling, Vicki says, is *time theft.* She glares around the room fiercely. I'm relieved I'm not the only one who looks guilty.

"It *is* considered stealing from the company," Vicki says. She has that weird Convergys accent, too, layered over a thicker Carolina one. "That is why you see a clipboard beside me—at the end of the day, I go through the Melody reports, and I *correct* 'em."

I look over to Jess quizzically. I haven't seen much of her and Anthone at home this week, but Anthone definitely looks better, so whatever antibiotics they got must be working. I vaguely remember the words *Melody report* from somewhere, but I've memorized so much stuff that a lot has leaked out. Jess shrugs, apparently also unsure.

"Now, I'm not going to be too upset about you toggling right *now,*" Vicki continues, "but you need to wean yourself away from that, because I'm telling you—if you go to the floor and you toggle like that, your TL* will write you *up* and log you *out.*"

"Second time, they'll fire you!" chimes in Kendall.

Vicki flicks off the lights and puts an extremely complicated spreadsheet up on the overhead projector. This, she explains, is a Melody report. The system sends her one for each of us, every day, showing what each of us has been doing for every second of our shift. It shows when you're on calls, it shows when you log in or out of the phones and the e-start time clock, it shows what programs and windows you have open and when—it shows every move you make on the clock.

Siempre va a te ver.

"Now, when I use the words *stealing from the company,* I'm not trying to make it out like you're a *thief,* okay?" says Vicki. "Sometimes we don't know what we're doing, and when we don't know what we're doing, we need to be educated on it, which is what I'm trying to do now."

But, she says, sometimes people know *exactly* what they're doing.

"I had an agent two groups ago whose Melody was really crazy, so I started paying attention to him. He made the mistake of sitting directly in my view for the whole entire day. And by the end of the day, he had *three hours and twenty-two minutes not logged in.*" There's a murmur of disbelief.

"He was literally sitting there with his headphones on *pretending* he was talking to a customer all day!" says Kendall, who clearly likes this story. We laugh.

"Literally talking with no one on the phone!" Vicki says, holding out her arms in the universal sign for *Can you believe this chump?*

I don't think I'd have had much sympathy for the guy a month ago. But now I *do* kind of get why he might have done it. I've actually considered it myself after a couple of particularly bad screamers.

---

* Team leader—our direct supervisor once we're totally out of training.

Destiny raises her hand. "I mean, did he not *know* that you can hear everything, that you monitor our calls?"

"No, he knew it! He hung *hisself,*" says Vicki with satisfaction. "We gave him *every* opportunity to get on the phones."

So after watching this guy pretend to be on the phones all day, Vicki says, "I pulled him by hisself and I talked to him. I wasn't ugly—I just said, 'I just want you to be aware that this is considered work avoidance, which is a form of theft from the company, because you are *stealing time.*' And he took 'stealing time' as me calling him a thief!"

"And this man went *crazy!*" says Kendall.

"I'm sitting down, and he's over top of me yelling, 'You're calling me a *thief?*'" says Vicki, still outraged. "It was all I could *do* to keep my temper."

Vicki goes on about toggling and the e-start time clock for a while, pointing out things on the sample Melody report. "Honestly, guys—I take my time with e-start, because that's your *money.* I like to make sure it's correct. I don't want it to be incorrect," she says.

I try my *What is she talking about?* face on Destiny this time. She also shrugs.

"For example," Vicki says, pointing, "*this* is when her open time was, but she didn't get here 'til *here.*"

"She was *seven minutes late!*" says Kendall.

"*This* is how much time she was online on the phones, and *this* is how much time she was *not* on the phones," Vicki continues, pointing to something else. "You see all this—logging in, logging out, logging in, logging out, logging in, logging out? You got two minutes, nineteen minutes, six minutes, an hour and twenty-seven minutes, twenty minutes..."

Destiny raises her hand. "Now, is all that logging-in-logging-out-logging-in-logging-out for when you go on your breaks and stuff, too?"

"Yes. See, here—this nineteen-minute one is a break," Vicki says. "She punched in back from break at 17:28, but she didn't log in to the *phones* until 17:31. So I would have to go back to her time card and correct it to 17:31—which is putting her *late.*"

"Vicki has the ability to punch you out for that time, so you don't even get *paid* for it," says Kendall.

I look around at what's left of my class in astonishment. For one, that's stupid—the computers are so ancient that getting everything up and running again after being away takes at *least* two minutes, and you'd be a fool to log in to take calls before you've gotten everything open.

But, more important, if Vicki's saying what I *think* she's saying—if it's part of her job to change our official time-clock records to reflect only the time we're logged in to the phones—that sounds an awful lot like wage theft.

"So the minute you punch back in, you should log in," says Vicki. "At the *same time*. Because I have to go back and correct it."

"Correct it... *how?*" asks Kolbi. The whole class seems pretty uneasy.

"Say you log out of your phone because you have break in five minutes, and you just sit there for five minutes?" says Vicki. "You've just used the first five minutes of your fifteen-minute break. Or say your break's at ten and you log out at 9:55. When I go back to correct your time, I *will* change you to 9:55—so you'll be five minutes late from break."

This is news to me and appears to be news even to the veterans. There's a concerned murmur.

"Uh, I'm kind of confused—"

"What does that mean—"

"You *change* it? Have you been—"

"Guys!" Vicki holds up her hands defensively, cutting us off. "Guys, if it was up to me, I wouldn't do it! But that *is* my job; I have to correct your time. That *is* part of my job. And I like my job and the fact that I can take care of my kids, so I'm not losing my job over you. I mean, I love you to *death,* but I'm *not* losing my job over you."

Destiny raises her hand. "What do you mean you *change* it—you change it in e-start?" she asks carefully.

"Yeah, I change it in e-start. I *have* to," says Vicki. "Because you are being paid to be here, *on the phone.* So when you log off the phones, you should be punching out at the same time."

I raise my hand. "So wait—does that mean we're not being paid when we're, like, in the bathroom?" Vicki glowers at me, and I shrink.

"You have an *hour*—fifteen-minute break, fifteen-minute break, thirty-minute lunch. I *know* Kimberly went over that with you. And they give up to ten minutes extra for you to go to the bathroom during the day. So an hour and fifteen minutes, *tops,* is what you should be off the phones." This doesn't answer my question, but Vicki's still giving me the stink eye, so I let it go.

You know what? I think as Vicki continues lecturing on the evils of time theft. *I think I've been here long enough.*

As we leave for the weekend, I apologetically tell Vicki that something's come up and I need to move back to Philadelphia by the end of next week. She doesn't seem angry, or upset, or even surprised. She just says okay. I guess she's probably had hundreds and hundreds of people quit on her. I mean, I'm the third just this week.

I go about my last few days at Convergys as if nobody's listening—as if metrics and call flows and sales mandates don't exist. I do this because I hate them, but I'm also curious what will happen if I just act like a normal human being who's not trying to juggle eight other things. And I fantasize about the next screamer I get—the possibilities for going out in a blaze of glory are endless.

But I don't get any.

Maybe I've gotten more competent. Maybe it's luck. Maybe it's the flip side of how Butch Patty's callers always smell her blood in the water—with my new *Office Space*–like detachment, maybe I sound confident and unafraid. But I'm pretty sure it's just that once I stop trying to juggle more balls than I can handle, I can talk like a normal human being again.

My very last call is a guy—I'll call him Ash—who's trying to figure out why he got such a hefty bill. That's an easy one. I pull up the data usage on his plan, and—yup—one of his two lines went way, way over its data limit.

"Oh, that's Sarah's line," Ash says glumly.

"Does Sarah play Pokémon Go, by any chance?" I ask.

"I think she might?" he says.

"I can't actually see what she used the data for, but I *will* say that a *ton* of people have called in this month because of data overages, and when they check with their kids, they find out they've been playing Pokémon Go, like, twelve hours a day." I give him some specific advice to pass on to Sarah about minimizing the data the program uses. The level of detail must give me away, because Ash asks if I play.

"Blue team," I admit.

"Me too!" says Ash. He begins excitedly talking about Pokémon Go with the single-minded enthusiasm and long-haul rhythm I generally associate with being somewhere on the spectrum.*

Last week I'd have tried to cut off this tangent and gotten increasingly stressed as he rambled on and on and my stats got worse and worse. Today I put my feet up on the desk, lean back in my chair, and embrace the opportunity. The 600-second warning comes up, then the 750-second warning; I dismiss them. They have no power over me.

Half an hour later, we've discussed every possible facet of Pokémon Go and moved on to relationship advice. Ash is still hung up on his ex, Sarah, who I'd assumed was his daughter. He's still paying her phone bill, though she broke up with him several months ago.

"But how can you get over somebody when you're in love?" he asks, dejected.

I tell him to hang in there—time helps, and so can exercising until you're too tired to wallow. I suggest a couple of albums to listen to, but say it sounds like he needs to make a clean break for a while. Maybe he should talk to Sarah about getting off his cell plan. We role-play some ways that won't make Sarah feel like a bad person.

Finally, I check the clock. It's 4:45 p.m.

"Okay, Ash—it's my last day of work, and my shift's over in fifteen minutes. Let's settle your overages before I have to go."

When Ash finally hangs up ten minutes later, I'm aglow with job satisfaction. *I helped,* I think, though I know it's dumb.

I don't feel like Russian rouletting whether one last call will take five minutes or ninety, so I log out of my phone. I type *cx very enthusiastic about Pokémon Go, cutting ties with Sarah for a while* into Ash's notations, save and quit, clock out in e-start, close the sedimentary layer of windows covering my desktop, shut down my computer, and exit the building for the last time.

There's nobody I know out at the picnic tables. That's not a huge surprise; most of the smoking crew has quit already. So I smoke a cigarette by myself, stare at the Buffalo Wild Wings sinkhole, and eavesdrop on a new

* I mean, that's not meant as an insult—speaking with single-minded enthusiasm and long-haul rhythm is one of my defining character traits.

class of newbies getting to know one another. They sound as optimistic and confident as Butch Patty did back on our first day.

Nobody I know comes out by the time my cigarette's done, so I just toss it and hit the road. I've already said my goodbyes, and I'm starting to feel an urgent need to get away from this place. I moved all my stuff back into the trunk and backseat this morning and left a thank-you card with two more weeks of rent in cash on the coffee table; I hope it'll help a little.

I get to leave, I think as I drive past the Baymont Suites. *I get to leave,* I think, driving past the Walmart, YMCA, and Barnes & Noble. *I get to leave,* I think, driving past the Chick-fil-A, Hickory Furniture Mart, and all the abandoned factories along the interstate. They all shrink to nothing in my rearview mirror, and the only thing I can think is *I get to leave.*

PART THREE

McDONALD'S

Number One

Hello!" I say, smiling at the next person in line. "How may I help you?"

First: I love McDonald's. My entire life, Chicken McNuggets have tasted like reward, consolation, apology, and prize, all wrapped up in one big greasy bag.

I got braces when I was nine or ten—pretty common in the middle-class-to-wealthy area of Virginia where I grew up. I remember the monthly visits to the orthodontist kind of fondly, actually. I got to skip a couple of hours of school, and there was an old Ms. Pac-Man machine in the waiting room. Best of all, my mom would usually take me to McDonald's afterward for my usual Happy Meal with Chicken McNuggets.

In middle school, I had a bunch of surgeries on my legs—one of the reasons I'd worried about making it through Amazon. I don't remember those couple of years of trips to Children's Hospital fondly *at all.* But after every episode of needle-centric tests or leg-brace fittings, my parents would stop and get McDonald's for me on the way home.

A few Februaries ago, my husband, Rajiv, sprung a hole in one of his lungs. I was already at one of the lowest points of my gray years of depression,* and with him in the hospital for weeks, I got stuck in a dark place where I couldn't write, or sleep, or do much of *anything* aside from staring at the ceiling in vague horror.

* This is the era that produced the "*Onion* article would be funny if life wasn't so goddamn bleak" headline I mentioned earlier.

Not great timing, as the investigative piece about Uber I'd been working on for months was already late and nowhere near done. When I couldn't get to sleep, which was a lot, I'd give up, log in to Uber, and drive around in the snow until two or three in the morning. I may not have been able to force any words onto the page, but at least I *felt* like I was doing something. I ate so much drive-through McDonald's on those cold nights that by the time I brought Rajiv home, the car smelled like a McNugget.

The point is, the more tired, sad, upset, or stressed out I am, the less I'm able to resist the siren call of the golden arches. *Here,* they sing. *This will make you feel better.* And it always does. At least, for a little while.

"Hi!" I say again, a little louder, willing the guy with earbuds in to look up from his phone and realize he's up. *"How can I help you?"*

A few days ago, after ringing up my first McDonald's sale—an Egg McMuffin—I surprised myself by hip-checking the register shut with professional ease. I didn't even think about it; it was as reflexive as if someone had tapped my knee with a rubber hammer.

My trainer, a short Latino guy named Erik, had given me a smile. "You've done this before?"

"Like riding a bike," I'd said with a shrug.

Erik had ERICA tattooed on his neck, and I wanted to ask about it—did Erik date an Erica? Does he have a daughter named after him? Is he named after his mother?—but decided to wait until I knew him a little better. I guess I'll never find out, because Erik wasn't there when I showed up for my third shift. Presumably he'd been called to show another newbie the ropes at one of the several other Bay Area McDonald's franchises owned by the same Asian businessman who owns this one in downtown San Francisco. Training was over.

Since then, it's been a week of just me and Candela working breakfast rush. I feel bad for Candela, the morning shift manager, who's stuck doing both her job and the 75 percent of my job that wasn't covered in training. Candela's a middle-aged, blond, apple-shaped Latina who's even shorter than I am. She opens the store on weekdays and is alone on counter until I clock in to the second of the four registers at 7:00 a.m.

My arrival every day is clearly a net negative for efficiency. To my left, Candela's her usual frantic whirl of motion, like a hypercompetent

Tasmanian Devil. She reminds me of Olivia, the hugely pregnant woman with the cotton-candy voice I shadowed at Convergys. Like with Olivia, I'm pessimistic about ever getting on Candela's level.

I can work the cash register just fine, but that's only a fraction of the multitasking hornpipe of working counter at McDonald's. I'd anticipated some parts of the job from my experience on the other side of the counter: Greet the customer with a smile. Push the appropriate picture buttons on my touchscreen, causing the order to pop up in real time on screens back in the kitchen and above the counter. Take their money and make change or have them swipe or insert a card. Hand over the tray or bag with the order.

But there's a lot of extra work I never noticed.

I hadn't noticed that the person who takes your order often assembles it, too—grabbing the food from various places, consolidating it all in a bag or on a tray, adding the appropriate combination of napkins, condiments, straws, etc.

She also makes a bunch of items herself—sodas, oatmeal, coffee, ice cream cones, shakes, McFlurries, smoothies—and fits that in between taking and assembling other orders.

She has to help the surprising number of people who can't figure out the credit-card machine, or who use coupons, or who pay with apps.

She keeps an eye on customers waiting for their food and figures out what happened if they've been waiting longer than a few minutes.

She deals with the new hassle of delivery services. I've been utterly shocked by how shoddy and badly planned food-delivery apps look from this side of the counter. McDonald's partnership with Uber Eats, for example, strikes me as *exactly* the sort of kludged-together monster you'd find at Convergys.

She clears orders from her register out of the queue once they've been handed off to customers.

She keeps an eye on how many condiments and napkins and cups and straws are out and restocks a couple of times each shift in between taking and assembling orders.

She makes sure she never, *ever* runs out of coffee.

She's on various steps of this dance across two or three orders simultaneously whenever she has a line. And I've had a line for all but about five minutes of the thirty-odd hours I've been flying solo at McDonald's.

I hope it's just because I'm new and slow. But I know in my heart that this is *exactly* the permanent state of emergency Kolbi described at Chick-fil-A. Ray Kroc's famous *If there's time to lean, there's time to clean* has actually become law here. Not *law* like *rule*—*law* like *physics* or *gravity*. It's so embedded in the place that nobody even has to say it anymore.

I work in a busy franchise in downtown San Francisco, blocks from the headquarters of a ton of huge tech companies—Uber, Twitter, Dropbox, Reddit, Craigslist, Airbnb, TaskRabbit, Pinterest, *Wikipedia,* Square, Yelp, etc. I've only been here a week, and I've already served countless people voluntarily wearing hoodies and T-shirts bearing the logo of their employer.*

As someone involuntarily wearing the logo of her employer, I find this bizarre. My uniform *is* mercifully tasteful, though. When I was hired last week, I was handed three plastic-wrapped dark gray T-shirts with a subtle white *M* over the heart and one black visor with a less subtle embroidered white *M* smack in the center of my forehead. I was instructed to keep these clean and to wear them with my own appropriate black pants and nonslip shoes.

At a franchise in another city, I might have been charged for the shirts and visor. Here, I'm not. In many ways, a McJob in San Francisco is about as good a McJob as you can get anywhere because of the city's worker-protection legislation.

At $14 an hour, I'm paid almost twice as much as the average McDonald's crew member—in November of 2014, voters overwhelmingly passed a ballot measure that would gradually raise San Francisco's minimum wage to $15. San Francisco has universal paid sick leave, and the biggest retail and fast-food companies can't schedule their San Francisco employees the way companies do most everywhere else. It's an attempt to disincentivize common practices like (A) employing a large staff of part-timers or temps instead of a smaller staff of full-timers to avoid paying for benefits and (B) scheduling in a way that's nice and flexible for the company but leaves workers unable to plan their lives more than a couple of days in advance.

---

* When I meet up with a high school friend who works in tech, I ask about this. He just rolls his eyes and says that the show *Silicon Valley* is basically a documentary.

But despite having one of the best entry-level McJobs in the country, I sometimes feel that by going with the very first place that called about my application, I've picked a uniquely exhausting place to work. Like how I have to constantly hold my last three or four orders in my head because Candela keeps wiping the goddamn order queue.

I assumed this was an accident the first time it happened, but then I *saw* her do it, clearly on purpose.

"*Nooooooooo,* why would you do that?" I moaned, desperately trying to recall the details of three orders that had just vanished from the counter-facing overhead screen.

Candela, amused by my theatrical despair, just laughed. "You go too slow!" she said, pointing to a small fractional number in a corner of the order screen—some sort of productivity metric I hadn't noticed.

"Wait—what does that mean?" I'd asked. But we were in the weeds. Candela was already on to the next customer, and I had to start digging myself out of all my orders disappearing. I now constantly hold my last three orders in the back of my head, though doing this all day gets almost as mentally exhausting as all the multitasking at Convergys.

But the biggest source of extra work here is the fact that nearly everything free for the taking in most franchises is kept behind the counter here—the soda fountain, condiments, utensils, creamer, coffee stirrers, etc. The only thing customers can get for themselves are napkins and straws, so on top of everything else I'm constantly filling tiny off-the-books orders for soda refills and condiments.

This must keep costs down, but it slows order assembly down a *lot*. Like, here's the steps I remember to assembling a Big Breakfast with Hotcakes and coffee meal, for here:

1. Go to the coffee station on the right side of the counter.
2. Grab the appropriate-size cup, fill it to the inside line with coffee.
    - If you use the last of a pot of coffee, swap it out for a fresh one; make a mental note to return when you're done to start the empty one brewing again.
3. Add however many creams and sweeteners the customer requested.
    - If you can't remember, check the order screen.

- If you neglected to put that information into the system because the interface makes doing this a pain in the ass, apologize and ask the customer to tell you again. She will usually be happy to do so.

4. Get a wooden coffee stirrer and stir.
5. Toss the stirrer, grab the appropriate lid, and put it on, double-checking that it's super secure—for reasons unclear to me, McDonald's keeps its coffee undrinkably, scaldingly hot, and a spill can burn you in seconds.
6. Pick up the coffee, grab a tray in your other hand, and carry them over to the hot box—the centrally located window connecting kitchen and counter.
7. Put the tray down by the hot box, put the coffee on the tray, then continue over to the fry station on the far left wall.
8. Using tongs, pop open a little paper sleeve, pick up a hash brown, and slide it into the sleeve.
9. Grab a napkin on your way back to the hot box.
10. Put the napkin on the tray.
11. Put the hash brown on the napkin.
12. Check the hot box for your Big Breakfast with Hotcakes.
    - It isn't there yet—Big Breakfasts are a pain in the ass for the kitchen, too.
13. Squat down and grab from under the hot box:
    - one syrup tub,
    - two butter packets,
    - two packets of the customer's choice of jelly (go back and ask if you don't remember),
    - two or three ketchup packets,
    - a salt packet, and
    - a pepper packet.
14. Put these on the tray, then check the hot box again.
    - Still no Big Breakfast.
15. Speed-walk over to the far right wall, dodging coworkers, to get a shrink-wrapped set of utensils (knife, fork, and napkin).
16. Speed-walk back and put them on the tray.
17. Check the hot box, which now contains your Big Breakfast.

18. Gently pick up the plastic container so the breakfast foods inside don't all roll to one side, then put it on the tray.
19. Make a final check that you haven't forgotten anything.
20. Carefully carry the loaded tray to the far right side of the counter.
21. Check the overhead order screen for the number associated with this order.
22. Yell the number until someone comes to get it.
23. When the customer steps forward with her order receipt, hand over the tray with a smile and hope she doesn't want anything else.

I assume we keep everything behind the counter because of all the homeless people, who are as much of an omnipresence in San Francisco as the western North Carolina accent is in Hickory.

I live in Philly and spend a lot of time in New York and DC, cities with homelessness problems of their own. But San Francisco is like nothing I've ever seen. It's hard to get good data, but a recent survey counted nearly ten thousand homeless people just in San Francisco proper. Nearly half of those were living in the downtown Sixth District, home to the Mission and this McDonald's. There's a particularly high concentration around my store, as one Yelp review complains:

> As many other reviewers have pointed out, this location ALWAYS has homeless people hanging around inside the restaurant or lurking/passed out directly outside. It is impossible to enter or leave without stepping over someone or encountering a panhandler begging for change. Now, I have gotten to the point where I simply won't go there if there are homeless people blocking the entrance. (Which means I don't go there at all anymore). MCDONALDS CORPORATE, PLEASE DO SOMETHING ABOUT THE HOMELESS LOITERING SITUATION AT THIS LOCATION!!!!!

There *are* often homeless people "hanging around" the store—because they bought food and are eating it like any other customer. But I wouldn't say the reviewer's sentiment is *wrong,* exactly. Nearly every review of my store mentions the homeless, because they *are* a very aggressive presence. Many are loudly and energetically mentally ill, very persistent about panhandling, strung out, or all three.

There's a surreality to the Sixth District because its huge homeless population coexists with the city's highest concentrations of skyscrapers, venture capital, tech workers, rich foreign tourists, high-end shopping, and, in my anecdotal experience, Teslas. The contrast between all the wealth and the homeless tent encampments, urine smell, and syringe detritus is truly bizarre.

I don't mind the *job* job of McDonald's so far. I have literally zero *time to lean* outside of what's mandated by law, but I do get genuine satisfaction from making customers happy, and that's a lot easier here than it was at Convergys.

In my peripheral vision, I notice some workers I still haven't met clustered around the time clock over by the fry bin—reinforcements for lunch rush already? I check the clock, and find I've already been here four hours. Time on the clock here moves *fast*.

You clock in by scanning your fingerprint, and, as at Amazon, the system won't let you clock in before the exact time on your schedule. So for a few minutes, the small area between the fry bin and the smoothie machine is crowded with several people about to start their shifts. Behind them, someone drops the day's first basket of fries into the deep fryer with a sizzle.

At 11:00 a.m. on the dot, the wall-to-wall screens behind me flicker. When they come back on, the Egg McMuffins falling in slow motion have been replaced by Chicken McNuggets and Big Macs falling in slow motion. Behind me, workers take turns pressing their fingers to the little square, then disperse. It's lunchtime.

I switch my touchscreen over from breakfast to lunch, weirdly proud that I don't have to get Candela or Lalo to show me how. *I'm learning.*

Lalo's the franchise's general manager, who usually clocks in around now. If you were drawing a cartoon of Candela, you'd start with a circle. If you were drawing a cartoon of Lalo, you'd start with a rectangle, like a brick stood up on its small end. She has a square jaw and an aura of *solidness,* reliability.

The schedule's constantly in flux, but the shifts tend to be roughly grouped by language—breakfast is usually staffed by Spanish speakers, dinner and nights by Tagalog speakers, and lunch goes back and forth. People with the least English usually work in the kitchen or cleaning up; people with the most are usually on register. I'm far from the only native English speaker at my franchise—the later Filipino shifts in particular have a lot of younger, unaccented first-generation workers, including one gawky young guy who sounds eerily like Sylvester Stallone. But as the sole white face at this franchise, I'm pretty sure I'm permanently stuck on register.

I like my coworkers so far, and they've all been friendly. But my Spanish is even worse than I remembered, and I didn't even know what Tagalog *was* until I asked. Even my first-generation coworkers often use Spanish or Tagalog to make each other laugh—I assume because most customers can't understand—and it's just harder to make friends when you can't participate in jokes.

It would have been tougher to make friends than it was at Convergys even if I spoke both languages perfectly—there's barely any time to chat at all. There's *always* a line; we're *always* in the weeds.

And that's everyone, not just counter workers. Managers like Lalo and Candela sometimes do paperwork in the upstairs office, but during the meal rushes that take up most of the day, they perform like the star center of a hockey team—going everywhere, covering wherever it's needed. And if Candela's fast, Lalo's like a Benny Hill video on fast-forward.

The average American worker doesn't get that many obvious demonstrations of why their bosses get paid more than they do. Here, at least, it's obvious that lower management is made up of the best and fastest women on the crew—though most McDonald's managers aren't paid that much more than crew members like me.

"Hi!" I say loudly. "I can help the next person over here!" The line is growing now that we're serving lunch, and it's starting to get noisy. I smile when I recognize the security guard who steps up to my register. He's a charming regular—black, probably ten years my junior, and *far* too attractive to have tried to get my number on my first day. It caught me so off guard that I briefly forgot how flirting works—I turned bright red, avoided eye contact, and waggled my left hand, mumbling something about being a married lady. He'd raised an eyebrow, grinning. "So?"

"Hey, if it isn't nothing but trouble!" I say, then laugh as he pretends to storm away in a huff. Hip-checking the register drawer closed came back immediately; it took a whole week to get back into the rhythm of asexual customer flirtation. But now that I have, I've fully relapsed into the habit of using vaguely maternal nicknames like "hon" and "darlin'."

I doubt the guy's attention has anything to do with me—I think he just likes all women in his life to smile when they see him and remember his weird drink order—half fruit punch and half Sprite.* When he finishes ordering and steps to the side, it's easy to access a genuine smile for the next person in line.

"Hi!" I say. "I can get the next person in line over here!"

"Do you have the McPick 2 with the two fish sandwiches?" asks the older black man who steps up.

I didn't expect to learn anything new about the McDonald's *menu* by working here—as I mentioned, I'm familiar. But I was only familiar with half the menu—the rich-people half. It's the obvious one, the one advertised on the customer-facing screens above my head. It's the one you order from if you haven't worried about overdrawing your checking account in a while. Items from this menu can usually be ordered using very few words—"Number 1 with medium fries and a Coke," maybe—and a meal generally costs between eight and twelve bucks.

But there's a whole *other* menu, for poor people. This one is more like Animal Style at In-N-Out—to order from it, you kind of have to already know about it. You *can* find it on the screens, but it's usually tucked away in a far corner. It was called the Dollar Menu when I was a kid: as I write this, they're calling it the Dollar Menu again. But while I'm in San Francisco, the poor-people menu is called the McPick 2.

"Sorry, no, we don't have the McPick 2 for $5 here—we do the McPick 2 for *$2.50*. Do you know what's on that menu?"

After a week on the job, the McPick spiel is already as automatic as the Nicene Creed—zero conscious thought involved. Different franchises

* I pick up a bunch of weird and extremely specific new stereotypes at McDonald's; one is that ordering a mixture of two different fountain drinks is a black-people thing.

participate in different deals, and the news that we don't have the McPick 2 for $5 here doesn't always go over well. But I can usually nip complaints in the bud by immediately launching into what's available *here.* Which I do now.

"So with the 2 for $2.50, you can pick any two things from that menu—there's a McDouble (that's sort of like a double cheeseburger), a McChicken sandwich, a small fry, and a four-piece McNuggets—you can pick any two of those, and it's $2.50 total. Add a dollar drink—whatever size you want, they're all a dollar—and you've got a whole mini meal for $3.50."

This time, my patter works. The guy places a McPick 2 for $2.50 order and moves off to the side, apparently pleased with the deal he's getting.

As I become more and more familiar with the semisecret menu, I've started to enjoy helping homeless customers get the most bang for their fistful of change. The dollar breakfast burrito is a good value; so is four McDoubles for five bucks. But the best deal by far, volumewise, is the twenty-piece McNuggets for five dollars.* When somebody comes in with more than five bucks and asks how much food it'll buy, I recommend it every time.

"Hi!" I say, smiling at the next person in line, a middle-aged black woman with dreads down her back. "I can get you over here!"

As she approaches, my eyes are drawn to the enormous, painful-looking burn scar covering most of her right shoulder and upper arm. *God, whatever did that must have been terrible.* After a split second I hope she didn't notice, I flick my eyes to her face and lock them there.

"Hi," I say, smiling. "How can I help you?"

She orders a small coffee. But as I turn to start making it, I hear Lalo yell *"Mamá!"* from over by the fry bin, where she's methodically popping open and filling cardboard fry containers.

Coworkers on both the Spanish and Tagalog shifts frequently get each other's attention with a generic *"Mamá!"* or *"Papá!"* I figured it was a thing among friends, but when I glance over, Lalo's looking right at me.

"Hey! *Mamá!*" she yells again. I point at myself and tilt my head in question.

---

* That's literally the same price as a ten-piece Chicken McNuggets. Only suckers get the ten-piece.

"Yeah, *you,*" says Lalo. My brief thrill at being in Club *Mamá* evaporates as she stabs her fry tongs at the woman with the burn scar, who's holding out her money. *"No service."*

"Huh?" I say, taken aback.

"*No service*—don't serve her," she says again, impatient, then addresses the woman directly. "*You*—you get out *right now. No service.*" And with that, Lalo turns and goes back to popping open and filling fry containers with practiced ease.

I look at the woman with the burn scar, who continues holding out her money as if nothing happened.

"I, uh, I... can't serve you, I'm sorry?" I hazard.

"And *why not?*" the woman demands. Her voice sends a Pavlovian stab of adrenaline through my body, though it's been months since Convergys. *Oh, fuck me,* I think. *It's a screamer! In person!* I have no idea what this woman did to get herself eighty-sixed from a McDonald's, but I'm pretty sure I know what she's *about* to do.

"I... I'm sorry, you heard my boss—I can't serve you," I say, bracing myself.

And, right on schedule, the woman with the burned arm goes full screamer.

"Why the *fuck* not? This is *bullshit,*" she yells at the top of her lungs. She turns and begins screaming about her civil rights to the line of customers.

There's things I might find interesting about this moment if the wave of fight-or-flight energy—which is even more overwhelming when the screamer's three feet away—wasn't making it so hard to think.

First, nobody on either side of the counter acts like this is out of the ordinary. People glance over when she starts, and some move a few feet away. But there's a general communal shrug.

Then there's the woman herself. I'm all too familiar with the auditory signals of a screamer after Convergys. Now I get the visuals, too. First there's the wide eyes and high eyebrows of surprise, which then fold down into the narrow eyes and furrowed brow of anger. Nostrils flare, to draw in air faster. Jaw thrusts forward. Lips go tight and thin. Hands become fists. Shoulder muscles tense.

"You tell that bitch I've got as much right to have a coffee as anyone else!" the woman demands, turning back around to stab a finger at Lalo, who's still pointedly ignoring her.

"I, uh—she's my *boss,* I..." I stammer, but the screamer's turned her attention to Lalo, migrating to the other end of the counter to yell at her more directly.

I look over to Lalo for guidance. But Lalo doesn't try to soothe the woman, or apologize, or keep her as a customer. She just ignores her. So I follow her lead, cancel the order, and pretend the screamer just isn't there.

And, my god—it feels *so good.*

The customer is always right policies are common in customer service, and they breed a particularly nasty type of despair. At Convergys, even when a customer was worth almost nothing to the company—the habitual liars trying to get fees waived, the clearly insane, the people months behind on their bills—the worst customer still had more value to the company than the best rep. So you'd better apologize, grovel, and swallow your pride, because your dignity is valued at *zero.*

Lalo ignoring this woman demonstrates that, officially, there are situations in which the customer is not right. Lalo's ignoring the screamer, and I can, too—while I may not be worth much, I'm at least not *zero.* It's hard to explain my rush of desperate gratitude about this. I'm kind of in *love* with Lalo for a few seconds. It's weird, intense, and a little embarrassing.

Don't be fucking grateful! screams a little voice in the back of my head. *When did you start seeing these pathetic scraps as something to be grateful for?*

It's been so long since my newspaper closed, since I had a white-collar job. When I left for SDF8, I would probably have said "since I had a *real* job." But I sometimes can't even remember what it felt like to take dignity at work for granted. Now, it's so precious and rare that even a tiny crumb like this makes me want to weep with relief. *Pathetic.*

"Hi!" I say in a loud voice, determinedly making eye contact with the guy who's probably next in line. He looks at the still-ranting woman nervously. I force a smile and mentally command him to step forward. "How can I help you?"

And the line starts moving again.

The woman with the burned shoulder runs out of steam after a few minutes but continues to lurk around the counter making trouble for a full half hour, threatening to call the health inspectors and shouting things like "Is that a rat back there?" and "That Mexican just spit in the fries—I saw her!" By the time she finally leaves, the intense fight-or-flight pounding has subsided into a solid case of the jitters.

That might be lack of food or nicotine, though—it's been so busy that I haven't had my lunch or either of my breaks yet. The next time I check the clock, I'm surprised to find it's already 1:30—if I don't start taking my breaks in the next half hour, I'll run out of minutes on my shift to take them. I look around for Lalo to let her know, but I don't see her, so I shove hunger out of my mind.

"Hi!" I say. "How can I help you?"

Half an hour later, I jump when Lalo taps me on the shoulder and tells me to take lunch. It's already two o'clock, so I'm going to have to squeeze my two federally mandated short breaks into the last half hour of my shift, which is annoying.

Picking up lunch here isn't the problem it was at Convergys, but breaks and lunches at McDonald's are the least relaxing of anywhere I've worked. Staffing is so tight that I rarely have a break at the same time as another coworker, so there's no chance to make friends then, either. And management is crazy serious about the time clock. I've already gotten yelled at *twice* for being one minute late clocking back in after a short break, once involving my favorite accusation, "time theft."

I go press my fingerprint to clock out, then dance my way through the claustrophobic obstacle course of the kitchen and up the stairs to get my stuff. By the time I get back to the front with my purse, jacket, phone, cigarettes, and a twenty-piece McNuggets I snagged on the way, the time clock shows that I've already been on break three minutes—it actually displays who's on break and how long each has been away. Your name changes color the second you go over your allotted break time, for easy identification.

I take off my visor and put on my jacket before ringing up my twenty-piece as a shift meal at my register—I've found if my clothes say "on break," I get fewer dirty looks from the line. The twenty-piece is an even better deal with the 50 percent employee discount—for $2.50, you get ten McNuggets for lunch and ten to take home for dinner, which has been excellent for my budget, though probably not my cholesterol.

Once I've set the transaction up, I look around for Lalo—a manager has to come type in her three-digit approval code before I can pay for my half-price McNuggets.

At first I was puzzled by how many common situations require manager approval, because flagging a manager down can really, really clog up the line. Take opening the register: People often pay for something that costs $8.05 with a $10 bill, then locate a nickel after I've already made change and shut the register. To reopen the register so the customer can get two dollar bills instead of one dollar and a handful of change, I have to get manager approval.

Or if I have to make more than five changes to an order—every change you make after that, you need manager approval. This can be infuriating in the situation it most often comes up, which is when I'm deciphering the order of a non-English-speaking tourist via charades and pointing—if there's five changes, there's probably going to be ten.

Or another situation that comes up a lot: a customer who's already paid with a credit card decides that she actually wants her for-here order to go, or asks for an extra honey mustard packet.* I'm supposed to ring up a whole new transaction for fifteen cents or a quarter, which is a pain in the ass *and* likely to make the customer mad—the most efficient way to piss people off is by asking them to pay for something they think of as free. The customer doesn't have fifteen cents on her, so she swipes her card again—but you need a manager code to run a card twice in a row, so she has to wait even longer.

At first it's baffling that so many common situations require manager approval, especially because once you flag a manager down, it's not like she

* I'm *always* supposed to charge for these. Paper bags in San Francisco cost fifteen cents—an effort to disincentivize trash—and extra sauces aside from ketchup are a quarter each. For a few days, if the transaction had already gone through and what the customer wanted cost a quarter or less, I'd just hand it over gratis. Candela noticed. "You have to charge for the bag every time, you have to charge for the sauce every time," she told me one morning—not exactly stern, but serious. "You can't hand them out free. They have cameras—if they see that, you'll get in trouble."

asks any questions—she just comes over and punches the code in automatically.

Then I started thinking about it from the point of view of Taylor—expecting the absolute worst of his workers—and it kind of makes sense.

I can't open the register at will because...I could steal? I can't make a lot of changes to an order because...I might add extra items, overcharge the customer, and pocket the extra money? I can't run the same credit card twice in a row because...I don't know—I could buy someone else lunch? I have to spend precious minutes of my half-hour lunch waiting for a manager to approve my damn half-price McNuggets because...I might give my friends the employee discount?

A couple more minutes go by before Marisol—*when did Candela leave and Marisol come on?*—can come over to authorize my McNuggets.

"You can't ring an employee meal up yourself—a manager has to do it," Marisol says, looking irritated. Marisol's an afternoon shift manager who's probably a couple of years younger than me and walks with a pronounced limp. Her accent is fully American, but she speaks fluent Tagalog and usually manages Filipino-heavy shifts. I'm still not sure if she has Resting Bitch Face or just doesn't like me.

"Sorry—I thought I'd try to save you the time...it's so busy," I stammer.

"Well, don't next time—just be patient," Marisol says, canceling the order and ringing it up again herself. I check the time—*twenty-three minutes of break left.* Marisol frowns at the screen. "See, this is exactly why—you didn't charge yourself for a bag. And anyway, you can't do a twenty-piece as an employee meal."

"Wait—I can't?" I say, dismayed.

"No, it's already on sale," says Marisol, her tone saying *I really need to be doing other things right now.* "Do you want it or not?" I sigh and pay the full $5.15, then duck under the counter, weaving my way to the exit through the line that's been constant since my shift started seven hours ago.

We're not allowed to smoke in front of the store, so I go around the corner before lighting a cigarette with a sigh of pleasure.

It's stupid to be this mad about $2.50, I tell myself as the sweet, sweet relief of nicotine hits my bloodstream. But of course I'm still mad, because obviously it's not about the $2.50. It's because my worth may be greater than zero, but I now also have proof that it's less than three bucks.

Or one minute. *Shit, I forgot to check the time clock again before I left. How many minutes did it take to pay for my food? I was at three when I got downstairs...* To be safe, I set my phone's timer for fifteen minutes.

As usual, I spend my last couple minutes of lunch killing time by the smoothie machine. The system won't clock me back in until I've had my full thirty minutes, but I always try to be back and ready to clock in a couple of minutes early, because I *will* get yelled at for being one minute late. I wish I could tell this to the people in line, who stare at my apparent idleness resentfully as I wait to press my finger to the square.

It's silly to feel *guilty* over being a minute late, especially when between a third and half of my lunch break is spent navigating the kitchen, washing my hands, getting my purse, navigating the kitchen again, paying for my shift meal, navigating the kitchen *again,* putting my purse away, washing my hands, navigating the kitchen one last time, and waiting around to clock back in. Plus, I'm legitimately working my ass off at an in-the-weeds pace almost every single minute of my eight-hour shift.

But I *do* feel guilty. My coworkers are working their asses off, too, and they're better at it than I am, *and* they manage not to be late. I *really* don't want to stick out as the late girl. So I always pad my breaks with a couple of extra minutes in case the narrow path through the kitchen is obstructed, and always aim to arrive twenty or thirty minutes before my shift starts, just in case the train is delayed. So do most of my coworkers. It doesn't seem like much, but all the unpaid minutes of padding I put in to make sure I'm *never* a minute late really start adding up when it's every single day.

When I clock out at the end of my shift and go upstairs for my jacket and purse, Lalo's in the storeroom surveying the boxes stacked up to the ceiling and making notes on a clipboard. I say I'll see her tomorrow, then have to ask.

"Oh, hey—what was the deal with that lady with the burned shoulder?" I ask.

"Oh, her? She's *crazy,*" says Lalo, rolling her eyes. That woman comes in, orders a coffee, and *always* throws it at something or someone. It's annoying enough that she makes a huge mess, but she's been known to splash or even aim at workers or customers, so—*no service.*

"Jesus," I say. Getting hit by a full fresh coffee could put you in the hospital for sure. "Uh, well, thanks," I say. Lalo nods and goes back to her clipboard, clearly short on time to lean.

The entrance to the nearby BART stop is crowded with a dozen homeless people, so many that it's actually hard to get down the stairs. None of them bothers asking me for money, because, as I've been fascinated to discover, my McDonald's uniform is like an invisibility cloak when it comes to panhandlers. The whole time I work here, exactly one guy hits me up while I'm in uniform—and I don't really count him, because his "Hey, spare a cheeseburger?" was clearly meant to make me laugh.

It isn't rush hour yet, so there's a bit of a wait for the next train, but at least it isn't packed when it finally arrives. I've worked a couple of later shifts, and standing for more than half an hour on a rush-hour train *sucks.* Today I get a window seat. The view of the Golden Gate Bridge as we cross the river to Oakland hasn't lost its novelty yet; neither have the large semi-permanent tent cities under every bridge and freeway.

My commute is a blessedly straight shot, no transfers. But I'm staying so far out in Oakland that I'm only a few blocks from Berkeley, so it takes about forty minutes to get to and from work. I hated my forty-five-minute commute at SDF8 so much that I was willing to sleep at Walmart to avoid another. But unless I wanted to join one of those tent cities, this was the shortest commute I could manage in the Bay Area—and it was a miracle it was this short. The coworkers I've had a chance to talk to so far actually live several stops farther away than I do, because the cost of living in the Bay Area is *completely insane.*

San Francisco added 373,000 new jobs between 2012 and 2017 but only issued permits to build 58,000 units of new housing. Unsurprisingly, San Francisco now has the highest rents of any US city. The person I'd planned to stay with in Oakland had an emergency the week before I was supposed to arrive, and rentals in San Francisco and the close parts of Oakland were *way* more out of my price range than I'd anticipated. Even subletting a tiny bedroom in a place with roommates would run me $3,000, *minimum.*

There's been some innovative, thinking-outside-the-box solutions to

San Francisco's housing crisis, including "coliving spaces," a.k.a. dorms for adults. A depressing number of listings I looked at showed barracks-like rows of bunk beds. I actually did look into a few coliving spaces, thinking it might be an interesting window into the broke wannabe startup life. But rent on a single bunk bed would have been roughly twice my mortgage, and my money situation wasn't any better than it had been in Hickory.

Just a couple of days before my flight, I was incredibly lucky to connect with a friend of a friend of a friend—Pete, a church music director whose compensation package includes a two-bedroom apartment above the church's basketball court. He lives alone with his cat, Bartholomeow, but sometimes opens the second bedroom to people working on projects he thinks are interesting. After talking on the phone and checking with his church, he offered me the spot for free.

My bedroom's smaller than McKenna's, with a twin bed, no internet, no AC, and no functional light fixtures. The apartment's shower doesn't work, so Pete and I use the ones downstairs in the locker room. Nightly pickup basketball games go on directly underneath the apartment: I usually fall asleep to the nearly unmuffled sounds of bouncing balls, squeaking sneakers, and excited men. And I'm pretty sure Pete didn't manage to get rid of Bartholomeow's fleas before I arrived.

Still, I can't think of a better place to stay.

I started accompanying our church choir as a pianist when I was thirteen; my dad eventually joined up, too, on banjo, mandolin, and bass. It was something we did together. After college I spent most of my twenties working as a church choir director part-time, and I have a lot of fond memories from both periods. When I first met Pete—a wiry, gentle, bearded guy around my age—he was sitting on the steps of his church, practicing banjo, and I felt immediately at home. I've signed on as a temporary alto in Pete's small choir, which reminds me so much of my old choir that it makes me a little sad. Singing with them will be one of the few things that bring me pleasure during my two months in San Francisco.

On my first day at Convergys, Kimberly had each of us introduce ourselves with our names, whether we were married and/or had kids, and any hobbies we had. I was the first one to go, and I rattled off a long list of hobbies—piano, singing, painting, writing, gardening. I felt increasingly ridiculous as nearly every classmate who followed said she didn't really have any hobbies or that her hobby was her kids.

And after I get hired at McDonald's, I have to quit the choir—my work hours are just too unpredictable to commit to rehearsals or even Sunday morning services. Our schedule at McDonald's is posted less than a day before it starts, and I never have any idea how many or which hours I'll be scheduled for. It would be tough to have hobbies under these conditions, and nearly *impossible* to hold down a second job. Yet again, I can't imagine how people with kids make this work.

Number Two

Hi!" I say, looking up for the next person in line. It's lunch rush, and my feet hurt. "How can I help you?"

My suspicions were correct—the line really never ends. I've been working nearly full-time* for a couple of weeks now, and 99 percent of my time on the clock has been spent in the weeds. But the line's been crazier than usual today; Candela even looked relieved to see me when I walked in.

After a couple of weeks, I'm almost fully functional as a crew member. I can make my own drinks, assemble my own orders, call my own numbers, restock—everything in the job description, I think. I can instinctively grab a Sausage McGriddle by the color of its wrapper instead of reading the label of every single sandwich in the hot box until I find one. The head manager of our owner's several franchises took the time on a visit to mention that she's heard I'm doing great, and that I should expect to keep getting lots of hours. People apparently said I learned quickly, was easy to work with, and was fast on register.

I *am* fast on register—I can already hold my own if I'm just ringing up orders. But I'm still nowhere near as fast at assembly as veterans. So when the line gets crazy like this, I'm usually instructed to just stay on register, ringing up order after order as fast as I possibly can. It's really cramped behind the counter, and during lunch rush, people constantly bustle around

* I've been getting scheduled for between thirty and forty hours a week since I started, though never the full forty.

inches behind me, assembling and handing over the orders I take. I try to occupy as little space as possible and stay out of their way.

As lunch rush sets in, the line's already almost out the door. We're moving it as fast as we possibly can, but there just aren't enough of us. As we get further and further into the weeds, the line gets more and more irritated. You can *hear* it.

"Hi?" I say again, louder, when nobody steps forward. "I can get the next person in line over here!"

"Open up another register!" someone yells. *I wish.* It's true that only three of the four registers are open, but it's not like there's extra workers stashed in the freezer. *Sorry, lady—we're all in the same understaffed boat.*

"Hi!" I say again, trying to pitch my voice to stick out over the angry buzz of the line. *"I can help the next person over here!"* Again nobody steps forward. Impatient, I scan the crowd for someone with headphones hypnotized by their phone. But no—next in line appears to be a large gaggle of Asian tourists, eyeing me uncertainly.

"Hi!" I say, smiling and waving, motioning them forward. A designated spokesman emerges, stepping up with a tentative smile. I try not to let my exhaustion show when it becomes clear that he doesn't speak a word of English.

I usually don't mind playing charades with the no-English tourists—I honestly find them kind of charming. They're usually so happy to just *be* here, no matter how long they have to wait in line. Today, though, I just want to keep the line moving before it turns on us.

The number of foreign tourists who come in took me completely by surprise. They come from all over Europe and Asia to—judging by their shopping bags—spend thousands of dollars on high-end clothes and Apple products. Then, they come to eat at McDonald's. I get the feeling that, to much of the world, McDonald's is the ultimate authentic American experience.

Foreign tourists always order off the rich-people menu—Extra Value Meals, usually a Big Mac or a Double Quarter Pounder with cheese, usually the largest size. And they always order for here, regardless of how crowded it is or how strong the homeless smell is that day.

"Is McDonald's, like...on the checklist of things to do when you visit America?" I asked after a young guy visiting from the Philippines asked me to take a selfie with him. He roared with laughter, eventually saying that yes, it is. He was perfectly nice, but this irritated the hell out of me for some reason—not enough to refuse to pose for the photo, but enough that I didn't smile.

"Order two eight three! Two eighty-three!" calls Marisol, crossing behind me with a tray of food. I desperately try to ascertain which video of food falling in slow motion Mr. Spokestourist is pointing at before it's replaced by the next video in the rotation.

"Two eight three!" Marisol has to shout to be heard. About eight different urgent-sounding beepers and buzzers have been going off unheeded for god knows how long, creating a nerve-racking *Das Boot* atmosphere. But I'm more worried about the ambient sound of the line, which has steadily been getting louder and more hostile for the past hour.

The line sometimes feels like an entity in itself, with moods. And right now, it's on the verge of going screamer. I can hear two unhelpful women somewhere in the crowd holding a loud, performative conversation about how long the line's taking, how something smells terrible, how this is *bullshit.*

When the line gets like this, I keep thinking of a passage from *Good Omens,* one of my favorite books when I was a kid. It's a comedy by Terry Pratchett and Neil Gaiman* about a Revelation-style apocalypse, and the opening introduces us to our demon protagonist, Crowley, who's been stationed on Earth in human form for six thousand years. Crowley's somewhat "gone native" after living as a human for so long, and the efficiency-based methods of soul corruption he's developed displease his more traditional demon supervisors, Hastur and Ligur.

The three meet up to share their recent accomplishments. Hastur tempted a priest: "He would have been a saint, but within a decade we shall have him." Ligur corrupted a politician: "I let him think a tiny bribe would not hurt. Within a year we shall have him."

---

* A Gaiman-helmed miniseries adaptation starring David Tennant as Crowley will premiere in 2019 on—where else?—Amazon Prime.

They both looked expectantly at Crowley, who gave them a big smile.

"You'll like this," he said.

His smile became even wider and more conspiratorial.

"I tied up *every* portable telephone system in Central London for forty-five minutes at lunchtime," he said.

There was silence, except for the distant swishing of cars.

"Yes?" said Hastur. "And then what?"

"Look, it wasn't easy," said Crowley.

"That's all?" said Ligur.

"Look, people—"

"And exactly what has that done to secure souls for our master?" said Hastur.

Crowley pulled himself together.

What could he tell them? That twenty thousand people got bloody furious? That you could hear the arteries clanging shut all across the city? And that then they went back and took it out on their secretaries or traffic wardens or whatever, and *they* took it out on other people? In all kinds of vindictive little ways which, and here was the good bit, *they thought up themselves.* For the rest of the day. The pass-along effects were incalculable. Thousands and thousands of souls all got a faint patina of tarnish, and you hardly had to lift a finger.

I often picture Crowley as the original designer of modern scheduling software, because it frequently feels like we've been understaffed at the precise levels that will maximize human misery on both sides of the counter.

Right after I got back from Amazon, I was talking with my sister-in-law, Radhika, a lawyer and former labor organizer, and her husband, Suresh, an economist, about deliberate understaffing, how widespread a practice it is in retail and fast food, and what a huge difference it makes to a worker's experience of her job.

"So when I was scooping ice cream as a teenager, the manager actually put the schedule together on paper—was it like that for you?" I asked. Radhika, who'd had an after-school job at Jamba Juice, nodded. Suresh just shrugged. He's been pushed to study, study, study his whole life. He ended up with a freakishly masochistic work ethic and tenure at Columbia, but he never experienced a traditional McJob.

"So a couple decades ago, technology got good enough at analyzing the hour-by-hour sales data from stores for patterns, so it could make better and better forecasts about what times next week were going to be busy or slow," I said. "At the same time, scheduling switched over from being written out on paper to being done by computers. So when you combine those two new things—the forecasts and the algorithmic scheduling—you can hypothetically schedule *exactly* how many people per hour you'll need to handle the predicted business. You never have workers standing around on the clock with nothing to do. It's, like, *maximum efficiency.*

"So at Jamba Juice or wherever—you had those crappy days where someone calls out sick at the last minute?" I'd asked. Radhika did; Suresh sort of did. "They'd never *close* the Jamba Juice because a couple people called out sick, right? It'd stay open, and the skeleton crew would just do the best they could. But it would *suck.*"

That's for workers *and* customers—they get slower service even as workers push themselves to work harder and faster than usual. Exhausted workers and impatient customers tend to create a feedback loop of frustration and negativity that makes for a really miserable day.

"So at some point, someone was, like, 'Well, if people can keep the store open when someone's out with the flu, why don't they just work that hard *all* the time?' "

"So, like—*lean?*"* asked Suresh.

---

* Meaning *lean production*—the business philosophy of creating more and more value for customers using fewer and fewer resources. It's an evolution of the Toyota Production System—the reason Japan started eating American manufacturing's lunch in the 1970s. Lean retains a bunch of Japanese words like *kaizen* and *muda,* which you may recall were plastered all over SDF8. Because Jeff Bezos, along with a huge number of tech entrepreneurs, is super into lean.

"Yeah, sort of!" I said. "Except, like, *pathological* lean. It's like dieting when you're overweight versus anorexia—you keep examining yourself for more fat to get rid of, even if you're seventy pounds and look like a skeleton.

"Like, look at Walmarts—you know how they always look kind of postapocalyptic these days? Like, everything's a mess and it looks like nobody works there? *That's* what I'm talking about. It's apparently been a staffing policy from Arkansas* to only give each store manager enough labor hours for a skeleton crew for, like, a *decade*. Stores may look like garbage and working there completely sucks, but if everybody's in this constant state of trying to catch up, nobody's wasting time on the clock."

"But...why would they work faster?" Suresh had asked, looking genuinely baffled.

Radhika and I stared back at him, equally baffled.

"If they keep working faster and faster to keep up with the understaffing, then Walmart doesn't have any incentive to *stop* understaffing," explained Suresh, who has literally worked on very admirable projects involving labor and Walmart.

"It's the *line!*" Radhika said.

"Yeah, it's the *line,* dude—everybody's standing right there, *glaring* at you."

"When you've got a huge line, you don't have time to think about the big picture. You just go as fast as you can so people don't yell at you," said Radhika.

The dominant theory of economics since back in Taylor's day has been based around the idea of efficient markets and rational actors—the idea that workers, employers, consumers, and producers will consistently act in their own rational self-interest. This theory is generally known as neoclassical economics.

In economics, the shorthand for the hypothetical self-interested human is *Homo economicus.* But because we already have a Wanda, I'm going to call her Ayn.

So if Ayn's an employer, the theory goes, she'll try to get as much labor

* If something at Walmart comes "from Arkansas," it means it's straight from the company's Bentonville headquarters.

out of her workers as possible while paying them as little as possible—like Taylor. If Ayn's a worker, she'll try to get as much money as possible for as little labor as possible—like Matthias and Zeb, fully aware that Amazon needed them too much in the final days of peak to fire them over taking a covert "third break." Employers and workers bargaining for their interests eventually reach a natural balance beneficial to them both. The rising tide lifts all boats, and the world prospers.

In the free-market theory of economics, everything is naturally drawn to a mutually beneficial equilibrium as if by gravity. Workers unhappy with their pay or working conditions will find a new job. Customers unhappy with their cell phone provider's pricing or customer service will switch to another provider. An employer who wants to stay in business will raise wages or improve conditions if she's losing too many workers, and cut prices or invest in better service if she's losing too many customers. It's all very clean and elegant.

Supporters of this idea could point to Henry Ford's Crystal Palace as evidence. When we left Ford, he was trying to solve the horrendous turnover problem caused by his debut of the assembly line in 1913—workers were so miserable that he couldn't keep the Crystal Palace staffed, and it was crippling production. So in 1914, Ford announced the famous five-dollar day—a raise in wages to nearly twice what you could make elsewhere in Detroit.

There's a lot of mythology about why he did this; anything attributing it to Ford being a nice guy or something is pure bullshit. Know this: Ford *had to* offer five dollars a day to make it worthwhile to put up with the miserable conditions of the Crystal Palace.*

---

* Amazon announced in 2018 that it would raise the minimum wage at all its US facilities to $15 an hour, including for white badges. I think this is absolutely a net good, but that it's due to a cresting wave of negative PR over fulfillment center work conditions, the first major cracks in Amazon's antiunion floodwall, and the knowledge that a lot of those better-paid workers will be replaced by Kiva robots in the coming years. I am very curious to see how it affects wages at jobs that compete for the same pool of workers. But anybody who believes "niceness" or "the greater good" ever motivated a business decision by Henry Ford or Jeff Bezos needs to read more.

But the markets worked—Ford's turnover problem vanished. Other factories around Detroit—and soon the rest of the country—had to raise wages to compete for the best workers. A comfortable middle class started to form. The free market worked.

The thing about this theory of economics is that while it's very elegant, it's pretty clearly not how humans actually work. It's obvious to anybody who's *had* a line that its power over workers isn't rational. It's *animal.*

However pretentious we get, humans are still, as I believe Shakespeare once wrote, "nothin' but mammals." Because Wanda's chances of surviving your backyard are much better living in a tribe or group than alone, she's developed these beautiful, incredibly complex social tools like empathy, patience, generosity, guilt, friendship, shame, and loyalty that help hold groups of up to a couple hundred people together even when there's internal disagreements.

Some of these social tools are so old and deep that they've become something we just *feel*—they're what we call our conscience, our sense of right and wrong. Most humans implicitly understand why they shouldn't murder, torture, or hoard food while neighbors starve. Those things just feel *wrong,* repulsive.

They aren't necessarily *illogical,* though. These systems we've invented to explain the world—logic, reason, and free markets—just aren't complicated enough to mathematically factor in the *many* messy human behaviors with roots in those social tools. Instead of copping to that, though, many devotees of logic, reason, and free markets just dismiss "feelings" as the recourse of hysterics and children, even though pretty much all scientific and anecdotal evidence says that the things we feel—love, friendship, fury, sadness—are by far the most important things in most people's lives.

Every so often, though, a member of Wanda's tribe is born without access to those social tools, and is thus only capable of caring about herself. The modern term is *sociopath,* or *psychopath,* and there's an estimated one or two in every hundred people. Let's continue to call this person Ayn, because her lack of empathy makes her a real-life *Homo economicus,* acting only in her rational self-interest.

Remember, this isn't any more Ayn's *fault* than if she'd been born deaf. And for most of our history, Ayn's lack of empathy would have made her a *complete loser.* If immediate-return hunter-gatherer tribes today behave anything like they did earlier in Wanda's week, Ayn would have been ostracized for most of human history. If shaming didn't work—and why would it?—Ayn might be kicked out of the tribe. In rare circumstances, she might even be killed by the tribe as a whole. A life without access to empathy was likely to be terribly confusing, lonely, and unhappy.

That's why people like Ayn are still so rare today. Logically, total devotion to your own self-interest seems like it would be a selective evolutionary trait. But until about thirty seconds ago on the Wanda timeline, it was the exact opposite.

All those social tools we developed only really work on the small scale, though—it's as if we only have enough true empathy to extend to a couple hundred people at a time.* To grow society beyond that, we've had to figure out secondary ways to hold larger groups of humans together. Taylor recognized that the old bonds of loyalty between employer and worker couldn't keep a factory of a thousand running efficiently, so he tried to replace those with math and authority. On the large scale, it's impossible to regard every human as anything but a number.

Which is why in our modern world of free markets, Ayn's lack of empathy actually makes her *better* at surviving. She's finally found a world in which she's a *winner.* Empathy and morality are clearly vital to our species, but they're often illogical within the simple framework of free-market capitalism. They drag Wanda down like a swimmer in a prom dress while Ayn, with none of that baggage, is free to pursue efficiency and productivity in ways that Wanda would be too squeamish to consider.

Maybe Ayn uses child labor in her factories—a concept as wispy and vague as "childhood" has no value to Ayn, but access to a labor pool that's half as expensive as one populated by adults sure does. Maybe she unilaterally decides workers should be moving forty-seven tons of pig iron a day. Maybe she installs pain-medicine vending machines, or markets Oxycontin as nonaddictive, or pays her workers much, much less than what it costs to live. This is the kind of innovative thinking that makes Ayn an apex predator of the free market.

---

* For more on this, read up on Dunbar's Number.

And with the interconnectivity of global capitalism, her methods spread *everywhere* quickly. Others have to adopt them or go out of business. And so life gets marginally crappier for workers everywhere. Because it's supposed to. It's *designed* to. We are living in Ayn's world.

In 1913, the Crystal Palace was a uniquely difficult place to work. Today, though, cyborg-job technology's increasingly hard to avoid—as if every factory in Detroit introduced assembly lines at the same time.

Today, corporations have weighed the costs of high turnover against the costs of making the experience of work less miserable, and, because workers and customers are both kind of stuck with them, they choose bad service, terrible work conditions, and high turnover. It's not because it's some law of nature—it's like this because the unskilled labor pool can't vote with their feet when *everywhere* sucks.

"One oh five! One oh five!" yells Marisol, speed-walking behind me with a bag in each hand.

After an eternity, I think I have the tourists' large order down. *Close enough for lunch rush—anyway, how would they even complain?*

"Okay, is it *for here*"—I raise my eyebrows and point at the counter—"or *to go?*" I point to the door.

Mr. Spokestourist gives me the blank, nervous look of a man who knows he's just been asked a question in a language he doesn't know.

I don't know what else to do, so I try miming again. *"For here"*—I point to the counter and mime handing over a tray—"or *to go?*" I point to the door.

"Ah!" the spokesman says, understanding flashing across his face. He mirrors my *for here* motion triumphantly. I run his card and hand over the receipt, making a big show of pointing out the number at the top.

"*Three six eight*—they'll call number 368 when your order's ready. *Three six eight,*" I say, making eye contact and trying to will the information directly into his brain. I tap my ear, then the number on the receipt. "Listen for *three six eight,* okay?" He nods intently, and his group begins shuffling to one side.

"Hi!" I say, already looking up for the next person. "I can get the next person over here!"

Somewhere out there, one of the two loud angry women declares that it smells like *piss* in here. The raw hostility in her voice makes me flinch. *God, please let me not get them.*

"Hi!" I try to keep the anxiety out of my smile as a middle-aged white guy in a suit steps up to my register. "What can I get for you?" He orders and pays for a Big Mac Extra Value Meal with blessed efficiency. The entire transaction probably takes me about fifteen seconds.

It's totally unfair, but I've started to resent customers who save money by ordering complicated combinations of stuff off the poor-people menu and using coupons, which is time-consuming on my end. I'm much happier to get rich customers, who usually order simple Extra Value Meals and pay with credit cards.

"Order one oh six!" yells Marisol, crossing behind me with a tray.

"Okay, here you go," I say, smiling as I pull the suit's receipt from the printer and hand it across the counter. "They'll call number 369 when your order's ready—thanks a lot!" My eyes flick up over his shoulder, looking for the next person in line.

"Actually," he says, not moving, "could you make the Diet Coke now? I'm really thirsty."

"Sure, no problem," I say, though it's obviously kind of a problem. I'm supposed to stay on register until the line lets up. And I've already put the guy's order through, so it's too late to note that I'm making his drink separately, which means it'll tangle up the workflow.

But I get it—I'm really thirsty myself, actually. I want to help him, to make him happy. So I spin around and step over to the drink station, grab a medium cup, dip it full of ice, then pause and wait for my turn at the Diet Coke spigot. I pivot to grab a lid in the meantime, which puts me right into Marisol's path as she carries two overloaded trays. She swerves around me, keeping her balance, but it's a close call.

"*No!* I said *stay on register,*" she says over her shoulder, frustrated.

"Sorry!" I yelp. I abandon the cup of ice and step back over to my register, where the suit stands, waiting.

"Sorry, I guess I can't," I say, giving a rueful smile that I hope will work. "They'll call your number when your order's ready. It'll only be a couple minutes, promise."

I look over his shoulder for the next person in line, but the suit raises his eyebrows and doesn't move.

"Uh, can't you just finish my drink?"

He had to have seen that; he was literally three feet away.

"Three six eight! Number three six eight!" yells Marisol, crossing behind me again.

"Come on come on come *on,* hurry *up!*" yells one of the angry women. She sounds close now.

"Oh—I'm really sorry, but my boss just told me I have to stay on register. They'll call your number in just a second." I look over his shoulder again, willing him to move.

But he doesn't. "Seriously? It'll take, like, two seconds."

I'm *not* getting any further onto Marisol's bad side so this dude can get his Diet Coke half a minute earlier than he'd get it otherwise.

"Three sixty-eight, three six eight!" shouts Marisol.

"Uh, sorry—I *can't.* I shouldn't have told you I could when it was this busy. Sorry," I say. "It'll be out fast, I promise."

"Three! Six! Eight!" yells Marisol.

"Come on," the guy says, looking angry. "Just give me my Diet Coke."

"No," I say flatly, then hold up a "one second" finger and turn to Marisol.

"Hey, *mamá!*" I point out the cluster of Asian tourists. "It's them, over there; they're 368—no English." I wave to catch Mr. Spokestourist's eye and try to mime that Marisol has his food, then turn back to the suit, who's glaring.

For a bizarre second, I draw a complete blank on why he's still standing there and what he wants. I rack my brain, panicked, and finally come up with *Diet Coke.*

"Sorry," I say, trying to make it sound final as I give him my very blankest stare. "They'll call your number." Then I pointedly look over his shoulder and yell, "Hi! I can help the next person in line!"

The suit gives me a shitty look but finally moves out of the way, grumbling. I don't have time to feel bad about being rude.

"Let's go, let's go, let's *go,* I've been waiting *forever!*" says the woman who steps up to my register. She's black, middle-aged, and wearing a security guard's uniform. Her voice is definitely the one that had been yelling that it smelled like piss in here. *Goddammit.*

"I'm *really* sorry about the wait. What can I get for you?"

The woman glares and starts dictating her order, which, to my dismay, involves a lot of special instructions.

A surprising number of customers seem to fundamentally misunderstand how fast food works. The suit will probably get his meal within a minute, even with this long a line—his order was simple and unaltered, and Big Macs are such a popular item that the kitchen always has a few extras ready to go in the hot box. I gather that some algorithm predicts the number of McNuggets, Big Macs, and other popular items we'll sell every hour of each day, and tells the kitchen exactly how many extra Big Macs to make so one's always ready to go when you reach for it, but not so many that any languish in the hot box for more than a couple of minutes.

This was Ray Kroc's original "assembly line" theory of fast food—simple and standardized, with food made in anticipation of customer orders rather than in response to them.

Henry Ford was able to achieve amazing production numbers with the Model T because every car was identical, with standard parts, constructed exactly the same way every time. Model Ts came in exactly one color, because black paint dried the fastest—a microcosm of Ford's fetish for standardization.

The menu Kroc used to take McDonald's national was similarly minimalist, with exactly three food items—Pure Beef Hamburger, fifteen cents; Tempting Cheeseburger, nineteen cents; Golden French Fries, ten cents. He aimed to make his burger construction line as standardized and closely measured as the Crystal Palace, decreeing, among other things, that McDonald's burger patties must weigh 1.6 ounces and measure 3.875 inches in diameter. Don't like a quarter ounce of onions on your burger? Too bad, just scrape 'em off—custom orders slow things down, and speed was the whole point. That's why they call it *fast food.*

Then Burger King countered with "Have it your way" in the '80s, and to compete, McDonald's started broadening its menu and allowing for special orders. Today, the average McDonald's menu has more than a hundred items, and special orders are commonplace. But customers never changed their expectations of miraculously instantaneous service to match the vastly more complicated menu crew members are working with.

So a lot of people who've experienced the magic of getting a Big Mac seconds after ordering it seem to believe there's some Star Trek machine in the back that zaps food into existence from nothing. At least, that's the only reason I can think of that customers like this lady get so mad when their special orders take an extra minute or two.*

"Come on come on come on come on come *on,* I've got to *go!*" the angry woman yells, startling me by slapping the counter for emphasis. My heart rate jumps into high gear, and I feel the blood rushing to my face. I try to breathe slowly and focus on getting her stupid ever-changing order through.

"If you can't get it out right away, just give me my money back!" the woman yells, though she hasn't even paid yet. She keeps making changes to her order, and, after five of them, I have to flag down Marisol for her manager-approval password. The short wait doesn't go over great.

Finally, I take the woman's payment and hand over her receipt and change, but she doesn't step to the side.

"*No!* I'm not waiting any longer!" She jabs a finger at me. "*You* get me my food, *right now!*"

I grit my teeth. I don't like rewarding asshole behavior, but *whatever.* I have to get this woman out of my face before I flip into overdrive, and it's not going to take much more yelling to do that. My hands are already shaking as I turn and hurriedly start assembling her order. This time, everybody gets out of *my* way—I get the impression everyone's been keeping a wary eye on the situation.

"Hurry up hurry up hurry *up!*" the woman yells, slapping the counter again as I put a lid on her drink, grab a tray, put the drink on it, and carry it over to the hot box. Her special orders, unsurprisingly, aren't out yet. I get her fries in the meantime, but that only takes a few seconds. There's still no special orders when I get back to the hot box, so I have to just stand there as the woman harangues my apparent idleness.

"Hey, *mamá?*" I yell through the window after a few seconds.

"Eh?" Crispina, a grandmotherly Filipina, hears the panic in my voice and appears in the little window between counter and kitchen. From my few brief exchanges with her, I gather Crispina isn't entirely fluent in

* Ditto customers who get mad because their Big Mac was premade and waiting in the hot box, a.k.a. "not fresh."

English, but she always greets me by name and is actively friendly—more than most people in this lonely, crowded place. I've gotten attached to her in the desperate way of the friendless.

"You got a special order coming?" I ask, jerking my head at the screamer, who continues to yell. Crispina peers past me, then gives a sympathetic grimace I interpret as *yikes.* She holds up a finger, disappears, and returns to the window with...oh, thank god, the woman's special orders.

"Thanks, *mamá!*" I say, relieved, plunking this last piece of the order onto the tray. Crispina smiles, giving me a thumbs-up, and disappears back into the kitchen.

I return to my register with the tray and try to hand it over to the screamer, but she won't take it.

"Never mind, this is taking too long—put it in a bag!"

I briefly wonder what would happen if I tried to charge the screamer fifteen cents for the bag and resolve not to find out. Instead I turn around, grab a bag, whip it open, and carefully start transferring her food into it. She supervises me with narrowed eyes as I bag her food. If my disgusting hands touch her fries, she says, I'll just have to go back and get her new fries.

Finally, I give her the bag, praying that she'll leave.

"Honey mustard! Get me honey mustard!" she barks, and my fists clench tighter. I am *definitely* not trying to tell this woman that dipping sauces are a quarter each, so I duck down under the register, grab a tub of honey mustard, lean over the counter, and hold it out.

"In the bag," she says, not taking it from me. I drop it into the bag.

"More than that," she says, glaring as if she's caught me trying to cheat her. I pause, transfixed by hatred, then whip back down under the register and emerge with a handful of honey mustards—more than anyone could possibly need. *Whatever; take it out of my paycheck.*

I lean forward to drop the fistful of mustards in her bag. My hands are shaking with fury, it's an awkward number of sauces to hold, and I'm moving fast, so it's not a huge surprise that one pops out of my hand and bounces across the counter.

The screamer gasps. Then, quick as a shortstop, she scoops it up and wings it at my chest, hard. The packaging explodes; honey mustard splatters all over me and the surrounding area. And I'm fucking *done.*

"HEY, *FUCK YOU,* LADY!" The yell comes from someplace deep in my brain stem as I jump back. "WHAT THE *FUCK?*"

"SHE THREW MUSTARD AT ME!" the woman screams, pointing at me. "EVERYBODY SAW IT!"

"I saw it! That girl threw mustard at her!" her friend yells from two registers over.

"I—DID—*NOT!*" I scream back, stepping forward, planting my clenched fists on the counter. This is *my* space. My body vibrates with more violent energy than it feels possible to contain. The only thing in the *world* I want to do is launch myself over the counter like a jungle cat and *show these fucking assholes that they can't just fucking treat people like this*—

I blink, and realize everyone's staring at me.

A single person screaming at the sky, pigeons, pedestrians, service workers—that's old hat in San Francisco. But when it comes from someone on the other side of a counter? Apparently, that's something to gawk at.

I want to scream "THE *FUCK* ARE YOU ALL LOOKING AT?" But my brain has reasserted control of my body. So instead I throw up my hands, turn around, and storm back into the kitchen, where I don't have to look at all their stupid fucking faces.

Alarms continue to go off in the kitchen like we're all trapped in a sinking submarine together. The noise is fucking unbearable; I keep walking back and back trying to escape it, going as fast as I can manage on the treacherously greasy floor. When I get all the way to the walk-in freezer in the very back, I go in and slam the door behind me.

Kolbi said that her Chick-fil-A crew went in their walk-in freezer when they needed to calm down; now I totally get it. The thick, insulated door cuts off the *Das Boot* beeping, and the only noise in here is the Zen-like perfect-fifth hum of the freezer and my rapid breath, coming out in little panicky clouds. I look around to make sure there's nobody else back here and realize my glasses are speckled with mustard. I try to wipe them on a clean patch of shirt, but the specks just merge into a sticky, blurry smear. This, for some reason, is more than I can handle.

"God fucking dammit! Fuck!" I scream, hoping the soundproofing works both ways. I can actually *see* the scream for a second, drifting upward as it

dissipates. My red-hot fight-or-flight energy is quickly dissipating, too; I can feel that familiar exhausted emptiness looming up in its place.

Idiot. You don't even have the self-control to make it three weeks without fucking it all up. And now you're going to cry at work. Again.

Feeling utterly defeated, I lean against the freezing wall and let myself weep with rage and frustration.

The cold definitely speeds the process of coming out of overdrive. As my heartbeat slows, the temperature gets less comfortable. After a minute or two, I'm shivering and feeling more and more guilty about deserting my post during lunch rush.

Your coworkers are getting slammed right now because they have to cover for a stupid, spoiled, selfish brat with no self-control. Get up, you fucking baby. Get up. Get up!

I fumble the door open with numb fingers and flinch as the wall of noise slams back into place. I can hear order numbers being shouted over the disgruntled white noise of the line and beeping alarms as I walk back up through the kitchen to poke my head out and survey the situation.

Mustard Woman seems to be gone, thank god, though I do spot her friend in animated conversation with Marisol, who's nodding and writing on a clipboard. With the crew down me *and* Marisol, the line has gotten even longer, and while nobody's shouting, the hive mind is audibly discontent.

Come on, you fucking baby. Millions of people do this every single day. Suck it up.

I force myself forward, dodging frantic coworkers carrying bags and drinks and trays at top speed as I work my way back into position behind my register. I stare down at the glowing touchscreen, weirdly mesmerized for a couple of seconds. Then I exhale and look up, searching, to make eye contact with whoever the fuck is next in line.

"Hi!" I say, but the word comes out a choked whisper. I clear my throat and try again. "Hi, I can help the next person in line!"

But I can't.

TIGER TIGER TIGER shrieks my body, nonsensically, as the next customer approaches. I feel my face flush and my throat close back up. I reflexively step backwards, barely registering when I bump directly into someone.

Keep it together, you spoiled fucking baby. How fucking hard is it to take an order?

"Hi, what can—" I try again, but the words come out halfway between a sob and a croak, barely understandable. I try to smile, but tension makes my face grotesque. I cough and pretend to duck down to fiddle with something under the counter, panicking at the possibility of crying in front of everyone. *In . . . out . . . in . . . out . . .*

I emerge a few seconds later with a handful of straws to restock the bin, then attempt another smile at the totally normal, unthreatening woman at my register.

"Hi, how may I—" But my throat again closes up halfway through the sentence. The woman looks confused.

"Excuse me," I say, taking another deep breath. "How can I help—"

Goddammit.

"I'm sorry—" I choke out, then turn around and flee back through the kitchen.

What the fuck?

I run all the way upstairs to the bathroom this time. I splash cold water on my face, then rest my hands on the sink and stare at my reflection. My face is mauve, my eyes are red-rimmed, and there's mustard in my hair.

When I come back downstairs, having gotten most of the mustard off, Marisol's waiting for me with her clipboard at the bottom of the stairs. She's writing me up.

My behavior was completely unacceptable, she says. We're in business because of customers, and we have to be polite no matter *what* they do. It reflects poorly on managers when something like this happens. How can they trust me when I can't control my temper? I have to be able to just walk away. I repeat "I'm really sorry; I know; it won't happen again" over and over, my voice still shaky with nerves.

Ninety-five percent of me really means it—my behavior *was* obviously unprofessional and unacceptable. I *am* ashamed that I let my temper get the best of me.

But a sliver of me whispers, *This is fucking ridiculous.* I'm outraged. I'm *furious. She* threw mustard at *me,* so *I'm* getting punished? *Fuck this.*

But I suppress that voice, telling Marisol over and over that I understand what I did wrong and that it'll never happen again. But I didn't *choose* to yell; I'm pretty sure I won't be able to choose *not* to yell the next time something like this happens.

Finally her tone softens a little, and she says she knows customers can be difficult sometimes. It's hard. But I *have* to be able to walk away. She hands me the clipboard and a pen, telling me to sign at the bottom, and looks impatient when I insist on reading it first. Her written account downgrades what I said to a mere "What the hell," a kindness that surprises me. But it also states that *I* threw food at the woman and doesn't mention that she threw food at me. It seems to be based entirely on the friend's testimony.

I know it doesn't really matter, but for some reason I'm *deeply* invested in setting the record straight. I insist that I didn't throw anything, and that it's pertinent that I lost my temper after *she threw mustard at me*. Marisol rolls her eyes but amends the report to reflect my side of the story, too. I still feel like I'm being set up but sign at the bottom anyway—we both need to get back to lunch rush.

"Has anyone ever thrown something at you?" I ask.

She looks at me with genuine surprise, as if she didn't realize I was *this* stupid, then says *of course* people have thrown stuff at her. And she *walked away.*

"How do you—like, how do *you* do it?" I ask. "When someone's up in your face screaming, when someone throws stuff at you—how do you keep it together? Is there...I don't know, is there a trick to it?"

She stares as if I've asked her if there's a trick to breathing, then sighs and drops the stern manager act for a second.

"You just *do.* You've got a family to support—you just think of your family, and you *walk away.*"

God, you're so spoiled, I think to myself, feeling worse than ever. *You don't have any real responsibilities—not like Marisol, not like Candela, not like everyone else here. You never learned to control your temper because you've never really had to.*

But that tiny, furious voice hisses, *No! That's bullshit! Nobody should have to trade her last scrap of dignity for her family. This isn't how things should be. This isn't right.*

One last time, I promise Marisol I'll do better. She looks me up and down, takes in my shakiness, and lets out an exasperated sigh.

"Just...take lunch now," she says.

"Okay," I say, immensely relieved. "Thanks." I turn to go back upstairs and get my stuff.

"No!" Marisol says, frustrated. "Go clock out first!"

"Right, sorry," I say.

The rest of the shift *sucks.* I feel hollow and exhausted, and it's hard to smile. The line stays angry the whole time, but I keep finding myself on the verge of tears during normal interactions with perfectly polite customers. I must look insane. I'm desperate to leave by the end of my shift.

Upstairs, Dalisay's eating while waiting to start her shift. She's part of the Filipino crew, and I'd guess she's in her midtwenties—I don't know her particularly well. But I know her a little better than most of my other coworkers. She speaks American-accented English, so we work side by side on register a lot, and she's always been kind to me.

When Dalisay sees me, her face goes sympathetic.

"Hey, I heard what happened! I'm so sorry!"

"Yeah, it sucked." Dalisay is the first person other than Marisol I've had a chance to talk to about Mustard Lady, and for some reason I really, *really* want to make sure the gossip record is straight. It all comes spilling out.

Dalisay stands up, her body language sort of suggesting she's offering a hug. I'm so desperate for one that I just go for it.

"I'm sorry," she says, patting my back awkwardly. "They can be so cruel."

Number Three

A lot of people have asked which of the three jobs in this book was worst. It's still tough to answer, because it's like apples and oranges, but I think I'd rank the maddening isolation and physical pain of SDF8 as slightly worse than Convergys's screamers and frantic multitasking.

But until Mustard Lady, McDonald's wasn't even in the running. I really do get satisfaction from helping people, even just with their lunch. I liked the regulars. I liked playing charades with tourists. I liked helping homeless people hack the menu. I liked teasing people who came in reeking of weed to order fifteen cookies. I liked becoming competent at my job. I liked making people happy.

After Mustard Lady, it's gotten harder to enjoy any of that.

For some reason, the news of my losing my temper spreads like wildfire. For a few days, every crew member I have a second to talk to wants to hear my version of what happened. I continue to really, *really* need my coworkers to understand that *she* threw mustard at *me* and not vice versa, so I explain over and over, somewhat defensively. But everybody who's worked register seems to have had a lot of experiences just like mine. In fact, they seem surprised that this was my first.

I start asking what people have thrown at *them*. The list encompasses pretty much everything in the store—wrapped burgers, unwrapped burgers, burger patties, McNuggets, smoothies, full sodas, napkins, straws, sauces, fries, apple pies, ice cream cones...I gasp when one woman says she was once hit point-blank by a cup of hot coffee. I wonder later if it'd been thrown by the woman with the burn scar.

I also start asking how people keep from losing their temper when someone hits them with food. Everyone has a lot of thoughts to share.* They're more sympathetic than Marisol, but their advice is the same: Think of your family and *walk away*. You can't let them get to you.

And I take their advice. After Mustard Lady, some part of me finally accepts that you need walls between you and the customers to survive here, and I start building them. I still do everything I'm supposed to, of course. I just... stop *caring*. Caring makes you vulnerable.

It's actually hard to break the habit at first. But going the extra mile just *doesn't make sense*. The extra energy it takes for me to do a *very* good job benefits the customers, our franchise owner, and the McDonald's brand—and I get nothing but exhaustion in return. Good-faith effort is just too complicated to measure, and therefore doesn't exist to the fingerprint time clock and staffing algorithms. Even if I were gunning for a promotion, managers barely earn more than crew members. The only reward is in owning a franchise, not working at one.

So I wise up. I become less sympathetic and more skeptical about customer problems—and it works. I get better at shaking off unpleasant customers like Mustard Lady. I get harder and more pragmatic, like my coworkers. Like Ayn. Like a robot.

But empathy is a two-sided coin. The shield protects me from screamers, but it also appears to filter out any satisfaction I used to get from making people happy. Without that, and without much opportunity to form friendships with coworkers, my shifts become hour after hour of mechanical movement at top speed, saying the same words and performing the same motions over and over and over. I start really dreading my shifts.

---

* One sweetheart assistant manager has so much sympathy and advice that by the time I extract myself from the conversation, I'm three minutes late punching back in after lunch and get yelled at by Marisol.

Chronic stress destroys the human body. What it does to the human mind is much more interesting in the context of postrecession America.*

A lot of the experimental research on the effects of chronic stress was and is done on animals, particularly rats. As you know, the stress response evolved so long ago that its neurophysiology is about the same in all vertebrates, and scientists can create very good models of human disorders like depression and PTSD in laboratory animals. Human antidepressants were developed through testing on depressed rats† because they work essentially the same way in both species. There's actually veterinary spinoffs of drugs used to treat stress, anxiety, and depression in humans—Prozac, for example—that are chemically the same as the human versions. The point here is that the effects of chronic stress on rats are *extremely relevant* to the effects of chronic stress on humans.

The study of stress as a physiological response originated when a young assistant professor, Hans Selye, discovered it by accident in the 1930s.

Selye had been running an experiment that involved injecting one group of laboratory rats with a hormone and injecting another control group with saline. He was puzzled when *all* the rats—control and experimental—had terrible stomach ulcers by the end of the experiment. Neuroscientist Kelly Lambert describes the realization that made Selye the father of stress research in her book *The Lab Rat Chronicles:*

> If [Selye] had to be honest with himself, he wasn't the most competent rat handler. While he was injecting them, he sometimes squeezed a little too tightly. Owing to his anxiety, he sometimes dropped the

---

* Because I do eventually need to get back to McDonald's, I'm barely grazing the surface in this section. If this interests you, the book *Scarcity: Why Having Too Little Means So Much* is a decent primer.

† For the scientists reading this: no, rats technically don't get *depressed*—that word is only applied to humans. For simplicity's sake, though, I'll sometimes use the term *depressed rat* when I mean *rat with an experimental model of human depression.*

> rats, which meant he had to chase them around the room with a broom so he could finish the experiment. Thus the rats in this study were getting more than a dose of a hormonal extract—they were getting a pretty heavy dose of terror as well. The control animals endured the same unpleasant circumstances as did the experimental animals, explaining why, regardless of the type of injection, all the rats exhibited similar symptoms.

Since then, much of our understanding of chronic stress comes from *intentionally* doing unpleasant things to rats that you obviously can't do to humans—giving them electric shocks, dropping them in a container of water with no way to get out, making them live with a robot roommate programmed to bully them, dissecting their brains, etc. And this kind of research has nailed down the crucial elements of body- and mind-wrecking stress: *lack of predictability* and *lack of control.*

To demonstrate, let's replicate a famous series of experiments done on rats by J. M. Weiss[1] in the 1970s.

Put Rat A in a box with an electrified floor and give her unpredictable shocks: she'll develop the same stress-related symptoms Selye observed in the rats he had to chase around the lab with a broom.

Now put Rat B in the same situation, except play a beep ten seconds before you shock her: she'll end up with ulcers, too, but far fewer of them. Rat B can't *avoid* the shock, but she at least can relax until she hears the dreaded beep. That predictability helps her deal with the stress better.

Now give Rat C the same setup as Rat B—box, shocks, beeps—but add a button she can push after hearing the warning beep that will cancel the shock: she'll end up with *dramatically* fewer ulcers than either of the other two. Even that little bit of control Rat C has helps her deal with the stress much, much better than either of the others.

Later experiments went beyond counting rat terror-ulcers into the subtler behavioral and chemical effects of stress. To test your cure for cancer on rats, you first have to give a bunch of rats cancer; to test an antidepressant on rats, you need a reliable method of giving rats a pretty good approximation of human depression.

This feels weird, even to me. Depression has always felt like such a complex, mysterious, *human* thing. The idea that a scientist can just *give* it to a lab rat like a virus feels wrong.

But it's not. There's actually lots of ways to "infect" a rat with depression, though some are more efficient than others. A frequently cited 1992 paper[2] reviewing the best methods concludes that you don't actually want to traumatize or terrify your rats, like Selye accidentally did. The closest approximation of the depression that plagues modern humans can be achieved by bombarding lab rats with mild but chronic, random, and inescapable stress. You don't have to terrify them—just remove predictability and control from their lives, and they'll eventually lose interest in pleasurable things. When they do, you're ready to test whether your experimental antidepressant will get them interested again.

"Losing interest in pleasure" so perfectly described my own gray years that it was kind of surreal to read it in the sterile, clinical context of a scientific paper about rats. I found the characterization of the best stressors as "mild" to be oddly affecting, too—I put off going to a doctor much longer than I should have because I didn't think I'd really "earned" the right to have PTSD or depression, a feeling that's apparently very common. I wasn't a soldier or a refugee—nothing *that* bad had happened to me.

But trauma *isn't* the best method of creating a model of depression. All you have to do is remove control and predictability—the exact things low-wage workers have been forced to sacrifice in the name of corporate efficiency and flexibility. Is it any surprise that it feels like the country's losing its collective mind? It would be more surprising if we *weren't.*

Number Four

"Hi," I say loudly, making eye contact with the next person in line. "I can get the next person over here!" A middle-aged white man in a suit approaches my register.

"Hi," I say again, smiling at him. My feet hurt. "What can I get for you?"

It's been another long day, but they're all long days. I've stopped being surprised by the never-ending line, too—the schedule is obviously engineered to keep a line all day, every day. Understaffing is the new staffing.

The man doesn't return my smile. Instead, he glares as if I'm in the principal's office.

"What happened to 'Hello, how may I help you?'" he asks, raising his eyebrows.

I stare for a second, keeping my face carefully blank.

One more rat fact: So put Rat A in a shock box with no predictability and no possibility of escape—she'll develop physical and behavioral stress ailments similar to those of humans.

Do the same to Rat B, but give her a stick to gnaw on* after getting a shock—she'll develop fewer stress symptoms.

Now do the same to Rat C, but instead of giving her a stick to bite, give her an incapacitated rat to bite—Rat C will develop even fewer stress symptoms than A *or* B.

The experiment doesn't mention what effect this has on the incapacitated

---

* Gnawing on sticks is the rat equivalent of a hobby.

rat that Rat C vents her frustrations on, but I sometimes deeply identify with her. I've been trying to develop more compassion for screamers, mostly in hopes that it'll reduce their ability to stress me out. I've experienced that spinning loss of control myself, after all, honking like a maniac as the precious seconds until Convergys's system automatically marks me late tick away. Screamers, I think, are just people under more stress than they can bear.

In my previous life as a newspaper reporter, it wasn't uncommon for people to flip out at public meetings or hearings and go true screamer on the school board or a zoning commission. *Every time* I'd strike up a conversation with that screamer afterward, I'd find that they were dealing with some combination of money, health, work, or family stress that left me speechless. It's as if going screamer was just briefly venting the constant hell inside themselves.

I look at the guy at my register. His suit isn't cheap, and he looks like he gets as much time at lunch as he wants. But maybe his kids don't talk to him anymore. Maybe he's underwater on his mortgage. Maybe he's dying of cancer. Maybe he's been closeted for decades. Maybe he screams into a pillow every night, or maybe this show of sanctimony is the only scream he's capable of. Maybe his interactions with service workers are the only times he feels in control of his life.

He's only biting you because his life is a series of unpredictable electrocutions, I tell myself. *His body thinks it's the end of the world, and you know exactly how bad that feels. Be kind.*

"I *said,* What happened to 'Hello, how may I help you?'" the guy repeats, louder.

My smile tightens. Empathy's well and good. But again, I get that feeling of total certainty: if I force myself to say "Hello, how may I help you?" to this man, a sliver of my soul will be tarnished in a way I'm not sure is reversible.

I think of Marisol. "You just *do,*" she'd said, as if I were an idiot. "You've got a family to support—you just think of your family and you *walk away.*" To work here this long, she must have chosen her family over herself countless times.

Since I was a teenager scooping ice cream, I've had a little voice whispering contrarian ideas in my ear.

This is some bullshit.
If buying a few drinks at a dive karaoke joint is a splurge, your job does not actually pay well!
If you describe your workplace as oppressive, you don't actually love your job!
People shouldn't have to live like this.
How can you not see that you deserve more?

The whisper comes from whatever it is inside me that gets angry when things are unfair, and thinks it's possible to change things for the better. It's what briefly hijacked my body to scream "HEY, *FUCK YOU,* LADY!" It's the part of me that likes to help people, and can be hurt by them. It's what makes me able to experience pleasure and fury—the exact part that went missing during my gray years of depression. It's the idea that the world can be *better.* It's the expectation that the world *should* be better.

I'd be a better employee without this little voice. If I hadn't graduated from a good college, or had been born below the middle class, or had children very young, I'd probably have spent the last decade and a half struggling to sandpaper this troublemaking part of myself down to nothing.

Che Guevara famously said, "If you tremble with indignation at every injustice, then you are a comrade of mine." But *goddamn,* indignation is exhausting, and it'll get you fired right quick. Comrades of Che wouldn't last a second in fast food—they'd get fired, quit, or end up about as sane as Mustard Lady.

But me? My cage has had a button marked *I get to leave* the whole time. So I haven't yet had to get rid of my little voice, my rage, my hope, my indignation, my unrealistic expectation of being treated like a human being. I'm not Marisol. I get to leave. So I don't have to stand here and let this sour-faced suit chip off a piece of my soul.

"Sorry?" I say. I smile apologetically, cupping a hand around one ear.

"I said, What happened to 'Hello, how may I help you?'" he says again, louder.

I give another embarrassed smile and lean closer, over the counter. "I'm so sorry, sir, I didn't catch that either—what did you say?"

"I *said,* What happened to 'Hello, how may I help you?'" he says, starting to look really irritated.

"I'm really sorry, sir, but I still didn't hear you," I say, my face utterly blank. "Try me one more time?"

Go ahead, fuckface—I can do this all day.

"Are you *deaf?* I *said*—" the suit begins, but then gives up with maximum melodrama. He throws up his hands, rolls his eyes, heaves a loud sigh, and mutters, *"Never mind,"* but then finally deigns to give me his order. I get it perfectly the first time.

I'm still pissed off long after the guy's gone, and I'm sure I passed that tarnish along to other customers. I'd guess other service workers and underlings he encountered that day also suffered the knock-on effects of my passive aggression. It's the price other people pay so I can keep that little piece of my soul.

We're never really *out* of the weeds here, but it's been so bad today that I don't get my lunch until, like, two o'clock. I'm ravenous by the time I take off my visor and start weaving my way through the crowd toward the front door, where a homeless man is digging through the trash bins.

This happens a lot, but it's usually quick and discreet. This guy, an ancient white man, is aggressively mentally ill, and he hums and babbles to himself while merrily pulling things out of the trash and tossing them over his shoulder. The sizable pile on the floor behind him suggests he's been at it for a while.

The customers are giving this frail guy a wide berth, which is no small thing. It might be the flying trash, or the sharp smell of weeks-old urine, or the disconcerting way his chatter sometimes gets startlingly loud for a few seconds. I don't recognize any words in the eerie half-sung monologue, though it might be because he's slurring and doesn't have any teeth.

I look back up to the counter. The line's blocking the view. The sizable pile of trash on the floor is starting to obstruct the door. I feel bad for Juan, who's going to have a bigger and bigger mess to clean up the longer this guy keeps doing this.

Do not even consider donating your unpaid lunch time to this.

I start to walk around him to the door, but then the guy lunges at a regular I like, yelling an indecipherable question and clearly frightening her. I look back up at the counter, but nobody's going to notice this situation anytime soon. I sigh.

You idiot.

"Hang on; I'll be right back," I say to the general area, then elbow my way back up to the counter. I feel bad for Juan and the customers, so I'll get rid of the crazy guy. I feel bad for the crazy guy, so I'll do it myself.

I've only had to kick homeless people out a couple of times—both of them in situations like this, when I was on my way in or out and ran into someone who was scaring customers or making a huge mess. Both times I felt so bad about the homeless person's obvious mental illness that I tried to do it as gently as possible. My coworkers' standard method—shouting and/or waving a broom—is much more efficient, and I'd have to drop this affectation for sure to work here long-term. But I don't have to.

"Hi," I say, approaching the guy cautiously. He's even older than I thought. I wonder if he has any family. The guy glances at me, scowls, and resumes digging and tossing.

"Hey, I brought you some water," I say, holding up the cups I grabbed from the fridge. Our free waters are comically tiny, barely bigger than Dixie cups, but you get what you pay for. He looks at me suspiciously.

"You know you can't be going through the trash," I say, trying to sound firm but nonthreatening. "You're scaring people, and you're making a mess. I was just about to go have a cigarette—would you walk me out?"

He takes the waters with narrowed eyes but puts them down and goes back to rummaging and tossing, increasing the volume of his nonsense song. I sigh, pretty sure this guy doesn't understand language anymore.

This is not your problem. Go eat your lunch.

But for some illogical reason, I give it one more try.

"Come on. Juan's gonna have to clean up this mess, and he's really nice," I say, gesturing to the door. "Somebody's going to come chase you out or call the police if you don't leave on your own. Please walk out with me?"

With a speed that startles the hell out of me, the guy sticks his face right up in mine and screams as long and loud as he can, like the T. rex in *Jurassic Park*. He screams all the air in his lungs directly into my face, going alarmingly red. But when he's done, he walks out, leaving me alone in a ring of staring customers.

Way to donate your break time and safety to a multibillion-dollar company, my little voice whispers. *You're such a team player. You've got such a great work ethic. You idiot.*

I don't know if it's crazy-guy germs or just bad luck, but a couple of days later I come down with a nasty cold/flu and have to call out of a few shifts. Candela is less than pleased, but because this is San Francisco, I *can* call out sick without fear of losing my job. If I'd been working there a little longer, I'd even have been able to call out sick without losing the day's wages.* But the next schedule after I call out sick, I only get fifteen hours instead of my usual thirty to thirty-five.

Cutting someone's hours is a common punishment in fast food and retail—and the subject of an important class-action suit currently in the works against McDonald's. In 2014, the National Labor Relations Board brought seventy-eight charges against McDonald's and some of its franchise operators for punishing workers who'd participated in Fight for $15 protests by, among other things, cutting their hours.

But this lawsuit, which is still in progress, is about more than just hours.

I've been serving the customers of huge corporations—Amazon, AT&T, and McDonald's. Those corporations have made the rules I follow, set the quotas I need to hit, and supplied the technology that gives them incredible top-down power to micromanage my days.

But I haven't technically worked *for* any of them. I was always employed by a third party—Integrity Staffing Solutions, then Convergys, and now this franchise's owner. Hypothetically, Amazon, AT&T, and McDonald's had no responsibility or liability for my work conditions, wages, or work-incurred injuries. The corporate-middleman phenomenon is a very common loophole to avoid accountability in the modern job market, and the McDonald's lawsuit might mark the beginning of the end of that.

My hours got cut. Who knows why? It could have been punishment for calling out sick, or the mustard incident, or my occasional minutes of

---

* Paid sick leave needs to be the law, *everywhere*. Whether it's *morally* disgusting to punish workers for staying home when they're sick is debatable, though I know what side I come down on. But the current situation, which incentivizes coughing, sneezing, contagious, open-MRSA-sores workers to suck it up and get that paycheck, is just objectively *disgusting*.

lateness, or my requesting a day off to attend a political protest.* Or maybe it's just that there's two new people training on register whom they want to get up to speed. It was always busy; I kept forgetting to ask.

Frankly, I don't miss the extra hours. I've gotten passably competent at the job itself, but my research has hit a plateau. I'm not getting any additional insight into the mysterious scheduling algorithms and tech that run the store—I just operate like an efficient machine for nearly every minute of every shift. I've asked a few questions during those rare minutes of *time to lean,* but the answer is always "Don't worry about it."

This is to say: I was pretty ready to go home *before* the fucking Szechuan sauce.

* Milo Yiannopoulos's second, abortive free-speech rally at Berkeley—his first appearance there a few months before had sparked literal riots in the streets, and I thought going might be interesting for the book. (It wasn't.) Under my no-lying policy, I wrote "protest" as the reason for my time-off request. Lalo approved it but looked at me like I was insane, then asked out of nowhere whether I had kids. Afterward, so many coworkers *also* asked out of nowhere if it was true that I didn't have kids that I suspect gossip may have pegged me as frivolous.

Number Five

Hi," I say, looking up at my first customers of the day, a group of young tech guys in hoodies. I swallow a yawn. The basketball game underneath my bedroom went late last night, and I dragged so much ass this morning that I didn't have time for coffee. Tech dudes at 7:00 a.m. on the dot are out of the ordinary, but they'd have to be literally on fire to wake me up. I smile.

"What can I get for you?"

A spokesdude steps up, looking eager.

"Do you have the Rick and Morty sauce?"

"The... uh, sorry? The *Rick and Morty* sauce?" *Is that that cartoon people keep telling me to watch?*

"The, uh, you know—the *Szechuan sauce?*" He leans forward, almost conspiratorial. "Do you have any?"

"Sorry, I have no idea what you're talking about. Hey, *mamá!*" I call over to Candela. "Do you know about any Rick and Morty sauce?"

"Any *what?*"

"Rick and Morty sauce? It's, like... a cartoon?"

"Szechuan sauce!" the young man interjects, which doesn't help. Candela dutifully checks around the counter for the mystery sauce, even heads back to the stockroom. Alone at the counter, I notice that the line looks... *longer* than it usually is this early. The phone starts ringing.

"Mind if I get the next person in line while she looks?" I ask. The spokesdude nods.

"Hi!" I say, making eye contact with...another dude in a hoodie? *Something is definitely up.*

"No, we no have," Candela declares, emerging from the back to pick up the ringing phone.

"Sorry," I say to the first spokesdude. His group turns to leave, disappointed, and the next hoodie steps up. I smile at him.

"Hi, what can I get for you?"

"Do you have the Szechuan sauce?"

It goes on like this *all day.* The line is horrendous, and not everybody is as easily turned away as the first group. A couple of people actually accuse me of squirreling this mystery sauce away for myself. The sauce seekers make the line move agonizingly slowly, so it's loud and angry all the way through lunch.

"Open up another register!" someone yells. It's me, Dalisay, and Rashard on counter for lunch, with one register left vacant to deal with the Uber Eats orders. But the line doesn't know that.

"What is going on?" whispers Rashard.

"I have no idea," I whisper back.

I've only had a couple of shifts with Rashard, one of the two new counter trainees, but I'm practically in love with him, because he makes jokes in English. He's a flamboyant, funny young black man; Candela and Lalo love teasing him and getting him to dance for them. I like chatting with Rashard when I can, though it isn't often—he makes me feel less crazy. He was as surprised as I was the first time someone yelled at him for being a minute late, and during a really nasty lunch rush, as Lalo clapped her hands and shouted her habitual *Vámonos, vámonos, vámonos!* at the kitchen staff, he leaned over to hiss, wide-eyed, "It's like *jail* in here!"

"Hi! Hello!" I half yell, waving my hand. *"I can get the next person over here!"*

"You should really open up another register," says the guy who steps up.

"Tell our owner," I say curtly, then feel bad. Telling the owner *is* the only thing that might have any effect on the staffing situation. But how would he know? I make an effort to give the guy a genuine smile.

"Sorry, long day. What can I get for you?"

I take his order, then reflexively check the coffee levels on the way to make his drink. If you find yourself with all four pots empty at the same time, it backs up the line for at least half an hour, and we *definitely* don't need that today. So, robotically, I quickly lift the metal pots in turn to weigh how much coffee's left in each. It's something I've done hundreds of times.

Today, though, the metal handle of the third pot comes loose. I feel something twist as I lift, and the whole thing somehow swivels and tips horizontally, soaking the right leg of my pants with excruciatingly hot coffee.

"GAH, FUCK!" I gasp, thankfully not dropping the pot. I quickly set it down and scrabble at my right thigh, desperately trying to get the scalding fabric off my skin.

The damp patch goes cold quickly, and it doesn't *feel* like I got burned particularly badly. Then I notice the truly surprising amount of blood on the floor and both my hands.

Like many pianists, I'm weird about hand injuries; I can't even watch them in movies.* Now I freeze, hypnotized by the red, red blood. I feel woozy and stupid, as if my brain's working at a quarter of its usual speed. *The handle... must have sliced... my finger? I should... stop making... such a mess...*

I hold my right hand up as if taking an oath of office. But it only works for a second—I dreamily watch the blood blaze a new path: *finger... palm... wrist... elbow... floor.*

I look around for something to stanch it. *Not the counter rag, that's dirty... not the napkins, I'll get blood on the counter... not the napkins under the counter, I'll get blood on the condiments...*

Stumped, I look to my customer for help. *What do I do?* But he's also frozen, staring wide-eyed at the very bloody right hand I'm still holding up, as if asking for a high five.

Lalo's suddenly at my side, encasing my hand in a thick wad of napkins,

---

* Including but not limited to: *The Hustler, Blade Runner, Heathers, The Handmaiden, True Grit,* and, oh, god, *The Piano.* I don't even bother with anything involving David Cronenberg or the yakuza.

hustling me away from the counter and yelling in Spanish for Juan to get a mop and bucket. She points me upstairs and gives me a gentle push, saying that the first-aid kit is in the manager's office, then rushes back into the fray.

By the time I get to the bathroom upstairs, the blood's soaked through the substantial wad of napkins. I toss them out and put my finger under running water in the sink. It hurts a lot, but underneath all the blood, I'm relieved not to see... I don't know, tendons or something?

As the wooziness wears off, my thigh starts to hurt, too. I rewrap my finger in several layers of clean paper towels, clumsily unzip my damp pants with my left hand, and examine the huge, angry-looking magenta splotch on my thigh. No blistering, though—just a first-degree burn, thank god.

That puts me in good company. According to a 2015 survey of thousands of US fast-food workers by the National Council for Occupational Safety and Health, 79 percent had been burned on the job in the previous year—most more than once. And not everyone got off as easily as I did.

"My managers kept pushing me to work faster, and while trying to meet their demands I slipped on a wet floor, catching my arm on a hot grill," said Brittney Berry, whose forearm was severely burned, to the point of nerve damage, at the Chicago McDonald's where she worked. "The managers told me to put mustard on it, but I ended up having to get rushed to the hospital in an ambulance." A third of fast-food workers surveyed had been told to treat burns with condiments like mustard or mayonnaise.

"One of my coworkers and I have to empty the grease trap without protective gear, and since we were never given the proper equipment or training, we just dump the hot grease into a plastic bag in a box of ice," said Martisse Campbell, who works at a McDonald's in Philly and whose hand was severely burned by boiling grease from a fryer. He was also familiar with condiment-as-salve suggestions—"Once, my coworker got badly burned, and our manager told him, 'Put mayonnaise on it; you'll be good.'"

Berry and Campbell are two of dozens of workers who filed OSHA complaints in 2015 over deliberate understaffing at McDonald's in twenty-eight cities—they claim that the corporate-supplied scheduling system understaffs stores. Crew members are then pressured to work faster to make up for it, which leads to hazardous conditions and injuries.

But the best-known burn at a McDonald's was one that affected a customer—the famed $3 million coffee spill of the early '90s. It was, and still is, held up as the epitome of stupid lawsuits. Of course, there's more to the story.

Stella Liebeck, seventy-nine at the time, was in the passenger seat of a car driven by her grandson, who was taking her to do errands. Because the car had no cup holders, she held the paper cup of coffee between her legs* to add cream and sugar. Trying to remove the lid, she spilled the entire cup onto her sweatpants and wasn't able to pull the fabric away from her skin as quickly as I was.

Liebeck was horribly burned. She had to be hospitalized for eight days with burns on 16 percent of her body. A third of those were third-degree full-thickness burns, which had to be treated with the superpainful process of debridement and skin grafting. The total medical bill for two years of burn treatment was more than $10,000.

I soak a wad of paper towels in cold water from the sink and put it on my thigh, deliriously grateful that I grabbed loose pants this morning.

Liebeck tried to settle for $20,000 with McDonald's, which would have covered her medical expenses and lost wages from the weeks her daughter had to take off work to care for her. McDonald's refused to go higher than $800, so the case went to court.

Food that is heated to a temperature over 140 degrees Fahrenheit will burn your mouth. When people make coffee at home, it's usually between 135 and 140 degrees. In discovery, Liebeck's attorneys found that McDonald's required franchisees to keep their coffee between 180 and 190 degrees, a temperature that supposedly gave pots of coffee a longer shelf life and saved McDonald's hundreds of millions of dollars.

But as anyone who's had coffee from McDonald's can probably testify, it also will burn the *hell* out of your mouth if you don't wait ten minutes or so before trying to take a sip. Liquids at 180 degrees can cause third-degree burns in two to seven seconds, and Liebeck's lawyers discovered seven

* Something I've totally done, by the way.

hundred previous claims from people who'd been burned by superhot McDonald's coffee.

In his ruling in favor of Liebeck, the judge called the company's conduct "reckless, callous, and willful"—as if McDonald's were capable of being ashamed of its behavior.

But McDonald's can't feel shame. It has even less access to human social stuff than Ayn does, because *it's not human*. Still, we tend to anthropomorphize huge companies, and ascribe things like compassion, loyalty, guilt, generosity, and empathy to their actions despite vast evidence that the only language corporations understand is money.

That's why in addition to a scolding from a judge and a $160,000 judgment for Liebeck's pain and medical costs, McDonald's was initially hit with the much-mocked sum of $2.7 million in punitive damages. The *only* stick or carrot humans have that's big enough to affect the behavior of a company as huge as McDonald's is a correspondingly huge amount of money. The idea behind the multimillion-dollar award was that docking McDonald's for just two days' worth of coffee revenues would be enough of a market incentive for McDonald's to lower the temperature of its coffee rather than keep getting sued every time someone was burned.

But despite the headlines and the outrage, the final award in *Liebeck v. McDonald's* wasn't actually millions. When Liebeck died—in 2004, at the age of ninety-one—the local newspaper ran a follow-up story on her case:

> The trial judge later reduced that figure to $600,000...[and] Liebeck wound up with an amount said to be close to $300,000. [Liebeck's daughter Nancy Tiano] says her mother was "never happy about the incident" and that "the burns and court proceedings took their toll." During her final years, Tiano says, her mother had no quality of life. The good news is that the settlement helped to ease the end of her life by paying for a live-in nurse.

Three hundred thousand dollars isn't even a mosquito bite to McDonald's, so it never changed the temperature at which its franchisees are supposed to keep their coffee. You still have to wait a while before drinking coffee brewed according to McDonald's standards if you don't want to get burned. And if you spill it on yourself—or if someone throws coffee at you—it'll cause third-degree burns in three to seven seconds if you can't get your wet clothes away from your skin.

To be clear, this doesn't make McDonald's or other big corporations *evil,* any more than Ayn is evil. They just are what they are. They aren't capable of being anything else.

But right now, we treat them like the guy in *Grizzly Man* treated bears—like they have the capacity for compassion, mercy, or shame. But believing that human social norms will constrain a corporation's behavior when it smells money in the water is just begging to get eaten alive.

Spots of blood are already starting to show through the new wad of paper towels. I think my leg's okay, so I rezip my pants, rewrap my finger, and go hunting for the first-aid kit.

It's the first time I've been in the manager's office. Papers and charts showing what look like day-to-day metrics plaster the walls. I open nearly every drawer in the room before I finally find the first-aid kit and select a bright blue finger bandage. It's serious-looking and perfectly designed for my injury. To my relief, it actually stops the bleeding.

I clean up the blood in the bathroom and start heading back downstairs, then pause. Looking both ways, I slip back into the office to examine some of the papers on the walls. Most are indecipherable, but I do recognize the mysterious fractions from the bottom corner of the order screens on one of them. The paper's titled "Manager of the Month Competition" and appears to record whose shifts have the best sales-to-labor and seconds-per-order ratios. *Oh, duh*—that's *why managers keep clearing the order queue. They're probably juking the stats.**

Back downstairs, it's still slammed, so I jump right back into the fray. All day, groups of hoodies back up the line to inquire about the stupid Szechuan sauce, and they're much less polite about hearing we don't have any after they've waited in line for fifteen minutes to get the news. One guy

---

* I later learn that managerial bonuses are frequently handed out based on metrics like this.

even accuses me of hoarding the stuff so I can sell it on eBay, an idea that sounds pretty fucking equitable to me after this day.

As I politely try to get the guy to fuck off, wishing my finger and thigh would stop hurting, I notice that Dalisay, on the register next to mine, has just pulled a full-on screamer. The woman's so unhappy about how long she had to wait in line that she won't even order—she just keeps lobbing personal insults. I try to summon compassion for her but wince as the monologue careens into the screamer's shitty thoughts about race and immigration. I look over to Dalisay to see if she wants help, but she's a pro. I watch out of the corner of my eye as she handles the screamer professionally and without ego, despite way more provocation than I could have put up with. *Why can't I manage that?*

But then there's a flash of movement, and Dalisay jumps back in shock as the fistful of sugar packets the woman just threw hits the floor around her.

"Hey!" I yell. But fight or flight takes over Dalisay for once.

"You get out, *right now!*" she yells, pointing to the door. I've never heard her speak this loud. Rashard and I look at each other, wide-eyed. *"Get out and don't come back!"*

Then Dalisay seems to realize where she is and immediately turns and walks away, back into the kitchen. The woman trails her on the other side of the counter, still yelling insults, but eventually gives up and leaves.

I want to go back and check on Dalisay, but we're still slammed. So I stay where I am and continue my robotic quest to clear the line that never ends. She reemerges a few minutes later, a little red-faced, and takes her place at the register next to mine.

"I'm sorry," I whisper, leaning over to touch her arm.

"It's okay," she whispers back, using her foot to clear the sugar packets out of the couple of square feet where she needs to stand.

"I can get the next person in line!"

When my shift ends, at 3:30, it's *still* slammed, with customers almost out the door. I'm extremely ready to not be here anymore but agree to stay a little longer. It's not in my rational self-interest. But Dalisay's had such a shitty day. I feel like I just can't leave her and Rashard to face the huge line alone, even though I barely know either of them.

I wish I'd been able to get to know people here better. I miss my smoking crew back at Convergys—though, as far as I can tell from Facebook, nobody from my training class still works there. Despite all the ways Convergys was miserable, at least during training there was time to make friends. It was a far less efficient workplace than this McDonald's is.

I remember a conversation Kolbi and I had about her Chick-fil-A once.

"Honestly, the only reason I stayed there so long was that I loved my coworkers. You become a family, no lie. You know how Kimberly says our class is like a family? Which—I do feel that?" She'd hesitated then, as if worried she might offend me.

"But we've only known each other for a few weeks, and you were there for, like, four *years,*" I'd supplied.

"Exactly," she'd said, relieved. "It's nothing compared to what I felt at Chick-fil-A. That's like your brothers and your sisters. You look out for each other, you hang out outside of work—the Chick-fil-A crew! That's what I loved about the place; that was the only thing keeping me there."

I finally clock out at five and go upstairs to gather my stuff. My finger and thigh throb as I sit down, take off my visor, and reach into my bag for my bottle of Advil and small (legally acquired) vaporizer pen. The company names its discreet cigarette-shaped pens after the feeling each particular mix of marijuana vapor is supposed to give you, like *Bliss* and *Calm*. This one's called *Relief.*

"There's an innate biological desire for *relief,*" I hear the addiction specialist's echo in my head. "And that desire is part of what motivates the substance abuse."

I tell him to shut up, furtively taking a couple of hits of the pen then swallowing two Advil. The Relief pen is so good at muting the constant dull background noise of my sore feet, legs, back, shoulders, and neck that I've become an embarrassingly late-in-life pothead over the last two months. Never while I'm working, of course—but I have taken to carrying the pen in my purse for the train ride home after a shift. I've never hit it at work before, but I could really, really use some relief right now.

Because I stayed into rush hour, the train home is crowded, with nowhere to sit or even lean. As I sway back and forth, exhausted and slightly stoned, it occurs to me to look up what the stupid Rick and Morty thing was all about. But I'm too tired to be curious, and my data plan sucks—and honestly, just thinking the words *Szechuan sauce* makes me want to die.

A couple of days later, I'm waiting for the train downtown for an afternoon shift. I scroll through podcasts with my left hand—my right forefinger is still bandaged—and find that Patton Oswalt, a comedian I like, is the guest on the latest episode of *Chapo Trap House*.* I might have guessed from the episode's title, "Lost in the Sauce," what it was about.

"Szechuangate" was a very big deal online, apparently. Oswalt asks the hosts if he's got the details right:

PATTON OSWALT: Correct me if I'm wrong, but *Rick and Morty* mentioned a Szechuan sauce that then people demanded from McDonald's, and McDonald's flippantly said, "Nah, we don't have it," and then it's caused a huge—it was literally the number one trending topic!

[CROSSTALK FROM THE SHOW'S FOUR HOSTS]

OSWALT: Okay, so tell me what happened!

MATT CHRISTMAN: In the premiere episode of the season... Rick mentions this Szechuan dipping sauce that was a promotional item for *Mulan* in 1997—it was basically a sweet-and-sour dipping sauce. He says, "It was delicious, Morty, and they don't make it anymore!" And at the end of the episode, he goes, "My mission for this season, Morty, is to *get that Szechuan sauce!*" Parenthetically, it was not mentioned for the rest of the season—it was a *joke*.

AMBER A'LEE FROST: Moreover, the function of the joke was that this is an *extremely* arbitrary and esoteric reference.

---

* Since the 2016 election, I've taken to sampling a wide spectrum of political podcasts, from hard right to hard left, to get a better idea of how different people are interpreting the news. *Chapo Trap House* is pretty hard left, and it's one of the few in my lineup that I actually enjoy.

CHRISTMAN: Exactly—the joke is that this is not worth caring about....But the fans of the show, tethered to reality as they are, decided that they really wanted this sauce that most of them were too young to have ever had themselves. And so I guess some idiot, who is going to be fired tomorrow, thought, "Hey, it'd be fun if we just put out some! Limited run—give selected stores, like, twenty packets and some posters and have a fun little promotion."

But when people found out that certain stores were going to have actual Szechuan sauce, they bum-rushed every location; there were two-hour lines all over the place. A lot of the stores didn't have it, and a lot of stores that did ran out immediately. So there were hundreds and thousands of insanely pissed-off nerds screaming about how McDonald's did not give them the Szechuan sauce that they'd been promised.

FROST: Never get between a virgin and their condiments.

VIRGIL TEXAS: People were fighting; the police were called at several locations to guard the McDonald's.

The train stops between stations underground, and a voice mumbles something about a delay over the intercom. People groan. With the seal on Szechuangate broken and an unclear amount of time to kill, I figure I might as well google it.

The Chapos aren't exaggerating—a lot of people drove and/or waited in line for *hours* in hopes of getting the sauce, and many of them got way, way angrier than anybody I'd encountered the other day. There actually *were* riots: people trashed stores, and police *were* called to several locations.

The most frequently posted footage was shot in the lobby of a store in nearby San Jose, about half an hour from where I work. In it, an angry, elbow-to-elbow crowd yells, "GIVE US THE SAUCE! GIVE US THE SAUCE!" I can hear the guy holding the camera laughing, but it's honestly kind of terrifying. In another video shot outside the same McDonald's, a line of what looks to be at least five hundred people snakes around the block, flanked by cop cars.

Almost all the coverage of Szechuangate focuses on the adventures and disappointments of fans trying to get the sauce. There's stories about Szechuan sauce packets posted on eBay for thousands of dollars and compilations of tweets from disappointed fans, like this one:

> @McDonalds drove 4 hours at 6am from Canada for that #szechuansauce—no sauce, wouldn't even give us a poster :(#iwantmymcnuggetsauce

There's multiple interviews with the idiot who drove from Canada, another with someone who did manage to get the sauce and traded it for a car, many analyses of what a PR disaster this is for McDonald's, and a feel-good story about one guy who got the sauce and shared it with random people in line.

But I can't find anything about what this all looked like from the other side of the counter, which is what I really want to hear. I skim story after Szechuangate story, looking for any hint of my own perspective, but the rare pieces that mention crew members at all do so in the context of speculation that we may have stolen sauce packets to sell on eBay.*

I'd understood in theory before this that a ton of people despise and resent "the mainstream media." But I'd always assumed that "media" meant cable news, or people who unironically use the words *flyover country*. I had zero problem with that, because I also despised and resented those people. That wasn't *me*.

I've also always joked that the world would be a better place if, like Mormons on mission, everybody had to work a terrible service job for a year or two. At the very least, it should be mandatory for anyone with aspirations in business, politics, or journalism. Because if you don't really know anybody outside your class, you can't really understand the embarrassingly

* This isn't *entirely* the media's fault: there was a very prominent, official-looking sign in the back of my store strictly detailing how to handle press inquiries—give them the phone number for the McDonald's corporate PR and *don't say anything to them*.

large disconnect between the actual working class and the kind of people who shape public opinion and policy.

For example, at my old newspaper—god, it seems like forever ago—I made $36,000 a year as a thirty-two-year-old senior staff writer with a decade of experience. That number is sort of doubly embarrassing—on one hand, I cringe imagining colleagues from the journalism world reading that I was willing to do so much for so little. On the other hand, I cringe imagining coworkers from Amazon, Convergys, and McDonald's reading that I was paid so much for such comparatively easy and rewarding work.

Whatever it means to others, $36,000 was a living wage to me—more than enough for a childless dirtbag like me to live in comfort. Most people in my social circle—my tribe—were also comfortable, as were most people I've met in journalism. Coming from a middle-class background, I'm still kind of on the scholarship-kid end of my generation of journalists—it's *rough* getting through the years of unpaid internships and might-as-well-be-unpaid freelancing without outside financial support, and the barriers have gotten even higher since I elbowed my way in a decade ago.

And, god, politics is so much worse. Before party officials from the DCCC* will even consider you as a candidate for national office, you have to pass a "phone test"—take out your phone, scroll through your contacts, and add up how much you think you could get each contact to donate. If you can get to $250,000, you pass. This is in a country where most people live from paycheck to paycheck. A recent survey found that two out of three Americans had less than $1,000 saved, and half of those had zero savings.

And so it's no surprise that poor people—or even people who *know* poor people—don't really get elected. Two out of five people in Congress as I'm working at McDonald's are millionaires. Their combined personal wealth adds up to $2.43 billion. And they'll spend half their time† in DC schmoozing even wealthier people for money.

---

* The Democratic Congressional Campaign Committee, the party organization that works to elect Democrats to the House of Representatives.

† In 2013, incoming lawmakers were informed by the DCCC that they would be expected to do four hours of "call time" on the phone with high-end donors a day.

When was the last time they worked a bad job, or one without insurance? When was the last time they had a personal conversation with anyone working at McDonald's, or an Amazon warehouse, or a call center? Do they know anyone who had kids as a teenager, or got MRSA from their job, or actually had to *use* Obamacare, or didn't go to college, or has been in prison? What does *in the weeds* mean to them?

If my newspaper hadn't closed, I think, I might have written a quick Szechuangate blog post, probably treating all the people going to insane lengths for an advertising gimmick as dumb but harmless. Those people in line looked pretty similar to people I knew—I'd have automatically extended empathy to them.

But, honestly? I probably *wouldn't* have tried to go out and get a McDonald's worker's perspective on record. It would have been a lot more work, but the truth is that angle probably wouldn't have even occurred to me. My understanding of fast-food workers was the same as that of the throng of rowdy people in San Jose and most other reporters—fast-food workers just weren't quite *real*. I think that's why people stared when I screamed back at Mustard Lady—it was the novelty of seeing a chair lose its temper, or a touchscreen, or a robot.

What right do these fucking children have to be screamers? They have the freedom to wait in line for hours on a weekday—unthinkable to most workers—and, like a pack of inbred French kings, they waste it on frivolous bullshit. Where the *fuck* do they get the nerve to riot over Szechuan sauce?

I suddenly really *hate* them, and I hate the media for not understanding, either. I *burn* at their complacency, their comfort, their naivete, their lack of curiosity. I'd never have predicted I could muster this level of raw emotion over dipping sauce. But here, stuck underneath the streets of San Francisco, I'm fucking *furious*.

Pissed off as I am, I get a lot of savage pleasure out of the *Chapo* hosts ripping the whole idiotic thing to shreds, because they alone *do* come at it from the point of view of the workers:

OSWALT: In a couple of months, there'll be a lunch rush on a Friday, and around 2:30, the new guy will turn to his manager and say, "Man, that Friday lunch rush is *crazy*." And it'll be like the *Night Watch* guy: [*NIGHT WATCH*–GUY VOICE] "Let me tell you about *Szechuan sauce*—that cold, howling night. It was a couple of months ago..."

FROST: I picture a Sam Elliott type.

[LAUGHTER]

CHRISTMAN [SAM ELLIOTT VOICE]: There were hundreds of 'em—nerds like you never seen!

OSWALT [SAM ELLIOTT VOICE]: That was the one day that I prayed to god—*and also was convinced he didn't exist.*

It's mostly satisfying because it's funny, but it does offer a point about something that really *had* bothered me. I've found that screamers usually have some source of stress that makes every day a battle. But having hours to fritter away on something this pointless now seems like the definition of stress-free living to me, and the Szechuan guys mostly looked like they came from the Bay Area's tech upper class. Why *did* all these people go screamer? What was *their* excuse?

CHRISTMAN: So this is the revelation I had about this—say you're a young subject of late capitalism. It doesn't work for you in any meaningful way. Your life is shit, you have three or four awful part-time jobs, you have no health insurance, you have half a million dollars in unsecured student-loan debt—

OSWALT: That you'll *never* pay off.

CHRISTMAN: —you have no future in any meaningful sense. All the avenues that you were brought up to believe were going to lead to prosperity and stability—*gone*. But the *one thing* late capitalism promises is that every stupid, shitty, nostalgic indulgence you can think of is *yours,* at your fingertips.

[And so the Szechuan seeker concludes:] "If my life is a neoliberal hell, but I *can't even get a fucking cup of Szechuan sauce?* Why the *fuck* am I still allowing this system to control me? We should *burn it to the fucking ground*."

After about fifteen minutes, the train finally starts moving again. I arrive at work five minutes late, in the middle of lunch rush. Lalo emerges from the frenzy looking frustrated. She tells me that I really can't keep being late like this.

And I quit.

Number Six

Hi!" I say. "I can get the next person over here!"

Nah, I didn't quit by dramatically walking out—I would have felt terrible doing that to my coworkers, even though feeling that way isn't in my rational self-interest. I just told Lalo I had to move back to Philly, and that I could finish out the shifts on the schedule but wouldn't be around after that. This was met with barely a shrug: people come and people go.

During my last few shifts, I steal moments to tell the coworkers I've sort of gotten to know that I'm leaving. Some look sad and say they'll miss me; others echo Lalo's shrug. Turnover is always high, they didn't know me that well, and they've got work to do.

My last shift is evening to night, working counter with Dalisay. I don't always love late shifts, which involve dealing with a lot of intoxicated people, but there's this magic hour between dinner and late-night munchies when things *do* chill out a little. The scheduling algorithms are still amazingly accurate, which means there's still barely enough of us to cover the customers, so it's not *down time,* exactly. But it *is* less frantic, and since the line is shorter, customers are in better spirits. There have even been a few brief, beautiful minutes when we actually cleared the line.

Two young women in party tops step up and order McFlurries.

"I'm really sorry, but there's no McFlurries today," I say. "The machine's haunted."

The soft-serve machine has been acting weird all week, and I've found that people are less likely to get pissed that they can't get ice cream if I say the machine is *haunted* rather than *broken*.*

Even when people do get mad, every day that the ice cream machine isn't working is a better-than-average day in my book. Everything involving ice cream is the responsibility of whoever took the order, and the ice cream items take what feels like *forever* to make.†

I'm also legit embarrassed by my hideous cones. When Dalisay makes one, she somehow coaxes the stream of soft-serve into neat, symmetrical coils. No matter how many times I try to replicate her methods, I always end up shamefacedly handing over something that looks like Jabba the Hutt unsuccessfully trying to perch on a fire hydrant.

The two party girls are disappointed about the McFlurries, but not upset. They order cookies instead. As I ring them up, their eyes suddenly go wide at something behind me. One lets out a little yelp, pointing.

Dalisay and I both spin around to find that the ice cream machine has somehow turned itself on. The chocolate-vanilla-swirl tap is at full throttle, happily constructing a ropy, free-form tower with alarming speed. Right as we turn, the tower hits some sort of structural limit and starts slumping forward in slow motion.

Like a slapstick comedy team, Dalisay and I shriek in unison and dive to catch the collapsing ice cream before it hits the floor. I'm closer and get there first, so I end up with my left hand sunk to the forearm in the massing ice cream as I frantically fiddle with the on-off lever with my right. Nothing happens.

I pound the lever with a fist. Nothing happens.

---

* I frequently get asked why the McDonald's soft-serve machines always seem to be out of order, which I didn't realize was a thing. In my experience, they are legitimately out of order. The machines have to be cleaned of all their gunk every day, and it takes hours, and this usually has to be done while the store's open for business—owners aren't paying someone overtime to stay late cleaning the soft-serve machine when it can technically be done during normal hours in our *time to lean*.

† At the time, there was some kind of "Free Cone Fridays" promotion offered by Uber and McDonald's that made me dread the end of the workweek.

Dalisay appears with a huge stack of cups. Without a word, I grab them, drop to my knees, and start shoveling ice cream into cups with my free hand. Above me, Dalisay thumps the side of the stupid machine.

"Oh my god, *what* have I been saying all week?" I pant, putting a full cup on the floor and grabbing a new one. As I do, the tower of ice cream starts to tip forward; I scream and prop it back up, getting ice cream all over myself.

I'm still panicking, but it's shifting into a giddy, silly sort of panic. I start to giggle.

Above me, I hear Dalisay giggling, too.

"I was *so right!*" I snort. "The stupid thing *is* haunted!"

"The *power* of *Christ* com*pels you!* The *power* of *Christ* com*pels you!*" Dalisay intones, thumping the machine in rhythm, and I laugh and laugh and laugh.

There *is* still a line, as always. But it's not too long. Besides, its pressure is temporarily lifted. The reason for the delay is, for once, right out in the open, and it's obviously not our fault. We're doing our best, and for the moment it's visible. Nobody's going to yell at us.

In another minute, Dalisay manages to dam the river of ice cream. But for that beautiful minute, we're free to giggle and shriek and be human beings. It's my happiest memory of working at McDonald's.

And then, finally, I get to leave the weeds.

Conclusion: Out of the Weeds

Imagine a great white shark, a solitary apex predator. Her evolutionary path involved *eating* other sharks, not living in harmony with them, so why would she have evolved something as human as a conscience? Her life is simple, *binary:* eat, or be eaten. The strong survive and the weak perish, as they should.

Now imagine Wanda. She's spent millennia developing a complicated set of emotions and social values that help her get along in groups with other humans—things like empathy, generosity, love, shame, guilt, humor, compassion. Wanda isn't simple at all—these things that govern human behavior are so complex that even all her amazing technology can only manage a crayon-drawing approximation.

Now dump Wanda out in the cold ocean, all alone. It's a much simpler world out here—eat, or be eaten. All those complex social behaviors seem irrational in the ocean. Befriending or showing loyalty to a shark won't work out here the way it does on land, after all.

So shout some helpful advice at Wanda as you sail away: *"Just be a shark!"*

But Wanda just isn't *good* at being a shark. She's only going to be slightly better at it than a shark would be at fitting into human society. She's certainly never going to beat sharks at their own game—she's not built to. On land, all Wanda's wonderful messiness helps her survive. In the ocean, those same traits drag her down.

Businesses used to accept Wanda's inefficiencies as a necessary part of their workforce—humans sometimes need to socialize, go to the bathroom, take sick days, drive Mom to a doctor's appointment, attend funerals, stay up until four with the baby.

But at this moment, techno-Taylorism, the decline of organized labor, automation, and the ongoing destruction of shark-cage worker protections have tipped the balance of power in the workplace way, *way* in favor of employers. It's gotten so out of balance that even many *workers* seem to truly believe that the things that make them less efficient than sharks or robots are weaknesses—moral failings, like original sin.

So millions of people battle millennia of evolution every day, desperately trying to be something fundamentally different from what we *are.* And when we inevitably fail, we torture ourselves with guilt over not being born a shark, or at least able to plausibly imitate one.

Fuck that. You're *not* a shark. You're a *human being.* It doesn't make you a bad person if your family and friends and dignity are more important to you than some job. That makes you *normal.* The true outliers are the Taylors, the Fords, the Bezoses, the Ayns—people whose work is their life and life is their work. People who thrive alone in the cold ocean. People who can't or won't understand that almost all other humans have very different values, needs, and priorities. People with massive control over how stressful our day-to-day existence is.

So why *is* America so crazy? It's the inescapable chronic stress built into the way we work and live. It's the insane idea that an honest day's work means suppressing your humanity, dignity, family, and other nonwork priorities in exchange for low wages that make home life constantly stressful, too. Is it surprising that Americans have started exhibiting unhelpful physical, mental, and social adaptations to chronic stress en masse? Our bodies believe that this is the apocalypse.

And on top of that, people with power seem totally blind to how dire life has gotten for much of the country. The state of the union is always strong. GDP is up. Unemployment is low. *Everything's fine.* They're so insulated from the real world that they don't or can't understand that, for most people, our current system is *obviously broken.* That's why Make America Great Again caught on while Clinton's counter that America Is Already Great didn't—people aren't *stupid.* They know something isn't right.

Like Zeb's carpenter grandpa back in Texas, who "worked his ass off for fifty years and done what you're supposed to do, and he's still sixty-five years old and poor as *fuck.*" That sort of cognitive dissonance drives people to search for a *why.* And I understand that. Losing my faith in the American

Dream my dad taught me about left me almost as spiritually adrift as losing my faith in a religion. The idea is so central to American identity that its absence leaves a huge hole inside you. And refilling it with a new way of understanding the world from scratch is an intimidating task.

Trump gave people a prefab *why* to plug that hole, much as I disagree with his analysis. And because the only other option provided was the same old "Everything's fine!" a lot of people just took Trump's story of *why* as the truth, because at least it wasn't the same old bullshit. I think that's what won him the election.

Do *you* want to win elections? Acknowledge that something's wrong and *offer people a different why.*

So, why can't employers find good workers to fill open positions? *Because the drawbacks of the jobs they're offering outweigh the benefits.*

Why is the country ready to riot over jobs—immigrants taking them, trade deals killing them, Wall Street destroying them? *Because these jobs suck donkey balls.*

Why do people vote against their self-interest? *Because when national politics hasn't truly improved the lives of the nonwealthy in decades and is covered like sports, why take it any more seriously than professional wrestling?*

If the data says everything's so great, why is America *freaking the fuck out? Because the systems we use to compile and analyze data don't consider America freaking the fuck out to be relevant information.*

So if the constant hustle of the modern economy makes you feel like you're losing your mind, try not to be too hard on yourself. Depression and anxiety are perfectly normal reactions to the insanely stressful world we've built for ourselves. Suppressing our humanity is exhausting. It's driving us crazy. It's ruining our experience of life. It's making us sick and terrified and cruel and hopeless. And it's *killing* us.

In the 1970s, Japan coined a new word—*karoshi,* meaning death by overwork—after businessmen in their thirties and forties started dropping dead from strokes, heart attacks, and suicide after working twenty-hour days for months at a time. Giving the phenomenon a name, starting to measure it, and imposing a nontrivial punishment on the companies driving it were the first steps in keeping *karoshi* from getting out of hand.

There's now words for *karoshi* in Mandarin, Korean, and other Asian languages, though today they're mostly applied to blue-collar factory workers, not well-paid businessmen. But there's still no word for it in English, even as stress-related illnesses become an even bigger health crisis than cigarettes. Until we recognize this, name it, measure it, and talk about it, things aren't going to get better.

Because society is going to change a *lot* as Wanda develops that technology we can't even imagine—particularly when it comes to what we think of as "work." Silicon Valley and Wall Street sure know it—half of them are libertarians looking into universal basic income, the least libertarian idea possible, and the other half are building themselves luxury apocalypse bunkers. They're well aware that there's way more of us than there are of them, and that if something doesn't change soon, everything's going to explode.

This isn't sustainable. More important, it isn't *right. Things have to change.*

But it's been so long since there's been serious political opposition to the idea that we *should* all be living like sharks that many of us have actually forgotten that the ocean isn't our natural habitat. We assume that this is the end of history—that our particularly carnivorous form of capitalism is natural, and literally the only option.

And that leads to the worst part of all: we've stopped even *imagining* other, better ways we could live.

One final rat fact. Take the rats from the experiments with the box and the shocks and the beeps. There's Rat C, who can press a button after hearing a warning beep to defuse the coming shock—she gets stress ulcers. There's Rat B, who can't avoid the shock but can at least relax until she hears the beep—she gets even more stress ulcers. Then there's Rat A, who's shocked at random with no warning or control—she ends up with the most stress ulcers by a mile.

Now take those boxes and put a dividing wall in each that's annoying (but not impossible) to climb over. De-electrify half the floor. Now, put each rat on the electric side of her box and start up the Rat A treatment—unpredictable, uncontrollable shocks.

All the rat has to do is climb the wall to the other side and she'll be free. Rats B and C will figure this out and clamber over to the other side pretty quickly; so will any random sewer rat.

But Rat A's entire life has been nothing but unpredictable, inescapable suffering, and it's crippled her capacity to imagine anything better. So Rat A will just sit there getting electrocuted forever, even when relief is a short climb away. It's a phenomenon called "learned helplessness."

Rat A is so tragic because her despair makes sense. All evidence in her life so far supports her idea that everything just sucks, *forever,* and there's nothing anyone can do about it. When she assures you that climbing the wall is a waste of energy, she's genuinely trying to save you the pain she knows firsthand.

You are going to run into a lot of Rat As out there, and they can be very convincing in disguising their despair as pragmatism.

Why bother trying to climb the wall? It'll never, ever happen. You're being unrealistic. The grass is only greener over there because you're young and don't know anything about the world. This is the least electrified floor in history, but you still feel entitled to a floor with no electricity at all? How are you going to pay for this, anyway? We should be focusing more on the problem of mice. Have you tried meditation? Xanax? I think it's less painful if you sit on your tail, but I'd need to gather some more data. Look what happened to the rats in Venezuela! What if the other side is actually worse? You should be grateful you live indoors instead of in a sewer—and these shocks could be way worse, you big baby.

Do not listen to this nonsense. Don't be cruel, but be firm. Escape *is* possible; things *don't* have to be like this. The current way we've arranged our society is not inevitable, and it's far from natural. America got this way because we spent the past half century outsourcing the running of society to technology, data, and free markets—even though none of those things can tell if everyone's miserable.

You're going to have to help Rat A at first, to give her back the hope that's been electrocuted out of her. Be kind; she's been through a lot. Paint her a detailed picture of life on the other side. Make her remember how it feels to walk on unburned paws, and to wake up after an uninterrupted eight hours of sleep.

But, first, you have to imagine it for yourself.

Try it. Be corny. Imagine a better world, one you'd like to live in. Imagine a world that's kinder and less stressful than this one, a world built on human rather than shark values.

Don't think about politics, or policy, or feasibility—there's experts for that. Don't handcuff yourself with pragmatism right now. Just imagine, in as much detail as you can, a world that's *better.*

It can sometimes help to work backwards from specifics in your life to a bigger picture. In my better world, for example, Jess and Anthone's daughter, McKenna, would never learn the definition of Fish Mox.

What would have to change to make that happen?
What would the steps be to there from here?
What would you be willing to give up for that better world?

Big changes are coming, sooner than you think. Automation will upend everything we think we know about work in the next ten to twenty years—and if you think techno-Taylorism isn't eventually coming for you, you're fooling yourself. I bet you can already recognize its tendrils.

It's *scary.* But, honestly, I've found a lot of hope in the idea that these big changes are inevitable. Because if change is definitely coming, it's just a question of who gets to decide what the new world will look like, and what it will value. At the moment, the people in control of the future worship sharks and stopwatches and free markets. Unless there's a strong vision of another option, the world of tomorrow is just going to be a slightly more efficient, polarized, *carnivorous* version of today.

So keep imagining that better world like a beacon always ahead of you—because "Let's go back to the nice way things were before" isn't going to cut it. Things *haven't* been particularly nice for the working class for a long time—it only seemed that way because they were easier to ignore. Going back to the way things were before will inevitably bring us right back to where we are now—*freaking the fuck out.*

President Trump isn't a fluke; strongman us-vs-them leaders emerge when the population of a country is under incredible stress. Chronic stress drains people's empathy, patience, and tolerance for new things. If your better world values those things, you'll need to start by taking action to make *everyone's* lives less miserable—even people you don't personally like, or feel deserve your help.

Because, seriously—it's up to *you.*

Yeah, *you, mamá.* You're a worker, too—just like me and Jess and Zeb and Candela and Kolbi and Miguel and Mustard Lady. We're all in this together against the stopwatches and the sharks. And we may be only human, but there's a *whole lot of us*.

So, what now?

It won't involve buying anything, or looking at a screen, or the word Cheeto. It won't involve anything that would be a good bumper sticker. It won't be anything you can do online, or alone.

So you'll leave the house. You'll meet other people who think the status quo is cruel and ridiculous—they're literally *everywhere*. You'll listen to *their* better worlds. You'll start discussing not what's stupid and awful, but how things can improve. You'll fall in with a group of people devoted to a better world that looks mostly—though not entirely—the same as yours. You'll come to feel a bond with them that's even stronger than friendship. You'll become part of something bigger than yourself—and, weirdly, you'll feel more in control of your life than you have in years. By working toward a better world, you'll gradually stop hating yourself for your failures as a shark. And, slowly but surely, you'll start feeling like a human being again.

You'll know what to do from there.

Acknowledgments

Thanks to the McPhersons, Pete, and Jess and Anthone for opening their homes to me. You made me feel welcome in an unfamiliar place, and I can't overstate how much that meant to me.

Thanks to the many, many workers who talked with me for this. I hope that even if I couldn't find room for your specific story—and, odds-wise, that's nearly all of you—you can recognize your own voice as part of the chorus that shaped this book.

Thanks to my classmates from Convergys. You made a difficult time in my life so much better than it could have been.

Thanks to my friends in Philly for listening to me ramble about the ideas in this book for more than three years—double thanks if you read a draft.

Thanks to my parents for raising me to work hard and treat everyone as a human being, for their immense help with the costs of going to college, for my good teeth, and for everything else.

Thanks to my sister, Caitlin, and my brother-in-law, Jason, for—among so many other things—letting me hole up in the woods to write.

Thanks to my wonderful in-laws and their bizarrely perfect skillsets for fact-checking my research in economics, psychology, labor policy and law, and the biology of stress. Extra thanks to Aunty and Uncle for letting me hole up at *their* house to write.

Thanks to Lydia Wills and Vanessa Mobley for shepherding me through this whole book-writing process, and for believing in me.

And, of course, thanks to my husband, Rajiv. I've told you many times that I literally couldn't have done it without you, but it bears repeating. I love you so much.

Selected Reading

An extremely incomplete list of books that helped shape my understanding of the situation we find ourselves in.

Start with

Nickel and Dimed: On (Not) Getting By in America, Barbara Ehrenreich
Good Jobs, Bad Jobs: The Rise of Polarized and Precarious Employment Systems in the United States, 1970s to 2000s, Arne Kalleberg
The Status Syndrome: How Social Standing Affects Our Health and Longevity, Michael Marmot
Mismeasuring Our Lives: Why GDP Doesn't Add Up, Joseph E. Stiglitz, Amartya Sen, and Jean-Paul Fitoussi
Hand to Mouth: Living in Bootstrap America, Linda Tirado
Why Zebras Don't Get Ulcers, Robert Sapolsky
Temp: How American Work, American Business, and the American Dream Became Temporary, Louis Hyman
Private Government: How Employers Rule Our Lives (and Why We Don't Talk About It), Elizabeth Anderson
Labor and Monopoly Capital: The Degradation of Work in the Twentieth Century, Harry Braverman
The New Ruthless Economy: Work and Power in the Digital Age, Simon Head
Do What You Love: And Other Lies About Success and Happiness, Miya Tokumitsu
HyperNormalisation (film), Adam Curtis

Selected Reading

On workplaces in this book

The Everything Store: Jeff Bezos and the Age of Amazon, Brad Stone

Fast Food, Fast Talk: Service Work and the Routinization of Everyday Life, Robin Leidner

The Furniture Wars: How America Lost a Fifty Billion Dollar Industry, Michael K. Dugan

Closing: The Life and Death of an American Factory, Cathy N. Davidson

McDonald's: Behind the Arches, John F. Love

On the history of work and management

The Principles of Scientific Management, Frederick Winslow Taylor

The One Best Way: Frederick Winslow Taylor and the Enigma of Efficiency, Robert Kanigel

My Life and Work, Henry Ford

I Invented the Modern Age: The Rise of Henry Ford, Richard Snow

Taylorism Transformed: Scientific Management Theory Since 1945, Stephen P. Waring

Contested Terrain: The Transformation of the Workplace in the Twentieth Century, Richard Edwards

The Machine That Changed the World: The Story of Lean Production, James P. Womack and Daniel T. Jones

The Managed Heart: Commercialization of Human Feeling, Arlie Hochschild

Blood, Sweat & Tears: The Evolution of Work, Richard Donkin

False Prophets: The Gurus Who Created Modern Management and Why Their Ideas Are Bad for Business, James Hoopes

The Second Shift: Working Families and the Revolution at Home, Arlie Hochschild

Reengineering the Corporation: A Manifesto for Business Revolution, Michael Hammer and James Champy

Just Enough Anxiety: The Hidden Driver of Business Success, Robert H. Rosen

The Lean Startup: How Today's Entrepreneurs Use Continuous Innovation to Create Radically Successful Businesses, Eric Ries

Gigged: The End of the Job and the Future of Work, Sarah Kessler

The Job: Work and Its Future in a Time of Radical Change, Ellen Ruppel Shell

On low-wage work and workers

The Working Poor: Invisible in America, David K. Shipler

Precarious Lives: Job Insecurity and Well-Being in Rich Democracies, Arne Kalleberg

The Disposable American: Layoffs and Their Consequences, Louis Uchitelle
The Overworked American: The Unexpected Decline of Leisure, Juliet Schor
Free Time: The Forgotten American Dream, Benjamin Hunnicutt
The Precariat: The New Dangerous Class, Guy Standing
Strangers in Their Own Land: Anger and Mourning on the American Right, Arlie Hochschild
The Big Squeeze: Tough Times for the American Worker, Steven Greenhouse
The Working Life: The Promise and Betrayal of Modern Work, Joanne B. Ciulla
The Betrayal of Work: How Low-Wage Jobs Fail 30 Million Americans, Beth Shulman
Nomadland: Surviving America in the Twenty-First Century, Jessica Bruder
Where Bad Jobs Are Better: Retail Jobs Across Countries and Companies, Francoise Carre and Chris Tilly
"We Are All Fast-Food Workers Now": The Global Uprising Against Poverty Wages, Annelise Orleck

On Wanda

Stone Age Economics, Marshall Sahlins
Behave: The Biology of Humans at Our Best and Worst, Robert Sapolsky
Scarcity: Why Having Too Little Means So Much, Sendhil Mullainathan and Eldar Shafir
The Panopticon Writings, Jeremy Bentham
Discipline and Punish: The Birth of the Prison, Michel Foucault
Snakes in Suits: When Psychopaths Go to Work, Paul Babiak and Robert D. Hare
Karoshi, National Defense Counsel for Victims of Karoshi

On tech, automation, and the future of work

The Second Machine Age: Work, Progress, and Prosperity in a Time of Brilliant Technologies, Erik Brynjolfsson and Andrew McAfee
The Glass Cage: Automation and Us, Nicholas Carr
Automate This: How Algorithms Came to Rule Our World, Christopher Steiner
Algorithms to Live By: The Computer Science of Human Decisions, Brian Christian and Tom Griffiths
Mindless: Why Smarter Machines Are Making Dumber Humans, Simon Head

Rise of the Robots: Technology and the Threat of a Jobless Future, Martin Ford
The Robots Are Coming!: The Future of Jobs in the Age of Automation, Andres Oppenheimer and Ezra E. Fitz
The Mythology of Work: How Capitalism Persists Despite Itself, Peter Fleming
Live Work Work Work Die: A Journey into the Savage Heart of Silicon Valley, Corey Pein
Confronting Dystopia: The New Technological Revolution and the Future of Work, Eva Paus

On economics

An Inquiry into the Nature and Causes of the Wealth of Nations, Adam Smith
Capital, Karl Marx
"Economic Possibilities for Our Grandchildren" (essay), John Maynard Keynes
The Great Risk Shift: The New Economic Insecurity and the Decline of the American Dream, Jacob S. Hacker
Capital in the Twenty-First Century, Thomas Piketty
The Economics of Inequality, Thomas Piketty
Who Gets What—and Why: The New Economics of Matchmaking and Market Design, Alvin E. Roth
Misbehaving: The Making of Behavioral Economics, Richard H. Thaler

Notes

Introduction

1. Carl Benedikt Frey and Michael A. Osborne, "The Future of Employment: How Susceptible Are Jobs to Computerisation?," *Technological Forecasting and Social Change* 114 (January 2017): 254–80.

Part One: Amazon

1. Spencer Soper, "Inside Amazon's Warehouse: Lehigh Valley Workers Tell of Brutal Heat, Dizzying Pace at Online Retailer," *Morning Call* (Allentown, PA), September 18, 2011, http://articles.mcall.com/2011-09-18/news/mc-allentown-amazon-complaints-20110917_1_warehouse-workers-heat-stress-brutal-heat.
2. Mac McClelland, "I Was a Warehouse Wage Slave: My Brief, Backbreaking, Rage-Inducing, Low-Paying, Dildo-Packing Time Inside the Online-Shipping Machine," *Mother Jones,* March/April 2012, http://www.motherjones.com/politics/2012/02/mac-mcclelland-free-online-shipping-warehouses-labor/.
3. Dave Jamieson, "The Life and Death of an Amazon Warehouse Temp: What the Future of Low-Wage Work Really Looks Like," *Huffington Post Highline,* October 21, 2015, http://highline.huffingtonpost.com/articles/en/life-and-death-amazon-temp/.
4. The Energy Project and Harvard Business Review, "The Human Era @ Work," 2014, http://uli.org/wp-content/uploads/ULI-Documents/The-Human-Era-at-Work.pdf.
5. Judith A. Merkle, *Management and Ideology: The Legacy of the International Scientific Management Movement* (Berkeley: University of California Press, 1980), 22–23.

6. Robert Kanigel, *The One Best Way: Frederick Winslow Taylor and the Enigma of Efficiency* (New York: Viking, 1997), 326.
7. At least that's the number historian Robert Kanigel cites in his four-inch-thick biography of Taylor, *The One Best Way.*
8. Kanigel, *The One Best Way,* 320.
9. Adapted with permission from the Economic Policy Institute, "The Pay-Productivity Gap, 1948–2017," August 2018, https://www.epi.org/productivity-pay-gap/.

Part Two: Convergys

1. A useful review of the recent literature can be found in Jong-Min Woo and Teodor T. Postolache, "The Impact of Work Environment on Mood Disorders and Suicide: Evidence and Implications," *International Journal on Disability and Human Development* 7, no. 2 (2008): 185–200.
2. Again, this is just one of *tons*—Monica Molino et al., "Inbound Call Centers and Emotional Dissonance in the Job Demands—Resources Model," *Frontiers in Psychology* 7 (July 28, 2016): 1133, https://doi.org/10.3389/fpsyg.2016.01133.
3. See Tom Simonite, "This Call May Be Monitored for Tone and Emotion," *Wired,* March 19, 2018, http://www.wired.com/story/this-call-may-be-monitored-for-tone-and-emotion/.
4. I'm using MIT's living-wage calculator for the furniture cluster—http://livingwage.mit.edu.

Part Three: McDonald's

1. J. M. Weiss, "Effects of Coping Behavior with and Without a Feedback Signal on Stress Pathology in Rats," *Journal of Comparative and Physiological Psychology* 77, no. 1 (November 1971): 22–30.
2. Paul Willner, Richard Muscat, and Mariusz Papp, "Chronic Mild Stress-Induced Anhedonia: A Realistic Animal Model of Depression," *Neuroscience and Biobehavioral Reviews* 16 (Winter 1992): 525–34.

Index

Note: "EG" refers to Emily Guendelsberger.

abscessed teeth, 218–19
addiction, 80–81, 194, 297
Aetna, 128
Airbnb, 240
Akasha (Amazon worker), 106–10, 111–15
Alaska, seasonal workers in, 95–97
algorithmic scheduling, 9, 261, 305
Amazon
- class-action lawsuit against, 38–39
- fulfillment centers. *See* Amazon fulfillment centers
- history of, 15–16, 17n‡
- market value of, 25n
- names given to normal things by, 15n, 32n*, 109n
- public image of, 24–25, 26
- total employees of, 17n*
- Walmart compared with, 23–24
- Walmart's lawsuit against, 24n*
- Zappos purchased by, 28

Amazon fulfillment centers
- attendance at, 19–20, 32
- CamperForce program of, 93, 94
- conveyer-belt joyride taken by worker preparing to quit in, 17n‡
- crying on the job as common at, 52n
- eighth-generation, 87
- GPS monitoring of workers at, 11, 22–23, 24, 35, 111
- low worker satisfaction at, 24
- media exposés of, 18–20
- minimum wage at, increase in, 263n
- negative comments from workers in online forums about, 20–23, 52n, 112
- pain workers experience at, 29, 37, 53–54
- peak at, 16–17, 17n*, 93
- positions at, 30, 109, 110–11
- repetitive stress injuries at, 21–22, 202
- robots as replacing humans in, 87–89, 263n
- SDF8
  - balancing parenthood with work at, 55, 86–87
  - breaks at, 34, 35, 36n*
  - building (origins) of, 17n†
  - on Christmas Eve, 103–5
  - clocking in at, 244
  - EG's biggest reason for choosing, 18
  - EG's exhaustion at, 50, 51, 54, 58, 59–60, 79, 94, 98, 109
  - EG's first day at, 15, 16–18, 39–42
  - EG's first real shift at, 48–49, 50
  - EG's pain at, 50–54, 58, 78, 79, 82, 94, 277
  - EG's recording of management at, x
  - EG's semipermanent bad mood during, 59–61, 98
  - isolation in mods at, 45, 52, 85n*, 277
  - modesty-wrapped items at, 25–26, 88–89
  - monotony in the mods, 52, 55, 78, 90, 91–92, 92n†, 92n‡, 98
  - noise at, 17–18

Amazon fulfillment centers *(cont.)*
offenses resulting in termination at, 37–38
opening of, 87
orientation for, 31–39, 83, 192
outbound packing complex of, 16n
pain-medication vending machines at, 12, 41, 47, 53, 58–59
physical description of, 15, 16, 17
pickers' dislike of assignment to fourth-floor in, 90–91
Power Hours at, 60, 84, 99
reputation in Louisville area, 28
Spanish-speaking workers at, 31n†
timeline of EG's employment at, ix
training, 41–42, 43–48, 157
See also jobs: of EG, overview of
security at, 25, 26
temperatures in, 18–19, 20–21, 29, 91
temporary workers used by, 16–17, 17n*, 18, 19, 28–31, 32n†, 33–34, 93, 103
termination of workers at, 22, 23
Time Off Task (TOT) by workers at, 34–35, 36n*, 37, 51, 85n*, 98–99
workers' schedules at, 29–30
See also Amazon
AMCARE, 21, 21n*, 37, 41, 53
American Dream, the, 4, 7, 37, 192, 309–10
American Machinist, 65
American Magazine, 72–73
amoxicillin, 219, 220
Anthone (Jess's wife), 189, 190, 191, 192–94, 218–20, 227–28
anxiety, 124, 125, 171, 279–80, 310
Apple, 24
Ash (EG's last caller at Convergys), 231–32
assembly line, 197, 198–201, 269
AT&T
Convergys Hickory site for, 129, 130, 132, 132n, 147–48, 150–51, 196. *See also* Convergys
FCC's fining of, 172n*
purchase of DirecTV, 152n*
Aunt Patty "Evil Patty" (Convergys worker), 119, 217
description of, 121, 136
on first day of training, 120, 132
as a top seller, 121, 137
automation of jobs, 11, 89, 309, 313

Baker, Emily, 154
Barnes & Noble, 127, 127n§, 162, 163, 186, 233
Batman, 152
Baymont Suites, 187, 189–90, 233
Bentham, Jeremy, 155, 156n
Berry, Brittney, 292
Bethlehem Steel, 67, 72–73, 84
Bezos, Jeff, 15, 17n‡, 24–25, 261n, 263n
Blade Runner, 291n
Blair (Amazon temp), 42–43, 60, 83–89, 92, 99
boss, as a recent invention, 63–64
Boston Watertown Arsenal, 1911 strike at, 75–76
brain, 10, 10n†
Brazil, 139
Brianna (Convergys worker), 119, 190, 218
Buffalo Wild Wings, 119, 119n*
Burger King, 269
burns
suffered by a McDonald's customer, 293–94
suffered by employees, 291–92
Busk, Integrity Staffing Solutions, Inc. v., 38–39
Butch Patty "Good Patty" (Convergys worker), 119, 167, 231
description of, 121, 136
on first day of training, 120, 131–32, 133, 233
graduation day award to, 217
panic attack of, 120, 121–22, 125, 226–27

Caldwell County, NC, 166
call-center workers
annual turnover rate of, 195n
elaborate scripts of, 76, 123
number of, 122
online stories from, 122–25
stress of, 124–25, 130–31
Campbell, Martisse, 292

CamperForce program, Amazon's, 93, 94
Candela (McDonald's shift manager), 252, 257, 275, 313
  on cameras monitoring transactions, 251n
  description of, 238–39, 244, 245
  reaction to EG calling out sick, 287
  during Szechuan sauce incident, 289–90
  wiping of previous orders from queue, 241
capital, 61–62, 77
  definition of, 61n
  industrialization and, 64–66
  Taylorism and, 66–72, 73, 77
capitalism, 64, 73, 265–66, 303, 311
Carter, Jimmy, 78
Caterpillar, 17, 46
Chapo Trap House, 298–99, 298n, 302–3
Chick-fil-A, 180, 181, 182, 183, 184–86, 233
Christman, Matt, 298–99, 303
chronic stress, 210–11, 217, 279–80, 309, 311, 313
Civil War, 165
Clarify, 131, 171, 173–74, 175
Clinton, Bill, 164
Clinton, Hillary, 106
Cogito, 154, 157
Colvin, Fred, 65
Comcast, 128
Congress, 301, 301n†
Convergys
  attendance at, 133, 140, 144, 146–47, 184
  on attitude, 140, 141–42, 144, 145, 146
  Butch Patty's panic attack at, 120, 121–22, 125
  calls recorded by, 153, 157
  clients of, 128–29, 139
  compulsive sanitizers at, 129, 134, 158–61
  computer systems of, poor integration of, 149–50, 149n*, 161, 170, 171–76, 172n*, 277
  customers valued over employees at, 249
  description of interior of, 195
  EG's Amazon SDF8 job compared with, 157
  EG's handling of calls on own, 169–76, 182, 225–26
  EG's interview for job at, ix
  EG's last call at, 231–32
  EG's stress response to screamers at, 174–80, 221–22, 223–25, 277
  EG's training at
    classmates in, description of, 121, 132, 136–37, 157–58
    first day of, 120, 126, 128–30, 233, 255–56
    graduation day of, 217
    orientation during, 134, 137–49
    on sales, 152–53, 159
    shadowing real reps taking calls during, 161–62
    with Vicki, 226, 227–28
  on escalations (negative customers), 147–48
  friends EG made while at, 157, 245, 297
  LGBTQ workers at, 189n
  lunches at, 180–81, 250
  management at, 135
  Melody reports at, 227–28, 229
  MRSA at, 158–60
  overview of, 126, 138
  policy on making sales offers, 132–33, 132n, 150–51, 153
  referral bonus offered by, 145–46
  restroom breaks at, 11, 140–41, 149
  salary at, 143, 226
  sales commission at, 143
  smoke breaks at, 119
  stress of, 130–31, 171, 217, 226
  timeline of EG's employment at, ix
  on toggling in and out of phones, 227–28, 229
  turnover at, 119, 133, 157n†, 169, 195–96, 226, 231, 297
  wage theft by, 229–31
  workers' negative comments about, 130–33
  See also jobs: of EG, overview of
corporate-middleman phenomenon, 287
Costco, 24
Craigslist, 240
Crispina (McDonald's worker), 270–71

Cronenberg, David, 291n
Crowley, 259–60
crying on the job by Amazon workers, 52n
Crystal Palace, 197, 198–201, 222, 263–64, 266, 269
cyborg jobs, 11–12, 266

Dalisay (McDonald's worker), 276, 290, 296, 305, 306–7
Damien (Amazon traveler temp), 95, 97, 100
Darryl (Amazon temp), 42, 44, 46, 56, 57, 85n*
DCCC (Democratic Congressional Campaign Committee), 301, 301n*, 301n†
Delivering Happiness (Hsieh), 49
Dell, 139
Democratic Congressional Campaign Committee (DCCC), 301, 301n*, 301n†
depression, 74, 124–25, 171, 279, 280–81, 310
deskilling of jobs, 76–77, 123
Destiny (Convergys worker), 119, 172
  description of, 136
  on first day of training, 132, 133, 134
  as a hard-core sanitizer, 134, 158
  on launch sequence, 161
  during orientation, 143–44
  on previous termination, 133
  as a top seller, 137, 175, 193
  in training with Vicki, 229, 230
dignity, 4–5, 10, 249, 309
Dion, Celine, 115
DirecTV, 144, 157, 191, 198
  AT&T's purchase of, 152n*
  as a client of Convergys, 128
  gathering information during calls for, 162, 162n
  training at Convergys on, 152, 159
Discipline and Punish (Foucault), 156
Dish Network, 128
Disney, 24
Douglas (furniture salesperson), 167–68
driving and texting, 170
Dropbox, 240
Dugan, Michael K., 166

Eastern State Penitentiary, 155–56, 156n
eBay, 17
economics, neoclassical, 262–64
Ehrenreich, Barbara, 4, 23
El Kentubano, 31n†
Eli (Amazon workamper temp), 92–94, 96, 99–102, 103, 106, 211
embodied cognition, 210n
empathy, 264–65
Energy Project, 63
Erik (McDonald's trainer), 238
eugenics, 201–2
Everything Store, The (Stone), 17n‡, 24
evolutionary timeline, stress response and, 202–7
ExxonMobil, 24, 139

fake names, x
Family and Medical Leave Act (FMLA), 160, 160n
fast-food industry
  deliberate understaffing in, 260–61
  equipment used to monitor workers in, 7–8
  stress of jobs in, 183
  workers burned on the job in, 292
  workers' hours cut as punishment in, 287
FCC, 172n*
Feast, Josh, 154
FedEx, 17
feudalism, 63–64
Fight for $15 protests, 287
fight-or-flight response. *See* stress response
Fish Mox, 218, 219–20, 313
FMLA (Family and Medical Leave Act), 160, 160n
Ford, Henry, 202, 213
  as an anti-Semite, 197n*
  assembly line of, 197, 198–201, 263, 269
  background of, 196, 197–98
  eugenics and, 201n†
  five-dollar day announced by, 263–64, 263n
  My Life and Work, 196–97, 198, 201
Ford, Tennessee Ernie, 116
Foucault, Michel, 156–57, 225

Index

Fred (Convergys site leader at Hickory), 135, 137–44, 146–49, 191
free-market theory, 263–64
Frost, Amber A'Lee, 298–99, 303
Frozen, 112
furniture industry, US, 163–64, 165–66
Furniture Wars, The (Dugan), 166

Gaiman, Neil, 259, 259n
Game of Thrones, 206n
GDP, 309
global trade, 78, 164, 166–67
Goldman Sachs, 24, 139
Good Omens (Pratchett and Gaiman), 259–60
Google, 24
Grizzly Man, 295
Guendelsberger, Emily
  Car Life while at Convergys, 126–28, 137, 162, 186, 188, 254
  church choir background of, 255
  commute to Oakland, 254, 297–98
  commute to SDF8, 27, 39–40, 254
  corrective surgeries on legs, 50, 237
  depression and, 213, 223, 237–38, 281, 284
  end of Car Life, 187, 189–90
  first real job of, 3–5, 260–61
  husband of. *See* Rajiv (EG's husband)
  job at Amazon. *See* Amazon fulfillment centers: SDF8
  job at Convergys. *See* Convergys
  job at McDonald's. *See* McDonald's: San Francisco franchise in downtown Sixth District
  karaoke with Amazon coworkers, 106–16
  knee issue of, 30, 39, 97
  migraines of, 46, 50
  as a newspaper reporter, 26–27, 283, 301
  paychecks of, xi, 168, 190
  physical preparation for Amazon, 44n
  Pokémon Go and, 162–63, 231–32
  PTSD and, 212–13, 212n, 281
  trip to Myrtle Beach, 218
  use of McDonald's to feel better, 56, 58, 80, 215, 237, 238
  visit to Amazon temps at RV park, 94–102
Guevara, Che, 284

Hailey (Amazon worker), 107, 108, 109–11, 112–15, 193
Hamilton, 186, 186n
Handmaiden, The, 291n
happiness market, 191–92
Harvard Business Review, 63
Hastur, 259–60
Head, Simon, 23, 24
Heathers, 291n
Henredon Furniture Industries, 166
Henry, John, 88
Hickory, NC
  accent of people in, 129, 157–58, 243
  cost of living in, 191
  heat wave in, 162
  history of, 126, 163
  motto of, 165n
  Pokémon Go and, 162–63
Hickory Furniture Mart, 163–64, 233
Hitler, Adolf, 197n*
HM Electronics, 8
Hobbes, Thomas, 206, 215
homeless people, 243–44, 247, 254, 277, 285–86
HP, 139
Hsieh, Tony, 49
Huffington Post, 20
hunter-gatherers, nomadic, 215–17
Hustler, The, 291n

I Invented the Modern Age (Snow), 200
"I Put a Spell on You," 115
"I Was a Warehouse Wage Slave" (McClelland), 19–20
"in the weeds," 302
  at Amazon fulfillment centers, 23
  definitions of, 3, 5, 12
  at McDonald's, 241, 245, 253, 257
  service workers as, 9, 11
  toxic effects of, 6–7
Indiana, ix, x, 17, 166
Indiana Army Ammunition Plant, 17n†
Industrial Revolution, 62, 64–66

Index

Integrity Staffing Solutions, 16–17, 18, 28–31, 83, 103, 111, 287
Integrity Staffing Solutions, Inc. v. Busk, 38–39
Intel, 79
International Jew, The (Ford), 197n*

Jamba Juice, 261
Japan, 78, 261n, 310
Jasmine (Amazon temp), 42, 45
Jess (Convergys worker), 119, 225, 226, 313
  crisis with Anthone's abscessed tooth, 218–20, 227–28
  description of, 137
  EG's stay with, 190
  former opiate addiction of, 189, 192, 194
  as a hard-core sanitizer, 158
  on Jordan, 195
  maternal concern for EG, 188–89
  monetizing of spare time, 192–93
  partnered calls with EG, 172
  as a top seller, 137, 193
job satisfaction, 63
jobs
  cyborg, 11–12, 266
  of EG, overview of, 10–11
    applying for and getting, ix
    high turnover at, ix–x
    productivity-enforcing technology at, 11
    recording management at, x
    timeline of, ix, 10
    worst of, 277
Jordan (AT&T head of training at Hickory), 135, 137, 139–47, 189, 195, 196
Juan (McDonald's worker), 285, 286, 292
Jungle, The (Sinclair), 72

Kahn, Albert, 197n†
Kaitlyn (Convergys worker), 119, 137, 158–60
kaizen, 78, 261n
Kalanick, Travis, 198
Kalin (Amazon traveler temp), 97
Kanigel, Robert, 68
karoshi, 310–11
Kendall (Convergys worker), 227, 228, 229
Kimberly (Convergys trainer), 159, 169, 189n, 230
  description of, 129, 130, 135, 226
  on first day of training, 120, 129–34, 157, 255, 297
  on graduation day, 217
  as a hard-core sanitizer, 134, 158
  log-ins and passwords given by, 149, 149n*
  on making sales offers, 153
  maternal concern for EG, 188
  during orientation, 141–43, 146–48
  random coaching with, 222
  on using CSP for call flows, 150–51
Kiva robots, 87, 263n
Kiva Systems, 87
Kolbi (Convergys worker), 119, 226, 313
  on Butch Patty's panic attack, 120, 122
  description of, 136–37
  in sales role-plays, 152
  on stress of fast food jobs, 183
  in training with Vicki, 230
  trip to Myrtle Beach, 218
  on working at Chick-fil-A, 181, 182–83, 184–86, 240, 272, 297
Kroc, Ray, 4, 240, 269

Lab Rat Chronicles, The (Lambert), 279–80
labor, 61–62, 77
  definition of, 62n
  deskilling of, 76–77
  division of, 73–74, 75
  industrialization and, 64–66
  outsourcing of, 164, 167
  reaction to Ford's Highland Park assembly lines, 198, 199–200
  reaction to Taylor, 75–76, 197
  Smith on, 73–74
  Taylorism and, 66–72, 73, 77–78, 198
  in the US in the early 1970s, 78
Lalo (McDonald's general manager), 250, 251, 288n
  description of, 244, 245
  EG giving notice to, 304, 305
  during heavy lunch rushes, 290

reaction to EG's injuries, 291–92
refusal of service to homeless woman, 247–49, 253–54
Lambert, Kelly, 279–80
Lane and Henredon, 165
lean production, 261–62, 261n
learned helplessness, 311–12
"Let It Go," 112, 113
Library of Congress, 15
Liebeck, Stella, 293–94
Liebeck v. McDonald's, 293–94
"Life and Death of an Amazon Warehouse Temp, The" (Jamieson), 20
Ligur, 259–60
"Like a Surgeon" (Weird Al Yankovic), 110
Lindsay (rep on Walmart and Sam's Club accounts), 124
Little Shop of Horrors, 110
Lockhart, Jeff, Jr., 20, 21, 54
logistics hub, 17
London taxi drivers, 76
Louisville, KY
Cuban immigration to, 31n†
as a logistics hub, 17
opioid crisis in, 79, 80

Madsen, David, 216
"Magical Number Seven, Plus or Minus Two, The" (Miller), 149
Mao Zedong, 78
Mara (Convergys worker), 178–79
Marisol (McDonald's shift manager), 278n, 284
description of, 252
during lunch rush, 259, 266, 267–68, 270, 273
reaction to Mustard Lady incident, 274–76, 278, 283
Marshall (AT&T project leader at Hickory), 135, 137–41, 143, 145–47, 196
Marx, Karl, 74
Massachusetts, furniture industry in, 165
Matthias (Amazon traveler temp), 97, 98–100, 115, 263
McClelland, Mac, 19–20
McDonald's
burns at, 291–94
coffee at, 242, 293–95
Dollar Menu at, 246
founder of, 4
"Free Cone Fridays" promotion by, 306n†
lawsuits against, 287, 293–94
operations and training manual of, 7–8
original national menu of, 269
San Francisco franchise in downtown Sixth District
as always "in the weeds," 241, 245, 253, 257–58, 285
breaks and lunches at, 250–51, 252–53, 278n
calling out sick at, 287
cameras monitoring transactions at, 251n
clocking in at, 244, 250, 253
common transactions requiring manager approval at, 251–52
customer flirtation at, 245–46
customer hostility during lunch rush at, 258, 259, 266–69, 270–72
description of, 240
EG quitting, 304, 305
EG's burn and coffee pot injury at, 291–92, 295, 297
EG's first sale at, 238
EG's last shift at, 305–7
EG's stress response to screamers at, 248–50, 270–74, 276, 283
extra work from free items kept behind the counter at, 241–43
foreign tourists at, 258–59, 266
interactions with homeless people at, 247–50, 277, 285–86
lack of chances for EG to make friends at, 245, 250, 278
lower management at, x, 245
McPick 2 (semisecret menu) at, 246–47
multitasking duties of working counter at, 239–40
Mustard Lady incident at, 268–69, 270–76, 277–78, 284, 287

McDonald's *(cont.)*
passive-aggressive interaction with man in suit, 282–85
salary of EG at, 240
satisfaction from making customers happy at, 244, 247, 277, 278
scheduling at, 11, 244, 256, 257n, 282, 287–88, 305
shaking off bad customers at, 277–78
shifts at, 244–45
stereotypes at, 246n
Szechuan sauce incident at, 288, 289–90, 295–96
timeline of EG's employment at, ix
training at, x
uniform at, 240
See also jobs: of EG, overview of
soft-serve machines at, 306n*
Uber Eats's partnership with, 239, 290
McDonald's, Liebeck v., 293–94
McKenna (Jess and Anthone's daughter), 189, 190, 191, 192, 193, 194, 218
McKinsey Global Institute, 23
McPherson, Katie, 27–28, 49, 79, 81–82, 83
McPherson, Sue, 27
media
coverage of Szechuangate, 299–300, 302–3
exposés of Amazon fulfillment centers, 18–20
Melody (Amazon worker), 107, 108–10, 111, 112–13, 114–15
Melody reports, 227–28, 229
metallurgy, 65
MetLife, 154
Michelle (Amazon SDF8 trainer), 41–42, 43–46, 47, 48
Michigan, furniture industry in, 165
Microsoft, 24, 139
Miguel (Amazon SDF8 orientation leader), 31–37, 38, 39, 192, 313
Miller, George, 149
Miller's Law, 149, 171
Mindless (Head), 23
miscarriages among XPO warehouses workers, 21n†
Misty (Convergys worker), 157–58, 188
Model T, 198, 199, 269
Monae (Convergys worker), 119
Morning Call, 18, 20
Mother Jones, 19, 21
MRSA, 158–60
muda, 78, 261n
Mulan, 298
multitasking, 170–71
Muppet Christmas Carol, The, 81–82
My Life and Work (Ford), 196–97, 198, 201

NAFTA, 164, 166, 167
Naknek, AK, 95–97
names, fake, x
National Council for Occupational Safety and Health, 292
National Labor Relations Board, 287
National Park Service, 15
Neal (Amazon traveler temp), 96, 97, 100
neoclassical economics, 262–64
New York
furniture industry in, 165
homeless in, 243
New York Times, 21n†
Nickel and Dimed (Ehrenreich), 4, 23
Nike, 24
Nixon, Richard, 78
Noll, Henry ("Schmidt"), 67, 69–72, 69n, 82, 84, 112, 161
nomadic hunter-gatherers, 215–17
North Carolina
first European settlers in, 164
furniture industry in, 165–66
recording own conversations in, x
trans bathroom bans of, 189

Oakland, CA, 254–55, 297–98
Obama, Barack, 152
Obamacare, 10, 302
Olivia (Convergys worker), 161–62, 239
One Best Way, The (Kanigel), 68–69
Onion, 213n*, 237n
opioid addiction, 79, 80–81, 194
orientation sessions, recording, x
"Original Affluent Society, The" (Sahlins), 215

OSHA complaints, 19, 292
Oswalt, Patton, 298, 302–3
outsourcing of labor, 164, 167
Oxford University, 12
Oxycontin, 79, 80

pain-medication vending machines at Amazon, 12, 41, 47, 53, 58–59
parents
  single, 86–87, 190
  working, 107, 108, 190–91, 192–93
peak at Amazon, 16–17, 17n*, 93
Pete (Oakland church music director), 255
Philadelphia, PA
  2016 Democratic National Convention in, 188
  Eastern State Penitentiary in, 155–56
  EG's violent encounters with teenage boys in, 212, 212n
  homeless in, 243
Philadelphia City Paper, 26–27
Philadelphia Daily News, 5
phone numbers, 149n†, 217
Piano, The, 291n
piecework, 65
pig iron, 67–72, 67n, 73, 202, 265
pin factory, 73–74
Pinterest, 240
Pokémon Go, 162–63, 188n, 231–32
Power Hours, 60, 84, 99
Pratchett, Terry, 259
Principles of Scientific Management, The (Taylor), 66, 67, 70–72
productivity-enforcing technology
  at Amazon fulfillment centers, 11, 22–23, 24, 35, 111
  as normal in the low-wage labor market, 25, 55–56
Prozac, 279
PTSD, 212–13, 279, 281

race, xi
Radhika (EG's sister-in-law), 260–62
Rajiv (EG's husband), 10n†, 27, 58, 219–20, 237, 238
Rashard (McDonald's worker), 290, 296
rats, experimental research on, 279–81, 282–83, 311–12
Reagan, Ronald, 78
Reddit, 123n, 240
repetitive stress injuries, 21–22, 202
restroom breaks
  at Amazon SDF8 fulfillment center, 35, 36n*, 51
  of call-center workers, 123–24
  at Convergys, 140–41, 149
retail industry
  deliberate understaffing in, 260–61
  workers' hours cut as punishment in, 287
Rhonda the Tank, 50, 54, 107
Rick and Morty, 289, 298
Roanoke Island, 164
Ryan, Paul, 7, 9–10

Sahlins, Marshall, 215
salmon processing plants in Alaska, 95–97
sample bias, 201n*
Sam's Club, 124
San Francisco, CA
  effort to disincentivize trash in, 251n
  homeless in, 243–44
  housing crisis in, 254–55
  worker-protection legislation in, 240, 287
Sanders, Bernie, 106
Savannah (Convergys worker), 181, 182, 218, 227
scheduling, algorithmic, 9, 261, 305
"Schmidt." *See* Noll, Henry ("Schmidt")
scientific management. *See* Taylorism
Selye, Hans, 279–80, 281
Shakespeare, William, 264
sick leave, paid, 240, 287
silicon computer chip, invention of, 79
Silicon Valley, 240n
Simone, Nina, 115
Simpsons, 64
Sinclair, Upton, 72–73
single parents, 86–87, 190
SiriusXM radio, 139
"Sixteen Tons," 116
slavery, 165

Smith, Adam, 73–74
Snopes, 188n
Snow, Richard, 200
sons, teenage, mothers' reactions to behavior of, 92*
Soper, Spencer, 18–19
South Carolina, 165
Sprint, 139
Square, 240
Steve (Convergys HR at Hickory), 135, 137–38, 143–46, 196
Stone, Brad, 17n‡
stress
  addiction and, 80–81
  from call-center jobs, 124, 125.130–31
  chronic, 210–11, 217, 279–80, 309, 311, 313
  of fast-food jobs, 183
stress response, 202–6, 209–11, 214, 217, 279
substance abuse, 80–81, 194, 297
suicide, call-center reps and, 124–25
Suresh (husband of EG's sister-in-law), 260–62
System X, 171, 171n, 173, 174, 175, 176
Szechuangate, 299–300, 302–3

Taco Bell, 76
TaskRabbit, 240
taxi drivers in London, 76
Taylor, Frederick Winslow, 265
  background of, 66
  The Principles of Scientific Management, 66, 67, 70–72
  on "Schmidt," 67, 69–72, 69n
  scientific management of, 66–72, 73, 75–78, 198, 199
  similarities between Ford and, 196–97
Taylorism, 66–72, 73, 75–78, 198, 199
techno-Taylorism, 76, 124, 308, 313
technological work speedup, 7–9, 11. *See also* productivity-enforcing technology
Teena (Amazon temp), 42, 47
teenage sons, mothers' reactions to behavior of, 92*
teeth, abscessed, 218–19
Telegence, 131, 171–73, 172n*, 179
telephone numbers, 149n†, 217
Tennant, David, 259n
Texas, Virgil, 299
texting and driving, 170
Tiano, Nancy, 294
Time Off Task (TOT), 34–35, 36n*, 37, 51, 85n*, 98–99
time to lean, time to clean if, 3–4, 7, 56, 63, 240
Tonya (Hickory Furniture Mart saleswoman), 163–64
TOT (Time Off Task), 34–35, 36n*, 37, 51, 85n*, 98–99
Toyota Production System, 78, 261n
Transamerica, 138
travelers, 94–95
True Grit, 291n
Trump, Donald, 28, 106, 152, 166–67, 310, 313
Twitter, 240

Uber, 25, 76, 238, 240, 306n†
Uber Eats, 239, 290
understaffing, deliberate, 260–61
unemployment, 166, 309
UPS, 17, 24
Utah, 216

Verizon, 128, 139
Vicki (Convergys trainer), 226–31
Virginia, 165

Wadsworth, Kelly, 196
Walker, Robert, 80–81
Walmart
  automated monitoring system used by, 23–24
  as a client of Convergys, 128
  EG's Car Life phase of parking at, 126, 127, 254
  internet urban legends about, 188
  lawsuit against Amazon, 24n*
  low worker satisfaction at, 24
  monitoring of reps' restroom breaks, 124

parking lots as safe havens for people to park in overnight, 127n*
understaffing policy of, 262
Walton, Sam, 127n*
War on Drugs, 81
Washington, DC, 243
water spiders, 109, 109n
Watertown Arsenal in Boston, 1911 strike in, 75–76
Wayfair, 17
Wealth of Nations, The (Smith), 73–74
Weiss, J. M., 280
Whole Foods, 24
Wikipedia, 240
workampers, 93, 94
workers. *See* labor
workers' compensation, 36
working parents, 107, 108, 190–91, 192–93

XPO, 21n†

Yankovic, Weird Al, 110
Yelp, 240, 243
Yiannopoulos, Milo, 288n
YMCA, 127, 233
Yolanda (Amazon temp), 42, 44, 46, 54

Zappos, 28, 49, 83
Zeb (Amazon traveler temp), 95–100, 101–2, 103, 263, 309, 313
Zone, 171, 171n, 173, 174

About the Author

Emily Guendelsberger has worked at *Philadelphia Weekly,* the *Philadelphia Daily News,* and the *A.V. Club* and has contributed to the *Washington Post, Politico* magazine, the *Philadelphia Inquirer,* and *Vice.*